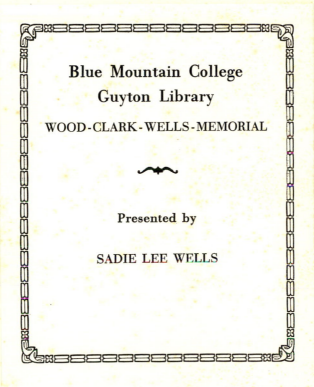

TEACHING SHAKESPEARE

TEACHING
SHAKESPEARE

EDITED BY

WALTER EDENS
CHRISTOPHER DURER
WALTER EGGERS
DUNCAN HARRIS
KEITH HULL

PRINCETON UNIVERSITY PRESS

Copyright © 1977 by Princeton University Press
Published by Princeton University Press,
Princeton, New Jersey
In the United Kingdom: Princeton University Press,
Guildford, Surrey

Library of Congress Cataloging in Publication Data will
be found on the last printed page of this book

Publication of this book has been aided by grants from
the Graduate School and the Arts and Sciences Division
of Basic Research of the University of Wyoming and
The Andrew W. Mellon Foundation.

This book has been composed in Linotype Baskerville

Printed in the United States of America
by Princeton University Press,
Princeton, New Jersey

For Richard Lionel Hillier,
SHAKESPEARE TEACHER

CONTENTS

Acknowledgments   ix

Introduction   *By Walter F. Eggers, Jr.*   xi

I. DESCRIPTIONS AND PRESCRIPTIONS

One. Shakespeare in the Classroom: Scientific Object vs.
Immediate Experience   *By Robert B. Heilman*   3

Two. Shakespeare Inferred   *By John W. Velz*   27

Three. The Presentation of Shakespeare   *By D. Allen
Carroll*   48

II. SHAKESPEARE AND THE ENGLISH CURRICULUM

Four. Shakespeare and the Graduate English Curriculum
By Norman Rabkin   67

Five. Deromanticizing the Shrew: Notes on Teaching
Shakespeare in a "Women in Literature" Course
By Winfried Schleiner   79

III. THE COURSE IN SHAKESPEARE: GENRE AND CANON

Six. On Teaching the Shakespeare Canon: The Case of
Measure for Measure   By A. C. Hamilton   95

Seven. "Things Climb Upward to What They Were
Before": The Reteaching and Regreening of *Macbeth*
By Albert Wertheim   114

Eight. Lear's Comic Vision: "Come, Let's Away to Prison"
By Paul M. Cubeta   138

Nine. Plays within Plays in Shakespeare's Early Comedies
By David M. Bergeron   153

IV. EXEMPLARY APPROACHES TO PARTICULAR PLAYS

Ten. Hunting for Clues in *Much Ado About Nothing*
By Ray L. Heffner, Jr.   177

Eleven. Teaching *Coriolanus*: The Importance of
Perspective   *By Brian Vickers*   228

vii

V. SEEING AND HEARING THE PLAY

Twelve. "This Wide and Universal Stage": Shakespeare's
Plays as Plays   *By Jay L. Halio*   273

Thirteen. The Teacher as Poetic Actor   *By G. Wilson
Knight*   290

Fourteen. Some Problems in Teaching Shakespeare's Plays
as Works of Drama   *By Bernard Beckerman*   305

Annotated Bibliography   *By Andrew M. McLean*   317

Notes on Contributors   334

Index   337

ACKNOWLEDGMENTS

WE ARE grateful for support in publication of this book to the Graduate School and the Arts and Sciences Division of Basic Research of the University of Wyoming and to The Andrew W. Mellon Foundation. We owe thanks for special help to Betty Bunch, Lu Ann Heward, Barbara Kissack, and Liz Stagner. The essays have been regularized in format, and all quotations from Shakespeare's plays are taken with permission from the *Riverside Shakespeare* (Boston: Houghton Mifflin Company, 1974).

INTRODUCTION

WALTER F. EGGERS, JR.

AUBREY's legend that Shakespeare was a teacher, a "school-master in the country," before he became an actor and play-wright is irresistible to Shakespeare teachers, who like to think that they would have his sympathy. Yet the only memorable teacher in Shakespeare's plays is Holofernes in *Love's Labor's Lost*, a vain and dogmatic pedant. To show off his learning, Holofernes devises a pageant of the Seven Worthies for the King and Court, and before he can get his own part underway, he is laughed off the stage. There may be a touch of sympathy for Holofernes when he complains to his audience, "This is not generous." Shakespeare seems generally to approve of the efforts of amateur actors, and Aubrey's schoolmaster-become-actor would have known that teachers are like actors, subject to a sometimes difficult audience and easily "put out of countenance." But the satire is stronger than the sympathy. We may assume that young Shakespeare respected his teachers—as we assume all good students do—but the only certainty is that he knew how foolish teachers can be.

The teachers who have contributed to this book, like the teacher whom we honor with its publication, are neither pedants nor pedagogues but "professors" in the rich sense of the word, whose authority rests on their special dedication to their subject, Shakespeare's plays. Many are prominent scholars, and all have extended their teaching beyond the classroom in critical books and essays. For this reason, their descriptions of what they do in the classroom should be not only useful to other teachers but critically significant. Their different ways of teaching reflect different personal styles but also different conceptions of Shakespeare's plays. Taken together, these essays offer the variety of critical approaches that we expect in Shakespeare studies.

Diverse though they are, these essays also share a particular concern for developing students' interests and skills beyond strict formal analysis—a concern which seems characteristic of the present moment in Shakespeare studies and in literary criticism in general. The kind of close reading that we identify with New Criticism remains a foundation for most of the methods of teaching described here, but this book also exhibits new or renewed attention on the part of Shakespeare teachers to the affective and historical dimensions of literature. All of the essays raise broad questions about the relationship between the text and its audience. Does "close reading" preempt the emotional experience of a play? What are the significant differences between the responses of a reader and the responses of a theater audience? Is it possible, and is it proper, to base our judgments of older literature on the sympathies and expectations of its original audience? What is the value for formal analysis of contextual concepts like genre and canon? These are by no means new questions; they are some of the questions that teachers have always had to answer for themselves, and in the most practical terms. But they were less conspicuous and seemed less important when New Critical theory held sway. In this book, most of the essays are oriented around questions like these.

The last section of essays, "Seeing and Hearing the Play," addresses the question most disputed throughout the book: what should the teacher do about the specifically theatrical aspect, the performability, of Shakepeare's texts? In that section are projects for classroom performances (by students and teachers alike) and examples of theatrical analysis; earlier essays, too, encourage the teacher to use whatever technical means are available—films, videotapes, records, Globe theater models—to impress students with the idea of the play in performance. There are limits to what a teacher whose degree is in literature can do with machinery even of the most sophisticated kind, and certain other essays are emphatic in arguing against wasting class time this way.

We have given the last word to the "theatrical" side not to resolve the dispute but to stress its importance. The teacher of literature should be warned that to conceive of drama as performance may mean to shift his fundamental assumptions about the stability and integrity of the literary text; he and his students will have to pay closer attention than they usually do to the effects on an audience of the moment-by-moment progress of the play. (Mark Rose recently described this shift in ideas at a meeting on "theatrical techniques in the classroom" during the Second International Shakespeare Association Congress.) Although not ostensibly "theatrical," two essays which do consider this most elusive aspect of dramatic texts are the "exemplary approaches" to individual plays. What makes them the longest essays in the book is that the teacher who tries to be comprehensive can be satisfied with no single, instantaneous view but must examine multiple perspectives on the play in its duration.

Performance is within the province of teachers of literature who recognize that the kinds of decisions they make as literary critics are involved in every theatrical production. In this respect, stage history or the history of productions, a burgeoning critical field, may become more and more useful for the classroom. Theater history offers yet another kind of resolution between "literary" and "theatrical" approaches: essays in various sections of the book point to Shakespeare's enhancing the poetry of his plays theatrically, by means of metaphors built into the structure of the theater, reflexive stage imagery, and even settings. Finally, theatrical contexts can be related to broader historical contexts: the image of cosmic and social hierarchy, for example, which is part of Shakespeare's Globe, had its counterparts in the fictional worlds of Shakespeare's plays and in the world outside the theater. Theatrical criticism can be reductive, but in ways like this it can also enlarge the text. A classroom is not a theater, and teachers who aspire to be actors should remember Holofernes' fallen countenance. The compelling argument for bringing the theater into the classroom is that the teacher who liberalizes his conception of the text to include its contexts expands the student's critical comprehension.

The same general argument obtains in a second section of essays dealing with contexts, the essays on "the course." Some important questions about Shakespeare's plays arise in a Shakespeare course and never so clearly outside it, for organizing the syllabus means coming to grips with the relationships between texts and with the subjects of genre and canon. Special discoveries follow, in which students can participate directly. The danger in this approach is that it is easy to promote glibness in students. Comparisons yield generalizations of the kind that can distract attention from the individual text, and some students find nothing so satisfying as a generalization. These are the students who moved one generation of teachers to call ideas of genre and biography critical fallacies. But comparisons can also be used as the platform for formal analysis. "This play is called a tragedy, and it was written shortly after that one: what do you make of the difference between them?" To allow leading questions of this sort, we must accept the idea that a student's capacity to analyze a text depends as much on experience as on intelligence. Something that any literature course can achieve as a course is refining students' expectations. To the degree that students can put themselves in the place of Shakespeare's audience they become expert in Shakespeare's plays, and even the first step in this direction is worth their taking. The contexts of genre and canon open out, as the context of the theater opens out, to the conventions and traditions of the broader context of history. Again, a more liberal conception of the object of literary study makes the objectives of the course more ambitious.

The collective argument of the essays in this book is that teaching becomes a way of learning for the teacher as well as for the student when the classroom is the focus for significant critical questions. It follows that discussions of teaching should be especially useful when they are tied to critical issues, as these essays are. Teachers of Shakespeare have received more of this kind of help recently at conferences and in journals (in the past two years there have been special teaching issues of *The Shakespeare Newsletter* and *Shakespeare Quarterly*). But we can help each other only so much, as all of these essays acknowledge. The true needs of the Shakespeare teacher are classes of reasonable size, a prominent place for Shakespeare in a strong curriculum, good texts and a good library.

Richard L. Hillier has enjoyed these advantages teaching Shakespeare at the University of Wyoming, and he is in large measure responsible for them, as a guiding light in this department for forty years. There can be no more appropriate tribute to his professional career than this book, as there is no better testimony to the joys of Shakespeare than his teaching. When I first came to Wyoming I was put on the spot by a colleague in the art department, a noted sculptor, who asked how I could look forward to teaching the same Shakespeare course year after year. I told him that some of the happiest people I knew were Shakespeare teachers. "Like Dick Hillier," he said.

I. DESCRIPTIONS AND PRESCRIPTIONS

ONE

SHAKESPEARE IN THE CLASSROOM: SCIENTIFIC OBJECT VS. IMMEDIATE EXPERIENCE

ROBERT B. HEILMAN

WHEN I think about the teaching of Shakespeare, a number of matters pop into my mind. Like all poppings, this one is not orderly:

1. Someone's aphorism, "Shakespeare is the most taught and the least read of all poets."

2. Someone else's aphorism (I heard it uttered): "When historians have had enough time to do their work, critics will disappear."

3. The counteraphorism would be (surely someone must have framed it long ago): "The critics begin where the antiquarians end."

4. Anyone who has ever had anything to do with a department's teaching schedule will know that almost everyone in a department, whatever his "field," feels able to teach Shakespeare, and that almost everyone wants to. Maybe this works out; at least the teacher may be supposed to be learning something. In my experience, the eighteenth century is the specialism least likely to produce volunteer adjutant Shakespeareans.

5. On the other hand there is the man, not without professional repute (some of it in Renaissance matters), who says he cannot teach Shakespeare because a decent mastery and management of the secondaries would take a lifetime, and he has not a lifetime to give for his countrymen in Shakespeare classes.

6. The image of a Shakespearean heading for class, slop-

3

ing a little to the left to counterbalance the burden in his right hand, his depot of dainty devices, his satchel of salubrious sound effects, the portable record player.

7. A Ph.D. candidate telling an adviser she hadn't got much into Shakespeare scholarship because her instructor in the Shakespeare seminar had said that what was important in the students' term papers was not what the secondaries said but what the students themselves saw, discovered, etc.

I shall not canvass such matters formally, systematically, or seriatim. They simply constitute a mass point of departure. They set up the situation (or, as one might proclaim in a burst of with-it jargon, delineate its parameters). They sketch (once again I have fought off "adumbrate") a range of attitudes in Shakespeare pedagogy. They remind us of the Shakespeare who can be packaged by specialists only, and of the Shakespeare who is everybody's meat, with everyman his own instant butcher; of Shakespeare as the center of a scholarly system outside of which he is unintelligible, and of Shakespeare as simply a stimulus to everyman's (and every age's) sensibility; of Shakespeare as an object in history who can slowly be identified, pinned down, delimited like an archaeological relic, an organism, a pattern of radiation, and of a Shakespeare who is fluid, evasive, and inconstant, and therefore equally accessible to everyone who goes at him with any kind of tools at all. These views imply, then, a diversity of pedagogical stances—from fear of defective comprehensiveness to faith in untutored insight, from seeking historical objectivity to telling the world, "This is how Shakespeare strikes me," from a rage for order to a contentment with bull sessions, from a sense of Shakespeare-through-facts to a settling for Shakespeare as sensory stimulus and excitement.

When one makes this kind of summary, of course, he may fall into oppositions a little neater than the unruly actualities that are one's primary theme. The problems in Shakespeare-teaching are a mixed bag that cannot all be conven-

4

iently lined up in antipodal, antithetical, dichotomous pairs. Insofar as I use opposites, then, they are a convenience, a way in, rather than a schema inalienably rooted in the nature of things; they open up various theoretical issues. Ideally we should reach theoretical solutions and derive a pedagogy from them. Yet things don't work out that way. Pedagogy goes on all the time, never waiting for theoretical edicts from professional supreme courts. What the instructor does implies pragmatic quasi-answers to theoretical questions; or, given the temperaments of many workers in the humanities, unplanned action comes first, and justifying theory is a sort of *a posteriori* tailpiece to the body of practice, wagging a philosophic echo to emotive-behavioral goings-on.

Pedagogy usually represents less a formal decision than a kind of drift—a drifting along with one's own personality, perhaps unidentified and probably unquestioned; or a drifting with the times or with those most successfully raised voices that appear to speak for the times; or a drifting along with older times felt, not as objects of demonic loyalty, but as voicing a quasi-permanent truth taken on trust and hardly in need of reordering or renovation. Many of us continue to float comfortably along on the current of historical study that rises in the postromantic fountain of some hundred fifty years ago (*Quelle*, that is). Many of us, perhaps even more, have felt the pull of the later current usually called "criticism," where the success of the voyages depends on the combined learning, sensibility, and discipline of the voyager, where novel fashions and fads in sailing equipment (literary Kontikis, lined barrels, inflated rafts, and even inner tubes) appear annually, and where the journey may establish a Columbus route good for other explorers, or may be a fantastic voyage on the strange inner seas of some wind-tossed special self. But by now the history-vs.-criticism match-up has been worked to death and cannot shed much light on what goes on in Shakespeare-teaching; in fact, as I will propose later, these two rivals have more to bring them together on a side than to make them challenge each other. We can get a better sense of practices and options, I think, by invoking—only, that is, as an instrument of exploration—another opposed pair that perhaps better describe the current problem: Shakespeare as scientific object and Shakespeare as immediate experience. At the risk of oversimplifying, let's say that in the former, we try to steer through Shakespeare; in the latter, Shakespeare floods over us. In the former, we turn a studious light on the object; in the latter, we are awash in him, as in a shower or sauna or tropical surf. In the former, we try to apply various principles and systems; in the latter, we submerge or we are surrounded or we are passive receptacles in an omnisensory vibratorium. But let me try to clarify my new dualism—Shakespeare as scientific object and Shakespeare as immediate experience—by some quick historical observations.

I

Romantic critics filtered Shakespeare through their own taste. Periodically men rebel against taste, even good taste (or perhaps especially against good taste, as more and more men—persons, of course—get into the act and generate egalitarian fogs over the literary landscape), and the chief postromantic alternative to taste was science: the move was from the personal intuition that persuades to the impersonal formulation that proves. If we want to be scientific, we naturally stick more and more to what is amenable to this kind of discrimination and ordering—to apparent causes and results and frequencies, to types, influences, forces, sources, and so on; to quantifiable matters within the plays or ascertainable or documentable ones outside them. I myself remember a long regimen in quartos and folios, acting companies, theaters and their structures, audiences, dedications, onlie begetters, historical allusions and parallels, local and contemporary analogies, etc. These were regarded, I gathered, as humanistic equivalents of enzymes, cell growth, amino acids, genes, blood types, dietary determinants, viruses, etc. The Shakespeare canon became a kind of anatomical specimen which dissection, essentially nonliterary, would show to have been of such-and-such a nature, and to have behaved in such-and-such a way, because it had had to because of such environmental and hereditary factors. Classes were fifty-minute transmission belts for all the varieties of laboratory equipage. The spirit of this never dies. In its more recent avatars Shakespeare science becomes typographic and compositorial, and Shakespeare seems a singular Feathertop conjured up by printer's devils —all this, of course, more for graduate teaching but also filtering down to undergraduate levels.

Deathless though it be, the view of Shakespeare-as-scientific-object is regularly needled, shoved, stepped on, and maybe modified by other concepts of what his works are and how to approach them. On rare occasions there is a tiny flash of skepticism even in the laboratory itself. I remember my shock when an apparently sound insider said (whispered, I'm sure) to me, "All this editional science is a great chess game. It doesn't amount to very much, but you can't say so." New textbook fashions all but did-in the Kittredge version of commonsensical pedagogical science: Kittredge would patrol the classroom—marching, strolling—telling what words meant and what the characters meant. Then paperbacks grew a glut of glossarial aids on every page, so classroom lexicographic science went down the drain, and the man behind the lectern had to resort to other laboratory materials and processes. One odd kind of subversiveness is the sudden outburst of nonscientific passion that can occur in an otherwise ordered world. I remember an authority who for some days had dictated to us all the quarto-folio-theaters-players business on Ben Jonson and then at the end, in an unfilled minute, suddenly declared, with abandon, "I like Ben Jonson, don't you? I hope you do." We were as shaken as if he had suddenly committed an act of indecent exposure.

ROBERT B. HEILMAN

From "I like Jonson" it may seem just a step to the post-1940 aesthetic analysis: from registering a response to explicating the structural conditions that make the response what it has to be, from saying "This is the way it strikes me" to accounting for the way it strikes me (and hence should strike others); from saying "I like Shakespeare" to saying "I find Shakespeare interesting because of his use of wit and irony." In some quarters it will indeed be believed that all we have here is two different versions—an earlier hasty amateur one, and a later more earnest and fancy one—of opting for personal responsiveness rather than impersonal responsibility. But I mention this apparent resemblance, or even identity, of earlier gusto and later widespread practice (psst, the new criticism) only as limbering up for a jump from appearance to reality. For the fact is that this critical movement has not really been an antagonist of the scientific-object credo. On the contrary it has been rather a translation of it into a new idiom: the object—the play—is not so much formed, like a geological entity, by the external pressure of temporal, societal, and theatrical habits, or identified as an imperfect assemblage of fragments to be integrated by editional and typographic evidence, as it is constituted by inner elements whose organic functioning can be so accounted for as to reveal what the play is. The move is not so much from science to feeling as it is from natural to biological science. And it is not biological science of a postmortem kind, for here, Shakespeare is not a cadaver inviting dissection, but a live body in which we try to see processes. The functioning elements may be poetic, actional, personal, conceptual, thematic; one may be predominant, but all may be active.

Though, in my view, this latter organic idiom is a more penetrating and productive one than the geological-pressure concept and its modes, still there is a strong family resemblance between them: for both, the play is an object that, whatever the resistance offered by its complexities, is still solidly there to be placed and understood. The struggle of

8

informed intelligence and imagination with mystery, constant but rarely triumphant, leads us to the gratifications that the play can afford.

II

So much, then, for this account of one pole of Shakespeareanism—a pole surrounded by a very large and diverse continent of Shakespeareans at work—where the Shakespeare play or poem is an object amenable to rational exploration and explanation and suitable for genetic, constitutional, or qualitative analysis. If so much diversity may be found here, what, then, is the opposite pole? To help identify it I hark back to my initial image of the instructor carrying the department record player off to class. This proposes a quite different treatment or use of the bard. But before we try to say what that is, we can note that the instrument-bearing instructor is only the electronic-equipment version of an earlier sound-effects type whom the profession has long known. I allude to the classroom actor who triumphs through a master's voice: less a taker of roles than a vocalist, to whom the usual tribute is "He reads so beautifully." What we get from him, in place of the dramatic object to be apprehended, is an aura of phonetic charm and acoustical seduction, an aural/oral (to borrow from science) hypnosis. Sometimes this laryngeal thespian will be a baritone of such resonance as to spread the benefits of his performance far beyond the immediate scene, especially if he is a devoté of the open-door policy; on the other hand I once knew an open-door man who could be strangely intimidated by a passing colleague and who tended, under the collegial eye, to make a visibly sudden shift from sound to sense. The "great reader," I suppose, is passé, a casualty of the general decay of spellbinding ("elocution") in these states. But the function he performed—ministering to a kind of passive seductibility—is not dead: what was once done by the professor as vocalist or verse choir is now carried

9

on by the professor as disc-jockey or, so to speak, as tape-worm. In place of live sound he offers recorded sound, the one-man cast gives way to the full company, the solo to the chorus, plugged into the wall or transistorized. The class, whether enthralled or asleep, need fear no more the heat of the questioning sun; the solar professor need have only a trace of electrical or mechanical talent. I once heard a colleague say, of this genial impresario, "He can't think of anything to say, so he plays records." Doubtless a naughty way of deflating a classroom performer who, in the eyes of the devoted, may be seen as a very pedagog. Human or pedagodlike, this provisioner of classroom goodies may insist, perhaps even without self-deception, that indeed he can think of something to say but that anything he might say is thin compared with the rich "total experience" of Shakespeare that he wants students to have. Well, why not? Shakespeare was meant to be heard rather than read (though even in Renaissance days, when hearing was more widespread than reading, stationers were never averse to rushing him into print), and to hear a decently spoken English may be desirable for ears corrupted by daily-life sound effects that pass for language. Profitable experiences surely.

But the question rarely asked about Shakespeare-by-ear is the question rarely asked about any proposal to get bright new materials into English studies. Someone says, "We *ought* to have a course in the black humor of the 1960s," or "We *ought* to have a course in English fiction from 1770 to 1800," or "We *ought* to have a course in the stereotyping of females by male novelists from 1860 to 1890." The loud *ought*, apparently deriving fire-power from the passions of the speaker, is mistaken for a valid imperative, and it intimidates. So no one ever asks the indispensable question, "In place of what?" I know I must avoid plunging into dismay at the multiplicity of asseverated, undefended "oughts" which, brought into curricular life at an Asiatic birthrate, have made English studies into a chaos of unrelated and unintegratable options with which the customer can deal only by convenience, preconception, gambling, grapevine, guesswork, and dope sheets on the charitableness and credulity of the faculty emcees. Still this overall state of affairs is the context in which to glance at electronic delights in class. *In place of what?* Though we can add English courses *ad infinitum*, we cannot add hours to the Shakespeare course, and every hour that goes for records and tapes is taken away from orderly discussion. Of course, one might ask another question: how many tapes and records? Once a term? Manageable, perhaps. But this is a little bit like planning to have a cold only once a year. What is catching is not amenable to rational limitation.

Records, in brief, are entertainment and, like productions of the plays, belong in outside-class time. The instructor can usually get people to devote outside-class hours to shows (on boards or screen), fun and games, nonparticipating semiattention uncomplicated by any sense that anything should be learned or known; he cannot get people to devote outside-class hours to critical study left unfinished in the regular class periods. The largest number of hours available in a term really does not allow ample time to get critically into even a few plays. If critical study, however oriented, is not going on steadily, there is little point in holding a Shakespeare class. Now to assert this, and to lift an eyebrow at electronic garnishings as deviations from a valid Shakespeare regimen, may sound pretty humorless and *ancien regime* on the one hand, or pretty panicky and Puritanical on the other—a neo-Grundyism in academic village-life. Yet the literal point that I have been making, though I do not shy away from it, is only part of the story. The electronic substitutions are perhaps more significant on the symbolic side. They are in the spirit of widespread developments that call for some eyebrow lifting.

I spoke a little earlier of "orderly discussion" as though it were a dependable reality of classroom life. But in recent years it has been threatened by a fun-and-games or emotional-volcano style begotten on hopeful innovation, the loose woman of the department, by unthinking good intentions, the perennial stud. Hence orderly discussion has not been in good repute. In its place we have had much welling-up of temperament, ejaculatory and often confrontational. The theme song tends to be, "What does Shakespeare mean to me?" or "How do I feel about or 'relate to' Shakespeare?" When even a rather sober instructor lets graduate students feel that what comes out of them is more important than the shaping of that what by thoughtful commentators, the private response gains primacy. It seems substantial and reliable, a burst of native woodnotes needing no modification or training by judgments that grow out of experience and reflection. We hear of instructors who believe that to provide educational tools and to direct classroom processes smell of "authority" and who prefer to present themselves as opinionless and thoughtless neutrals, or even as eager neophytes, barely monitoring the random ebb and flow of student opinion. Such an instructor fears lest dignity impede education, and so he tells his class, "Just call me Gary." He refers to this palsy sideline passiveness as "letting the students educate each other," thus—if he believes it—mistaking the unaimed crossfire of Roman candles of opinion for genuine illumination. Hence classroom bull sessions, predominantly casual and directionless, and often madly mistaken for exercises in group therapy. Thus we take out our hang-ups rather than take in what might help make things hang together (or hold seances in which student-mediums make the dead Shakespeare behave and speak just like those who call him up).

Relationships appear. Taking in sound effects is the converse of sounding off, listening to records the converse of recording inner rock, receptivity to broadcasting the converse of broadcasting the soul within: the passive and active modes of a style that is auditor-centered rather than Shakespeare-centered. In this there is a strange uncritical egoism, a naive reliance on spontaneous and uncriticized feeling.

We sum up the style when we accept "gut reactions" as a sound source of insight and judgment. Our age has coined this term, and thus it reveals what the general problem in Shakespeare-teaching, as in humanities-teaching, is. Critical thoughtfulness has hard going in an age which likes to route itself by what we now call "vibes" (the common man's version of Housman's spinal shivers). Such direction-finding is of a piece with the astrological dowsing of life, the rush into quickie new Jerusalems, and the dash into instant dimestore mysticisms. Pulsings, tinglings, vibes, rays: tune in, and be divine. The sad cry for "relevance" is a natural happening in this academic massage-parlor: if it doesn't make me feel the same as I feel now in this age, out with it. Hence our shift from the scholarly squares' dance, which encircled Shakespeare in his own times and forbade him to break out, to the new Kottillion, in which the constant blithe improvising movement makes Shakespeare successively the partner of every modern figure, not to mention in every figure from the danse macabre to the watusi and the funky chicken.

In this age it is too easy to apostasize from the true engagement with Shakespeare. In that engagement, the personal impulses are constantly modified by energetic study of a great reality which one neither wholly masters nor is wholly overwhelmed by. The apostasy leads to what one observer has called "the Shakesperience hour." This is what is healthful for neither history nor criticism; it reveals what they have in common, and need to preserve, and resist.

III

In historical terms I have been describing the last swing in a seesaw of styles of dealing with Shakespeare that has gone through two counterbalancings since the seventeenth century. The neoclassic period approached Shakespeare through a set of principles which had, the age felt, absolute validity; it was a Newtonian world which discovered quasi-scientific laws for literature. The age had an objective sense of things; truth was invariable; the problem was to get Shakespeare into conformity with the eternal decencies and rules. Then subjectivity made its first culture-wide claim in the romantic movement, and Shakespeare was mediated through individual personalities who despised rules, found a Shakespeare beyond laws, and enthusiastically intuited the boundless Shakespearean spirit that gave form, life, and brilliance to words and scenes, actions and agents. Next, a rebound to objectivity and science again: but the nineteenth-century version differed from the neoclassical in that it was heuristic rather than judgmental. The new objectivity took its stand not on evaluative principles applied to a given Shakespeare but on documentable facts that, once we got enough of them, would give us a substantive Shakespeare such as we had not had before. Final swing of the seesaw: twentieth-century neoromanticism, the radical subjectivity in which guts and vibes replace a factualism deemed sterile and, voicing the individual soul, declare its responsiveness the only Shakespearean truth. In sum: the two objectivisms (neoclassicism and scientism) had more in common than the two subjectivisms (romanticism and our own neoromanticism): both times the longing for the solid immutable induced, though I think it need not do so, a centrifugal movement and a tendency to settle for peripheral matters. The eighteenth century made a great deal of the unities, poetic justice, decorum; the nineteenth- and twentieth-century objectivism has been enormously concerned with genetics, pressures, congruences, the familiar externalities that for the most part do not open doors to the essential literary object. The subjectivisms are of course rooted in the sensibilities of the observer, but there are sensibilities and sensibilities. A century and a half ago the romantic voices of sensibility were gifted, registering a taste trained by a wide experience in contemporary and various earlier literatures; in our neoromanticism it's anybody's sensibility, and all are equal, except for the disposition in some quarters to count

14

the sensibility of the unread and the untutored as peculiarly adapted to the penetration of literary mysteries, Shakespearean and other. Since all sensibilities are equal, it also follows that anyone can teach Shakespeare.

The role of this shorthand history and these very quick comparisons in an essay on teaching Shakespeare is this: if each of us is aware of these historical swings in attitude, he is less likely to be taken in by the habits or the vogue of the moment and to regard them as final and irresistible. A historic sense will increase his mobility; he will be less a sucker for the bad fashions that represent one of the basic attitudes gone wild. Equally important, he may perceive where he has been coming in on the wide spectrum of possibilities that extends from the objective terminus (Shakespeare as scientific object) to the subjective terminus (Shakespeare as experience, as arena for any sensibility); or, to change the perspective, from the institutionalized Shakespeare transmitted via the received doctrine of the schools, to the divine Shakespeare approachable through private visions entertained in lonely cells. Once the teacher sees that he has options and sees what he has been opting for, he has a clue to the corrections that every good man wants to make. He might well want to find a balanced style, a working practice, a set of procedures that, while they obviously have to gratify his own passions and habits of mind and sense of fitness, can still be publicly defended. (The defensible practice is what we ought all to urge on ourselves, painful as it may seem to a profession saturated by a sense of the inviolability, that is, the nonaccountability, of each pedagogical personality.) "Publicly defended"—before what court? Not, I think, any jury of one's peers; one could simply be at the mercy of current practices. But imagine a "blue ribbon panel" of Shakespeareans who are outstanding and yet who do different things or do things in different ways: how would one look before such a group? To go through such an imaginary exercise may be salutary and, as a quasi "public defense," even more effective than a real hearing, which always tends to stimulate the most stubborn self-justification.

"A balanced style," I have said, and the phrase is not casual. It implies something of a middle ground in which, by having some regard for both the objectivist and subjectivist positions, one may check scientistic and sensibilitarian excesses that equally diminish the literary object. If one starts with an objectivist bias, "middle ground" means, for one thing, making some sort of tentative or pragmatic concession to the "gut reaction." Here and elsewhere I have rebelled against enthroning the intestinal carillon as the *arbiter elegantiarum* (what say your bowels on the bard's vowels?), so for the nonce I am partly admonishing myself. We can reasonably distinguish, however, between the guts as aesthetic supreme court and the guts as the source of an innocent, uncalculated responsiveness that can be utilized. As supreme court or any other kind of court, the guts are a neobarbarous dirty joke. But the gut-born naive responsiveness is all the novice has to start with (it's all we all have to start with in a relationship with a new work), and we may as well concede it to him. The viscera are fallible, but they may be useful—*if* the owner can learn to regard their messages as the start of a journey rather than the end, *if* he can recognize that the rumble in the belly is less likely to be the call of an unspoiled young god than it is to be a symptom of flatulence. Here comes the teacher's hard task of getting the gut-reactor to test his private vibrations against the hard evidence of the text, which may deny his visceral affirmations, modify them, or partly support them. Cleanth Brooks does this better than any teacher I have known; he seems born with a combination of patience, tact, and a sharp eye for an ingenious path from a student's gut reaction to the textual realities. I myself do not do it well; I tend either to be impatient with the gut signals, or, guarding against impatience, to be overly hospitable and to concede too much. The job of leading the student from feeling to the textual sources of feeling, especially to those misread or passed over, is indeed a "hard task"; one cannot be glib about it. Each instructor must find his own way of convincingly demanding, "Be specific. What passages do you have in mind? What about these other passages that have a bearing on what you say?"

What I want most to stress here is the importance of detailed textual work: individual words, lines, and passages, looked at singly (as sound or sense, as bearer of thought or index of character, as image, or metaphor, or symbol) and then brought together as amply as one may be able to do. These construct and thus define and render examinable the literary object to which we attend and which must be the test of all subjective responses. The text, the text, I keep wanting to say, and want to keep saying. In the main, we approach it, as we have to, by reading and discussing it. It is probably worth the time to have students do some reading aloud, painful as this usually is; here the "sound effect" and "experience" methods invoke, not a passive submission with little or haphazard awareness, but an active participation where the attention and effort may make some return to the individual engaged in reading a part or a part of it. I must acknowledge, too, some faith in memorization; for at least some individuals this will salt away a few lines for a lifetime—as touchstones, as sources of pleasure or meaning in some other context, or merely as material for the innocuous pleasure of some oneupquotesmanship. I value examinations which focus on the text: if students know that exams will contain spot passages, they will eye the text with a productive care hardly elicited by the expectation of such a hotline question as, "Do you think Richard II would have lost the throne if he had had Henry Kissinger to mediate with Henry Bolingbroke?" The coming at Shakespeare through precise and concrete, even if limited, elements of the work is one possible remedy for the curse—a stagey word, but I believe dramatically appropriate—the curse of Shakespeare study, as of English studies generally: the topics

ROBERT B. HEILMAN

and questions which are taken to be a "challenge to the imagination" but which, I have come to see, result principally in vaporous generalizations, self-indulgent pronouncements, and, from the cleverer, ingenious exploitation of fragments of Shakespeare as fieldhands on the plantation of the writer's mainly unconscious *amour propre*.

I turn to a more difficult operation: trying to describe a palatable "middle ground" for the determined subjectivist —fearful of "structure"; all for feeling, warm hearts, spontaneous responses, excitement, outflight of inpassion (agenbyt of inwit sentimentalized), "experience," group seances, circles of comforting togetherness; trying to combine ejaculation with communion, perhaps hand on hand or bottoms on floor (the indoors great earth mother). The instructor who devises such a theater may simply be beyond salvation. But one has to hope that in time the instructor may see the folly of this laboriously contrived dream of "ease and naturalness." The folly lies in a misconception of the nature of classroom life. The big problem is to get conductors of classrooms to recognize that classroom procedures are by nature "unnatural," and necessarily so—artificial, structured, fragmented or partial, postponing an overall, deep, rounded responsiveness. I try to get classes themselves to understand this from the beginning: what we are doing here is studying, not reading as we want to; carefully taking apart and partly putting together, not immediately mastering a whole. A class is not a theater; it cannot be and should not be. Studying a play cannot be like seeing it on the stage (or hearing it on a disc or tape). It cannot be immediately satisfying, gratifying, fulfilling as can be the whole or finished play. In class we stop, focus, repeat, go back, examine and reexamine, look about, look under, search, test, give up, start over: everything that we cannot do in a theater. What we do in a class is "unnatural" and "abnormal"—*if*, that is, the process is compared with seeing a play, or even with an ordinary reading of it. But what we do in a class is not final; it is not an objective pursued for

18

its own sake. To risk an analogy, the unnaturalness and abnormality of the classroom are like those of the medical examining room or the medical regimen. What goes on in these is, by the standards of ordinary active life, very strange, discontinuous, artificial; one is painfully in oneself rather than savingly carried out of oneself by the narcotizing routines or the stimulating special occasions of existence. But the specialized, uncomfortable, interruptive concentration of the medical experience is only an interlude and a prelude; it lasts only a limited time; and we expect it to lead to a better and fuller normal living. Likewise the classroom process, which I have willingly, if riskily, called "unnatural" and "abnormal": it is temporary, it takes only a small part of life, and, above all things, *it is not an end in itself but a means to an end.* Let's omit the grand ends sometimes claimed for humanistic education and assert only one: the ampler, happier, more satisfying, more gratifying subsequent experience of plays as wholes, whether read, listened to, or seen on stage. In class we analyze, dissect, use microscopes, laboriously trace out connections, and do all other grubby, painstaking, contrived tasks by which we learn; the payoff is the more meaningful *spontaneous* entry into the total life of the play when we are decently prepared for it as art—not wholly shorn of its mystery, but still vastly more accessible because of our trained grasp, through a fully alerted imagination, of the methods it uses and the substance the methods lead us to. (All right, any sick humor that crops up may be to the point. The medical interlude, we know, is not always followed by "better and fuller normal living." Likewise the classroom may inadvertently be a clinic revealing incurable cases of ignorance, irreversible addictions, and congenital defects of mind and imagination.)

What the feelie-gutborne-experience school tries to do, then, is to bypass the training and leap directly into the rewards of training. It tries to substitute the ultimate experience for the indispensable preexperience, the major course

ROBERT B. HEILMAN

for the prerequisite. This kind of classroom adventurism flatters the novice, but, as he cannot know, guarantees that he will remain a novice for life. Or to change the figure: premature snatches at heaven usually land the snatcher in another place.

IV

For both the native and a converted objectivist, if there be any of the latter, there are problems to which one does not find easy answers. Of course, the kind of objectivist whom I have called "geological" is wholly free from one problem: he will never run out of material in the field of formative pressures. Always, available for tapping, there will be a mountain of Elizabethan and Jacobean pamphlets and manuals on ecclesiastical doings, royal expenses, archery techniques, Jesuit-detecting, hog-feeding, corn pathology, farriery, and Italian crime; pre- or post-doctoral diggers can mine this range indefinitely (exhausting this natural resource seems improbable) and show how such matters pushed Shakespeare into meaning what they now reveal he has to mean. I present that cheery note with pleasure. But whether one's bent be geological (external forces as primary) or biological (internal structure as primary), there will always be the problem of the relationship between the primary literature that we teach and the "literature" that grows in mad luxuriance in "the field." Here the two extreme options have built-in difficulties. If we read only the literature that Shakespeare wrote, we have to teach entirely by the seat of our pants, and the risk is that the equipment, though tailored by a good Ph.D. outfitter, won't be good enough: sudden holes in the britches. But if we try to read all the "literature," we will have precious little time left for the literature. (Reminder: my initial image of the man who for this reason felt he couldn't teach Shakespeare.) It may encourage us to know that an eminent Shakespearean has said that nine-tenths of Shakespearean "literature" is junk, and that, if it were all tossed into the ocean, the profession would be better off. But alas, we don't know what the savable and saving one-tenth is. Anyway, even the one-tenth is gargantuan, and it grows hyperkinetically. The man of conscience needs help; even if he does steady, unabated sampling, he can't be sure he's getting much of what he ought to be getting. The recent system of abstracts acknowledges the problem, and the indefatigable many-sided *Shakespeare Newsletter* tries to compress volumes of discourse into manageable thumbnail sketches.

I propose that the art of annotated bibliography, so assiduously practiced as a benevolent and protective aid for the order of researchers, be applied with equal thoroughness in the teaching domain. There would, however, be one big difference: for researchers, the compiler includes everything; for teachers, he should exclude as much as possible. We could have a Committee on Materials for Teaching Shakespeare, or, maybe better, a single dévot should make a lifetime operation of this (like a good-eating guide, who samples all spots and tells us where to go for what). His job is not to spread out over the landscape a frightening wilderness of 10,000 titles, but to inspect them, tell what they say, systematize them, rank them, and get rid of most of them (as valueless for teaching purposes). He could use an approach something like this: here are several basic books on Shakespeare that the teacher could profit from, here are one or two key works on the different types and periods, here are a few titles (maybe books, but mostly articles) on individual plays; this is the kind of thing that they say, and that the teacher might get from them. Aside from that, he would tell what's in a lot of other secondaries that the teacher would not have time, and should not try to find time, to read for himself, and what they might be good for in this or that pedagogical approach. He should get out a new edition of his basic Guide every three or five years; he should probably limit himself to a set number of "recommended titles" to force himself to make an excision for each new recommended addition and thus to protect himself against the vampire of inclusiveness. Such a work might be one solution to the menacing problem of the "literature."

Within the objectivist fold, classroom options are numerous; though one might endeavor to rank these, he would hardly report his own doings as imitable, for a sense of his own failures would curb the exporter's impulse. Presumably each teacher will have a general plan of what ought to be accomplished; as for the details, he will probably depend somewhat on his personal studies. If so, he ought to cultivate a tough sense of whether private preoccupations make defensible public occupations in the classroom (oh, the esoteric Ph.D. subjects that blossom forth anew, with April cruelty, in honors seminars, special topics courses, and graduate seminars!). For some years I studied the structural role of imagery in plays; this can lead to some good things in class—at least it means sticking to detailed textual evidence—but a side-effect may be an underemphasis on actional structure. More recently I have been interested in problems of genre—in objective criteria for generic forms, and in looking at plays in the light of these criteria. The risk here is that explorations of different tendencies in a play may be taken for taxonomic drills or lessons in pigeonhole markmanship. Nevertheless, some attention to generic modes seems a workable classroom means of pulling plays together; this is especially true when Shakespeare employs notably diverse kinds of effect—in *Comedy of Errors* and *Taming of the Shrew*, for instance, complicating the basically farcical with the romantic versions of experience, the mechanical with different kinds of the emotional, and, conversely, in *Cymbeline* suddenly injecting the farcical into the apparently disastrous. Such consideration of the modal may work better with lesser plays, with their lesser degrees of oneness; yet surely *Macbeth* can be seen as an extraordinary portrait of a man who flees from self-recognition—a key event in tragedy—and takes refuge in a nontragic self-fortification: "stonewalling" it to the end. But granted, generic assessment can drift into labeling. In thus sketching

certain actual or possible misfirings of two classroom procedures based on my own interests, I am trying to make
concrete the need of that self-monitoring which every Shakespeare teacher ought to accept as a primary obligation.

Other problems keep floating into view. When we say that
Shakespeare is most studied and least read, do we impute
another failure to the teaching? Maybe, in a contrary view,
we should simply rejoice that, in view of our national habits,
it's lucky he's taught as much as he is, and should forget
about the reading. Maybe Shakespeare is a secular analogue
to religion as it is generally known among us: respected
in the abstract (except for those bold nay-sayers), ritually
practiced on Sunday, and otherwise left in peace, not exact-
ing intense attachment, but vaguely felt to be, in some not
really definable way, quite good for us. By a British army
officer whom I once got to know, Shakespeare was, on the
contrary, most read and least studied; my friend was always
easily and naturally doing Shakespeare himself, and clearly
my paperback edition of one play seemed to him, courteous
as he was about a presentation copy, a supererogatory tool-
kit. What does Sandhurst have that West Point doesn't?
Or what clientele does it draw on that West Point doesn't?
Do these schools symbolize indefinable national differences?
Or was my friend exceptional in the British scene? Maybe,
if Shakespeare isn't read, the nonreading only reflects an
extension into adult life of national student habits. One of
these is the obsessive fear of reading more than is required;
if six plays are on the list, and the student mistakenly reads
a seventh, he feels cheated and defeated and is fair game for
the taunts of his peers.

> The world's unsunny;
> I need a crutch;
> I paid my money,
>   But I read too much.

When this everyman-as-undergraduate shifts from econom-
ics to aesthetics, he says that Shakespeare is "sarcastic" when
he means "comic" or "ironic" or "unillusioned" or "despair-

ing." Can we ever hope to go beyond dictionary exercises? Or if we let that dreary headliner get into the course offerings—"Sexism in Shakespeare and in Shakespeare Criticism and Instruction"—we know that it will be a moneymaker: once again the lure of the simple easy-to-grasp melodrama of good and evil.

V

Of all the problems in Shakespeare-teaching that we might talk about, the last one I want to talk about is that we probably talk about teaching too much. In one sense it is a Dantesque penance for an ancestral habit of not talking about it at all (the unto-the-third-and-fourth-generation principle). Doubtless in some distant past, now and then, here and there, teaching came in a poor second to research and writing; some instructors made teachers in general vulnerable by indifference, vanity, and arrogance in the classroom, and thus provided grounds for grumbling. But such past misdeeds never had the magnitude which would explain, much less justify, the turnabout from instructor as divinity to instructor as drudge or lackey. I do not think the latter terms are too strong: what they image is our anxious sense of serving a master that has to be pleased, placated, on his/her own terms. It is this disturbing sense of the student body as a kind of electorate, I believe, that accounts largely for the almost obsessive profession-wide huddling—conferring, inquiring, soul-searching, guilt-feeling, proposing, and sawdust-trail-hitting—about teaching. To shift the metaphor, we talk principles, but the underlying issue is promotion and sales: how win, or at least appease, the public? I hasten to add that I am in no sense debunking or chastising; I mean merely to describe, and to register regret. If we were once casual and thoughtless about teaching, we are now overly self-conscious; there is a burdensome excess of how-to-do-it blueprinting and plan-making. One side effect of this, incidentally, is a decline of the ease and spontaneity which are very important in all teaching.

Academic courtship of a public reflects, in part, a general situation in the culture. Commenting on magazines that seek to attract youthful subscribers in larger numbers, the essayist Joseph Epstein asks whether this desire is not produced by a culture "preternaturally concerned with the young." In a sense we cannot separate ourselves from a society "preternaturally concerned with the young." But one of our functions is the criticism of society, and we may justly turn a skeptical eye on this excess of anxious parental hovering. Maybe all we need to do is talk less about myriad pedagogical adjustments to the young and get on with the business, assuming that, granted conscience and knowledge in the teacher, plus a moderate self-awareness and the experience for which there is no substitute, the teaching gets done. It would also be reasonable to go a step further and say that the teaching gets done *if* the students are open to and ready for it. I count it no very cynical asperity to assert —though we hesitate to assert it lest we seem only to be grousing in ancient academic style—that large numbers of them are not open to it and ready for it. (How grateful most of us are to find in our class a thirty-five-year-old woman who is coming back to complete an interrupted education, now doubly ready for, open to, and equipped by experience for a much better reading of literature.) What is worse, in recent years the not-open and the not-ready have come into a new sense of power—they have learned to con and to intimidate—to say what teaching should be, and to distribute rewards when it conforms to their predilections or punishments when it does not (to have a hand in promotion, in tenure, and even in appointment). From Germany and South America we hear harrowing tales of the impact of "student power" on universities. The point is that we better keep all this in mind and see whether it has not inflated the agonizing over teaching. I have no easy answers. One thing is sure: the situation will not be cured or even improved by thinking up new pedagogical gimmicks, carving up the literary materials into new and "more attractive course offerings," and debasing the grading system.

We cannot forget this larger context when we talk about teaching Shakespeare. Fortunately, Shakespeare continues to seem charismatic and almost magical and therefore to exact respect, and perhaps a touch of reverence, even from those "not open to and ready for" a substantial academic regimen. Further, the plays are not so easy as some literary materials to cut up and reassemble in chic, topical, hot-headline course offerings. These advantages are not ineradicable, however, and we can easily squander them if we decide that we ought to listen to voices that identify the true with the new, or first-rate materials with cut-rate prices. All the dangers are rooted in the recent academic sad fad: adjusting the goods to customer demand or foolish faculty fancies. Though I do not really know how to survive the danger, I do know that all survival courses are tough. And I do know that our survival depends on our not losing sight of the essential principle that Shakespeare does not answer to the expectation and feeling and consciousness of the public.

If he has any effect at all, he changes expectations and feelings and consciousness.

TWO

SHAKESPEARE INFERRED

JOHN W. VELZ

ONE difficulty of teaching Shakespeare is epitomized in the chastening question that crosses my mind at the beginning of each semester: "How can I ever say it all to them in fifteen weeks?" None of us ever does, of course, say it all to them; we are defeated by riches: Shakespeare's creative use of inherited (and his own invented) genres, his linguistic and prosodic subtlety, his responses to an array of intellectual backgrounds, medieval, classical, and humanist, his complex and developing dramaturgy. To know that there is more to the Shakespeare canon that we can fully impart—in a semester or in a lifetime—is to be aware that the plays and poems are worth the effort we put into teaching them. But the sense of frustration lingers. Over the years I have worked out some ways of encouraging students to infer a part of what I do not have time or talent to do justice to in lectures or class discussions; perhaps some of this illative pedagogy will seem usable to others.

I

Selection and arrangement of materials can be a heuristic strategy, as pedagogical tacticians have known since the time of Socrates. In a one-semester undergraduate Shakespeare survey I have to come to count on the arrangement of the syllabus itself to suggest Shakespeare's thematic concerns, his sense of genre, and his growth in artistic complexity, whether in characterization, prosody, dramaturgy, or structural design. The curriculum speaks most plainly when it juxtaposes early and late attempts at the same materials. *The Comedy of Errors* and *Pericles* are both plays in which children are restored to their parents and the parents themselves are reunited in an Ephesian religious setting, both plays in which patience in an absurd world is the harmonious antithesis of madness, plays in which shipwreck and identity are thematic. To recognize in the later play Shakespeare's reversion to materials he had worked with less graciously, less profoundly, some twenty years before is to discover something about the genres of New Comedy and Romance, to be given a context in which to specify by contrast the maturity of the mature Shakespeare, to see that the Shakespeare canon has what J. M. Nosworthy once called "integrity,"[1] and perhaps to watch Shakespeare judging his own early work by implication when he makes a later try at the same materials.[2]

Other pairings of the kind come immediately to mind. *Errors* makes an equally good companion to *Twelfth Night*, sharing with it twins, shipwreck, the mistaken giving of a purse of money, and an alien treated as an enemy of the state by a threatening duke. John Manningham, who saw *Twelfth Night* in 1601, recognized right away Shakespeare's debt to his earlier play and to the ultimate source in Plautus.[3] The roundness of Viola by contrast with Luciana's flatness will readily call attention to itself, suggesting how far Shakespeare had transcended by 1601 the stereotypical characterization of New Comedy. Then there is the familiar yoking of *A Midsummer Night's Dream* and *The Tempest* as plays about magic and a providential supernature, about the contrast between rational sprite and earthbound beast-man; both plays multiply analogically related plots to enforce a theme.

[1] "The Integrity of Shakespeare: Illustrated from *Cymbeline*," *Shakespeare Survey* 8 (1955), 52-56.

[2] My interest in Shakespeare's implicit self-criticism goes back to 1964 and Virgil K. Whitaker's stimulating paper, "Shakespeare's Rough Drafts," at the Marlowe-Shakespeare Festival at Rice University.

[3] See E. K. Chambers, *The Shakspere Allusion-Book* (London: Oxford Univ. Press, 1932), I, 98.

A less obvious juxtaposition but an even more seminal one places *Measure for Measure* immediately after *Romeo and Juliet*. The two plays are responses in different keys to the same paradoxical equivalence of clandestine love and death. It is clear enough that such an implied comparison is justifiable: Shakespeare seems to have had the earlier play on his mind (if only subconsciously) when in *Measure for Measure* he chose "Juliet" as a name for a young woman who consummates her love secretly and "Escalus" as a name for a governor who alternates between leniency and rigor as he copes with a disordered society. The two plays juxtaposed ask the students to ask themselves serious questions, these for two instances: How much of the difference between the earlier tragic resolution and the later comic resolution is to be traced to the competence of Friar Lodowick by contrast with the well-intentioned fumbling of Friar Lawrence? How may we account for the fact that *Measure for Measure* is darker in tone than *Romeo and Juliet* despite its telos of forgiveness and restitution—what, indeed, does tone have to do with genre here (or generally)?

A still more rewarding (less paradoxical) instance is a juxtaposition of *Richard III* with *Macbeth* as two versions of tyrant drama, both making use of infanticide (the murder of the princes in the Tower comes in Act IV, just the place where Shakespeare later elects to introduce the slaughter of Macduff's pretty chickens), both making use of eschatological imagery, both focusing moral worth in an antagonist who emerges into prominence only late in the action, both emphasizing the progressive isolation of the villain-hero, both inverting in Act V morally significant imagery introduced in Act I.[4] That the plays are truly comparable is suggested by the fact that the protagonists

---

4 In *Macbeth* the sere and yellow leaf and the unnaturally moving forest invert the imagery of planting and growth that Act I introduces; in *Richard III* Richmond speaks of fecundity and lineage in Act V, inverting Richard's talk of winter and unnatural parturition in the soliloquy that opens the play.

select the same metaphor when they muse beyond the half-way point in each play on the truth that there is no turning back from a life of crime:

> *Ric.* Uncertain way of gain! But I am in
> So far in blood that sin will pluck on sin.
>
> (IV.ii.63-64)
>
> *Mac.*   I am in blood
> Stepp'd in so far that, should I wade no more,
> Returning were as tedious as go o'er.
>
> (III.iv.135-37)

By juxtaposing *Macbeth* and *Richard III* students see these similarities, but they also can quickly be made to recognize the differences—the absence of a real counterpart in *Richard III* to the roles of Lady Macbeth and Banquo as foils to Macbeth, Macbeth's gradual yielding to temptation by contrast with Richard's decisive commitment to evil at the outset, the prominence of introspection in Macbeth and the contrasting direct self-revelation of Richard, the prevalence of verbal irony in *Richard III* and of dramatic irony in *Macbeth*. These contrasts are best defined in generic terms —the earlier play is a melodrama, the later one a tragedy. To teach genre in this way, empirically, as it were, is to put students in a position like that of an audience: generic distinctions are apperceived, not imposed by authoritative fiat.

One further juxtaposition can illustrate the possibilities for inferential learning when more than two exemplars are to be related to an informing principle, thematic or generic. *Much Ado About Nothing, Cymbeline,* and *The Winter's Tale* are a trio of interesting variations on a plot in which a jealous man's erroneous suspicions cause a "death" for his wife/fiancée that is as illusory as her putative infidelity was. In each case (Friar Francis, Pisanio, Paulina) benevolent competence or unrewarded service (or both) contrives the apparent death as a means to anagnorisis and penitence for the gullible and unjust husband/groom. If *Othello* is inserted in the grouping (either chronologically or *ex post facto*), students will be prepared to infer a tragic syndrome that, though it goes deeper, begins perhaps with the absence of a benevolent manipulator[5] and with the implications of Desdemona's momentary resuscitation in V.ii—life at this moment in *Othello* is an illusion as death is in the other three plays. A class may go on enriched by what now is becoming a Shakespearean tragicomic convention and its tragic inversion to the bitter scene in which Lear believes mistakenly that Cordelia is reviving. To take the four or five plays together as suggested here is to arrange exemplars of symbolic structures that range broadly across the canon and therefore to engage in expository criticism in the guise of curriculum design; more exactly—and better—it is to make heuristic critics of serious students, placing them where they must think of the canon as Wilson Knight thought of it in *The Shakespearian Tempest* or as Northrop Frye thought of it in *A Natural Perspective* or in *Fools of Time*. Pedagogy and literary criticism are at an interface in such teaching: the curriculum itself contributes to the stimulation of consciousness and to the discrimination of elements in a pattern of replications.

II

The curriculum that teaches by juxtaposition works very well in drama-as-a-genre courses. In spring 1975, for example, I began with the juxtaposition of *Richard III* and *Macbeth* suggested above in an honors course called "Tragedy, Shakespeare to Arthur Miller" in which the emphasis fell on exemplification of dramaturgical possibilities and variations on such tragic themes as exploitation and perversion. (The course employed juxtaposition repeatedly; *inter*

---

[5] It may be worth recalling the contrast suggested above between the ineffectual benevolence of Friar Lawrence and the competent providence represented by Friar Lodowick.

alia the students looked backward at Marlowe's *Doctor Faustus* as they wrote about Goethe's *Faust I*.) I have long felt that despite the linguistic problems Shakespeare poses it is appropriate to teach him also to lower-division students as an introduction to drama,[6] and it is in an introductory course, where perspective, consciousness, and sensibility are the desired ends, that juxtaposition works most effectively.

As the examples of section I above may suggest, the method can also be made to work well in an upper-division Shakespeare survey—indeed I have sometimes used it there. But another approach, grouping plays chronologically by genres, is more effective in giving intermediate or advanced students a comprehensive view of the Shakespeare canon, at the same time encouraging subtle distinctions within genres and emphasizing Shakespeare's gradual development as a dramatist. In this alternative arrangement, the emphasis falls crisply on genre, on Shakespeare's growth in capacity to realize the possibilities of a dramatic form, where in the juxtapositional approach emphasis falls on the replication of themes in various tones and various forms. The implicit teaching in a developmentally arranged course is more overt than in the case of subliminal juxtapositions, but arrangement in such a course is nevertheless still an invitation to perception. Moreover, arranging the canon developmentally by genres does not preclude juxtapositions that shock students into recognition.

Allotting a week to each play in a fifteen-week term, I prefer to follow five comedies with five histories and five tragedies, each group arranged chronologically. It has seemed to me best to take the comedies first not because they are more easily talked about[7] but because it is apparent

---

[6] At the University of Texas a graduate program to prepare teachers for community and junior colleges is now being developed—it is planned that methods of teaching Shakespeare will be an integral part of the curriculum.

[7] They are not, actually, as is suggested by the paucity of critical books on the comedies in contrast to the plethora of readings of the tragedies.

in comedy what Shakespeare was beginning from. The argument still goes on about whether Shakespeare himself invented the English history play, and the backgrounds of Shakespearean tragedy are still being sketched;[8] but in comedy it is pretty clear what Shakespeare inherited and synthesized into the various subgenres (romantic comedy, problem comedy, dramatic romance) that are thought of as his special achievements.[9] Any given semester, therefore, is likely to begin with *The Comedy of Errors* (which is structurally a predecessor of framed comedies like *A Midsummer Night's Dream* and *As You Like It*) or *The Taming of the Shrew* (an example of skillful multiple plotting), proceed to *Dream* or *The Merchant of Venice* (also a fine example of skillful multiple plotting), from there to *As You Like It* or *Twelfth Night*, on to *Measure for Measure* or *All's Well*, and then to *The Tempest* or *The Winter's Tale*.

After this developmentally arranged set of generic variations (admittedly a mere skeleton), the curriculum returns to Shakespeare's early work with *Richard III* (or *1 Henry VI*, which is a different kind of history play, more epic than dramatic in design), and moves from there to *Richard II*, to *1* or *2 Henry IV*, to *Henry V* (another and more successful attempt to couch an epic conception in dramatic form), and then to *Henry VIII*. The presentation of *Henry VIII* largely

[8] In 1967 J.M.R. Margeson proposed Mystery cycles, more often thought of as divine comedies, as a contributor to the Elizabethan sense of the tragic in drama. See *The Origins of English Tragedy* (Toronto: Univ. of Toronto Press, 1967), ch. I. More light may remain to be thrown on Ovid's stylized horror as a background to tragedy, though Eugene Waith mapped the ground in "The Metamorphosis of Violence in *Titus Andronicus*," *Shakespeare Survey* 19 (1957), 39-49. The real meaning of Seneca to the Elizabethans is still being debated.

[9] See Leo Salingar, *Shakespeare and the Traditions of Comedy* (Cambridge: Cambridge Univ. Press, 1974) for the backgrounds. Salingar proposes that there was a late-medieval tradition of staged romance; otherwise his book offers new insights on a familiar set of backgrounds: New Comedy, Italian comedy, narrative romance. See Northrop Frye, "The Argument of Comedy," *English Institute Essays 1948* (New York: Columbia Univ. Press, 1949), pp. 58-73.

ignores the authorship arguments and focuses on the interesting relation the play bears to *Richard III*; Buckingham
sees his *casus* in *Henry VIII* Act II as a bitter parallel to
his father's, portrayed in Acts IV and V of *Richard III*, and
the structure of the later play up through Act III is closely
modeled on that of *Richard III*. *Henry VIII* also is much
like *The Winter's Tale* (a wife on trial for her marriage, the
birth of a new and redeeming generation, loyalty and service
as sustaining virtues, tableau, pageant, and moral icon as
meaningful texture); therefore *Henry VIII* makes a good
play to teach two-thirds of the way through a Shakespeare
survey course as a focal point, thematically retrospective
and generically eclectic.

This second quintet of plays is at least as provocative and
as varied as the first, since there seems good ground for
arguing that Shakespeare never settled comfortably on a
single generic conception of the history play any more
than he settled on a single kind of comedy. Some of his
plays on English history are tragic, looking back, for instance, to Marlowe's *Edward II*, as *Richard II* does, or to
de casibus narrative and the tragic morality, as *Richard III*
does. Others are comic: the *Henry IV* plays and *Henry V*
suggest a salvific pattern for a son thought (*only* thought)
to be a prodigal; *Henry V* concludes with a marriage that
students will recognize as an analogue to the denouement
marriages of the romantic comedies they'll have read earlier
in the term; and *Henry VIII* (as the remarks above on its
affinity both to *Richard III* and to *The Winter's Tale* may
suggest) is tragicomic in conception, working from the tragic
falls of the first three acts around a moral hinge to the
festivitas and fertility and reconciliation of the last two acts.
The generic eclecticism of Shakespeare's English history
plays makes them a good bridge between the comedies and
the tragedies.

It has often worked well to take *Romeo and Juliet* and
Julius Caesar as the first two of the five tragedies. *Romeo
and Juliet* is in form a romantic comedy of the Terentian

34

sort warped into tragedy,[10] and the students will recognize for themselves that Old Capulet is a stock father-of-the-heroine from the comedies they know and that the mooning pre-Juliet Romeo is an echo of the mooning Lucentios, Orsinos, and Orlandos of the early weeks of the semester. *Julius Caesar* is a Janus-play, looking back to the form of the histories Shakespeare was writing in the 1590s[11] and ahead to the tragedy of introspection and moral dilemma of his Jacobean period.[12] Another advantage to selecting *Julius Caesar* as one of the five tragedies is that late among their fifteen plays the students ought to read one that they studied in high school; without a word from the teacher they are made forcibly aware of how far their sensibilities have ripened since tenth grade if they read *Caesar* after studying eleven or twelve other Shakespearean plays.

And where after that? It is extraordinarily difficult to choose. *Hamlet*, of course, makes its own claims, not least of which is that it, too, is a Janus-play, looking back to vendetta tragedy and ahead to subtler moral issues; I nearly always teach it when *Caesar* is omitted. *Othello* contains in its first act a telescoped romantic comedy (like the first three acts of *Romeo and Juliet*). *King Lear* commends itself to illative purposes in that the questions it raises about kingship and personal virtue, about ceremony and suffering, are analogues at a deeper and more anguishing tragic level to what students will have seen repeatedly in the English history plays (abdication in *Richard II*, the King as scapegoat in *Henry V*, true kingship as opposed to mere pomp in *Richard II*, *Henry V*, and *Henry VIII*). *Macbeth* can claim

[10] I have argued this generic approach to *Romeo and Juliet* in a recently completed essay called "Shakespeare's Comitragedy."

[11] See Moody E. Prior, "The Search for a Hero in *Julius Caesar*," *Renaissance Drama*, n.s. 2 (1969), 81-101; John W. Velz, "Episodic Structure in Four Tudor Plays: A Virtue of Necessity," *Comparative Drama* 6 (1972), 87-102.

[12] See G. Wilson Knight, "Brutus and Macbeth," *The Wheel of Fire* (1930; rpt. London: Methuen, 1949), 120-39; Northrop Frye, *Fools of Time* (New York: Oxford Univ. Press, 1967), p. 27ff.

the advantage of implicit comparison to *Richard III* discussed above, and since it was for many years in the high
school curriculum I often in the past have done the play in
semesters when I bypassed *Julius Caesar*. An argument for
Coriolanus proposes that it inverts the usual syndrome of
Shakespeare's political tragedies, moving as it does from war
to civic affairs, not as the others move from politics to violence; moreover, Coriolanus represents a hero out of epic
(a Turnus or an Achilles, invincible but vulnerable), and
the students who have seen Henry V as an epic hero[13] may
respond to this tragic variation. Finally, there is *Antony and
Cleopatra*, which Maynard Mack has spoken of as a tragedy
of sunlight to be contrasted with *Macbeth* and *Lear*, tragedies of murky darkness and grotesque distortion.[14] *Antony
and Cleopatra* also relates to the last plays in its supple and
complex prosody and its paradoxical thematic tension between decadence and fertility. And, of course, a grouping
that begins with *Romeo and Juliet* may fittingly end with
another tragedy of *Liebestod*.

The riches to choose among in Shakespearean tragedy
have encouraged my Department to offer an advanced
Shakespeare course in the tragedies only (including the
tragic English histories); when I teach it I apply, *mutatis
mutandis*, the principles of curriculum design suggested in
this section for comprehensive Shakespeare surveys.

III

There is more to heuristic pedagogy than curriculum arrangement, obviously, important as arrangement is.[15] Examinations, for example, can do as much implicit teaching as

[13] See J. H. Walter's commentary on Henry V as Aeneas in the introduction to the Arden edition of *Henry V* (1954), pp. xxiii-xxxii.

[14] See his introduction to the Pelican edition of the play.

[15] Conversely, there is more to Shakespeare (and to curriculum design) than heuristic pedagogy—the reasons given above for selecting one
or another play are only a part of the rationale. No one must think
I value *Othello* only or primarily for its first act or *Lear* only or primarily for its tacit echoes of Shakespeare's English histories.

overt measuring if they are calculated to do it—leading students just beyond the periphery of what has been overtly codified and specified in class to what remains to be perceived and synthesized. Examinations of this kind are difficult to devise; I am usually uncertain of having done a good job "this time," transgressing the borders of what has been mapped in class enough to challenge without confusing or merely frightening them. The examiner may be on trial at least as much as the students; it is not a good idea to give "pedagogical" examinations unless the class is large enough to offer assurance that the exam is at fault in a given case, not the students.

Because there is anxiety enough in an assault on what they half-know to make adrenalin flow, I prefer to minimize memory by giving an open-book, open-notes exam if I have had other means (quizzes, class discussion) of determining that students have read the plays closely and remember them well. Then the questions ask the students to test a proposition they have not encountered before by holding it up to evidence that they themselves will provide. To make the propositions immediate and provocative I often invent a quotation, as in the question on anagnorisis below. The examination ought to follow the intellectual current the curriculum has taken, proposing juxtaposition (as in the question on *The Merchant of Venice*, *Cymbeline*, and *The Taming of the Shrew* below) or ranging across a group of plays, generalizing about characters, themes, genres, or dramaturgical strategies, sometimes developmentally (as in the anagnorisis question below). Designed in this way the examination forces students to articulate the sort of relationship they have only apperceived before and therefore the examination serves doubly as pedagogy: it holds one last set of discoveries to be made and it asks that once made they be articulated (and therefore shaped), perhaps for some students the first of the many apperceptions of the semester to be fully examined, judiciously weighed, clearly expressed.

The sample questions are given here with some hesitation,

37

partly because it seems probable that this approach is a common one and partly because the questions cannot in themselves convey the heuristic possibilities to someone who has not witnessed the course approaching but not quite embracing the intellectual territory the question surveys. Nevertheless at the risk of being nugatory I offer these typical questions.

1.   All that glisters is not gold,
        Often have you heard that told;
        Many a man his life hath sold
        But my outside to behold.

Apply this quotation from *The Merchant of Venice* (II.vii.65-68), either to *Cymbeline* or to *The Taming of the Shrew*; analyze the play you choose to show to what extent one might consider the quotation a valid statement about the meaning of that play.

2. Henry VIII and Prospero both learn lessons about governing properly. Specify and discuss the lessons each man learns to show that they are themes presented (in one form or another) in one or more of the history plays Shakespeare wrote in the 1590s.

3. "The tragic heroes of Shakespeare's plays before *Hamlet* do not experience a real anagnorisis; they meet their ends no wiser than when they began a tragic course."

Is this statement true, or should it be challenged or modified? What sort of wisdom does anagnorisis, when it comes, afford a tragic hero? Is it true, as this quotation implies, that *all* the heroes of Shakespeare's *later* tragedies experience anagnorisis?

Examinations have been spoken of here as terminal discovery. Preliminary discovery is at least equally important; unless the cast of mind necessary to critical perception can be inculcated at the outset, all the insights a student gains will be second hand and prescriptive. I try to embody discovery in the short exercises I assign in the early weeks of any undergraduate Shakespeare semester. Working papers are sets of ten or a dozen specific and interrelated short-answer questions contrived to make students discover and marshal the evidence for an interpretation which they intuit, since it is never specified in the exercise itself.

A working paper demands brief and very specific factual answers; no opinions, elaborations, or generalizations are admissible. I emphasize the pedagogical and minimize the judgmental by grading them only $\sqrt{-}$, $\sqrt{}$, $\sqrt{+}$, telling students these grades "don't count," and stressing that getting help defeats the whole benefit to them. They are urged to take them seriously, but not too seriously—to spend no more than an hour on a working paper once the play has been read. The number of working papers at the beginning of a semester is flexible; we go on to conventional critical papers once most of the class has caught the intellectual drift and can easily turn in a $\sqrt{+}$ paper.

The purpose of working papers is not only to encourage inference but also to make students think evidentially—students are manipulated into inducing a critical thesis from the data of the play, though they are not asked to state that thesis in the exercise.[16] The empirical posture forced on them is an appropriate posture for literary criticism, which at its best is inductive and heuristic.

Working papers also offer incidental benefits. The full-fledged papers that a class writes later in the semester are more likely to be evidential and substantive if they are preceded early in the course by two or three working papers on other plays, other theses. Then, too, students enjoy the exercises—they are limited, manageable, and moreover a taste of the treasure hunt is involved in the search for evidence and the implicit guesswork about "what the teacher is up to this time." Class discussion is usually lively the day a working paper is due, since everyone has an answer (and a thesis, too, perhaps) ready to hand. Some years of using working papers have persuaded me entirely that they are worth the effort it takes to make them out.

[16] It will readily be seen that working papers can be used in any literature course in which the emphasis falls on analysis.

It is not so easy to make a useful working paper as one might think. The virtue lies in the constellation of the questions around the controlling but never explicit thesis, and the challenge is to encourage the students to jump to that thesis, but not too readily. It was a revealing experience for me one semester in an honors Shakespeare class to ask the students to devise working papers themselves after they had shown in two or three working papers that they all had √+ ability. The results were surprising; the class could leap with assurance to the right conclusion when I precontrived it but they were unable to devise questions that would indirectly force me to think *their* thoughts. Perhaps the gap between the roles of student and teacher is suggested here; certainly the experiment was a revelation to me—though not the revelation each student was supposed to force on me.

The two working papers given here may illustrate the principles. The one on *The Merchant of Venice* came from an early week in a general Shakespeare survey and led in subsequent class discussion to a questioning of the nineteenth-century view that this is Shylock's play which ought to end when he departs the action. The *Julius Caesar* paper is from the second week of an upper-division course in Shakespeare's tragedies; it is based on a set of theses to be found in an interpretation I once made of the play.[17]

Working Paper #3

The Merchant of Venice

1. What ideas are connected with night in V.i? [3 or 4 possibilities]
2. What other scene(s) in *The Merchant of Venice* takes/take place at night?
3. What does Lorenzo say of the character of a man who dislikes music? What region of the universe is he associated with?

[17] " 'If I Were Brutus Now . . .': Role-Playing in *Julius Caesar*," *Shakespeare Studies* 4 (1968), 149-59.

4. Who performs a morally significant action in *The Merchant of Venice* in the presence of music? What is it?

5. Who besides Lorenzo talks to Jessica about music in the play? When?

6. What idea(s) associated with Orpheus (other than the music alluded to at V.i.80) is/are potentially relevant to this play? [Check a mythological dictionary]

7. After saying he has lent his body as security for Bassanio, Antonio offers to pledge himself again; what does he propose as security in this second bond?

8. What news is in the letter Portia brings with her to Belmont? Where did she get the letter?

9. What other mysteries or mystifications has Portia been responsible for or associated with in *The Merchant of Venice*? [as many as 3]

10. What literary genre gives prominence to the kind of mystery/mystification you mention in question 9?

WORKING PAPER #2

Julius Caesar

1. When does Cassius imagine himself in Brutus' place?

2. Who else imagines that he and Brutus have changed places? Where?

3. Who actually claims to *be* Brutus? When? [2 possible answers]

4. What role is Brutus asked to play by the Plebeians?

5. What family role is Brutus asked to play by Cassius?

6. Where does Octavius claim that he is "another Caesar"?

7. Show that just before the Battle of Philippi Cassius expects history to repeat itself.

8. Caesar offers the Plebeians "his throat to cut" (I.ii.265-66). What other characters offer to let others kill them? Give brief references to the text.

9. Antony reassures Caesar (wrongly) about Cassius (I.ii.196-97). What other misguided reassurance(s) about political opponent(s) can you cite in the play?
10. Antony makes a political application of Caesar's fall at the base of Pompey's statue (III.ii.188-92). Who makes a political application of another fall elsewhere in the play? Where?
11. Antony calls history "the tide of times" at III.i.257. Where else in the play are there references to tides, floods, waves, and the like? [perhaps half a dozen possibilities]

IV

What is true, in the three preceding sections of this paper, of undergraduate courses is true, *mutatis mutandis*, of graduate courses also; advanced students, indeed, infer meaning from curriculum arrangement and challenging examinations even better than undergraduates do to just the extent that greater experience has alerted and refined their sensibilities.

Moreover, there is in the study of Shakespeare's sources an inferential possibility open to graduate students that is largely closed to undergraduates who must master the plays themselves and haven't time to concern themselves with Shakespeare's raw materials. The observant study of Shakespeare's sources is among the most exciting avenues to literary criticism. To put it metaphorically and simplistically, if one subtracts the source from the work of art one is left with the creative process. To compare a sentence or a paragraph in a prose narrative with its transmutation into metrical dialogue in a dramatic scene is to learn a great deal about prosody, about dramaturgy, about genre, and above all about the way Shakespeare's mind worked. Juxtaposition is, of course, the frame of perception in source study, as it is in the approach to curriculum suggested in section I. Or, conversely, the undergraduate in a "juxta-position" course is put in the position of regarding the first play of each pair as a "source" (more exactly as a template) for the second play in the pair.

The possibilities of source study are illustrated very well in the juxtaposition of Sir Thomas North's prose account of Cleopatra's meeting with Antony at Cydnus and Enobar-bus' verse recollection of the event. I have often given grad-uate students North dittographed and, preparatory to a class discussion that will focus on what Shakespeare added to his prose source, asked them to annotate the passage in *Antony and Cleopatra* II.ii. Students see for themselves quite readily the elevating prosody, the punctuation of Enobarbus' monologue by Agrippa's exclamatory interrup-tions, the addition of descriptive detail, and other altera-tions that verse and drama encouraged or dictated. The astute student also sees for himself other kinds of additions Shakespeare made. One is the language of love in pathetic fallacy (the winds and water are not "love-sick" or "amor-ous" in Plutarch). Another is hyperbole (there are no equivalents in North for Cleopatra's "O'er-picturing" of Venus or for the barbering of Antony "ten times o'er"). Shakespeare's conception of the world of the play was ob-viously so "Brobdingnagian"[18] that it infected even this passage in which he was following North's already vivid and fully usable account of the scene very closely.

The implications of the passage and its source for the larger meaning of the play go yet deeper, for there is nothing in North to match the paradoxes Shakespeare sprinkles through this speech of Enobarbus. In Shakespeare Cleopatra "make[s] defect perfection" and "makes hungry / Where most she satisfies"—to cite two familiar instances from among the half dozen Shakespeare added. We can if we wish interpret such intrusive paradoxes in the passage

[18] This apposite term for the language of the play is from S. L. Bethell, *Shakespeare and the Popular Dramatic Tradition* (London: Staples, 1944), pp. 117-20.

43

as characterization of the speaker, who is a witty ironist and who will later in the play himself become a paradox, a loyal deserter. One of the number, however, suggests that all the paradoxes in this set piece are more meaningful, central to Shakespeare's conception of the whole play. In describing the dimpled Cupidlike boys on the barge, Enobarbus unconsciously echoes the paradox with which the play has begun:

> [the boys had] divers-color'd fans, whose wind did seem
> To glow the delicate cheeks which they did cool,
> And what they undid did. (203-5)

At the beginning of I.i, Philo has set a tone for the play by using the same paradox to describe Antony, who "is become the bellows and the fan / To cool a gipsy's lust" (9-10). Enobarbus' paradoxes contribute to and replicate a larger pattern—it is apparent that to Shakespeare paradox is at the very heart of the story: in the character of Cleopatra and in the ennobling decadence of Antony's desire for her. To observe Shakespeare tampering with his source in this passage in II.ii is to gain an insight no other critical stance can offer quite so well into the largest meanings of *Antony and Cleopatra*.

The pedagogical method is equally effective on a larger scale. In a seminar called "Shakespeare and His Sources" in spring 1974, for example, each student selected a play and made a detailed and comprehensive reading in light of the sources. Two students focused on the creative process, the conflation of discrete but analogous sources in Shakespeare's creative imagination (a memorable paper on *Cymbeline* and a fine one on *The Merchant or Venice*); one worked out a reading supported by hints from the sources (a neglected theme in *The Two Gentlemen of Verona*); one took "sources" broadly enough to embrace "analogues" and made of Heywood's *Iron Age* a very useful critical platform from which to observe *Troilus and Cressida*; one emphasized genre (New Comedy—Plautus' *Rudens*—as back-

44

ground to *The Tempest*). It was a highly successful semester; the excitement of discovery infected the whole class.

Source study in or out of the classroom tacitly calls attention to aspects of the creative process in Shakespeare inaccessible by any other means. One of them is alluded to above as "conflation of discrete but analogous sources in Shakespeare's creative imagination." This is the phenomenon Kenneth Muir pointed to cogently in a series of articles in the 1950s;[19] it is sometimes called "polygenesis" or "coalescence." Attention to multiple sources can show us and our students not only how a passage can be interpreted but something also of Shakespeare's mind. He had an extraordinary memory which worked by association;[20] it was not, however, photographic, and when we catch him recalling imperfectly we get not only the explanation for some anomalies in the texts of the plays but also evidence about his working habits. To put students in touch with sources is to offer them the possibility of some very exciting inferences. Contrary to traditional belief Shakespeare did not write with Golding's Ovid, Holinshed, North's Plutarch, and the Geneva Bible stacked up beside him. A recent short article explains a strange crux at the beginning of *Julius Caesar* IV.i as traceable to Shakespeare's unconscious confusion of a passage on the Proscription in the "Life of Marcus Antonius" with a passage that immediately precedes the corresponding account of the Proscription in the "Life of Marcus Brutus."[21] A student alert enough to catch discrepancy, curious enough to read wherever Shakespeare may have read, can sometimes in effect look over Shakespeare's shoulder as he writes. We don't have nearly for

[19] See, e.g., "Pyramus and Thisbe: A Study in Shakespeare's Method," *Shakespeare Quarterly* 5 (1954), 141-53; "Shakespeare Among the Commonplaces," *Review of English Studies* 10 (1959), 282-89; "Menenius' Fable," *Notes and Queries* 198 (1953), 240-42.

[20] John Erskine Hankins offers a detailed demonstration in *Shakespeare's Derived Imagery* (Lawrence: Univ. of Kansas Press, 1953).

[21] John W. Velz and Sarah C. Velz, "Publius, Mark Antony's Sister's Son," *Shakespeare Quarterly* 16 (1975), 69-74.

Shakespeare what John Livingstone Lowes had for Coleridge, but the road to Shakespeare's Xanadu is not closed.

Advanced students have often noticed allusions in one play to the sources of another Shakespeare did not write until a year or two later; the evidence is there that he read and digested well in advance the material he planned to use —that he did not write as "Fancy's child," but with premeditation and after reflection. Macbeth's comparison (for one example) of himself with Antony and of Banquo with Octavius (III.i.54-56) shows plainly that *Antony and Cleopatra* was on Shakespeare's mind a year or more before he wrote it. The process also worked conversely; Shakespeare did not set a play aside when he had finished it, but drew on its sources in later plays, just as he might draw (as suggested in section I) on its motifs and situations and symbolic structures. There was, doubtless, something retentive, something *ex post facto*, about Shakespeare's temperament, despite his brilliance in innovation. In 1970, Ramon Saldivar, an undergraduate student in my honors Shakespeare class, discovered a striking instance of Shakespeare's looking backward at a source. The character of Tullus Aufidius, only lightly sketched in Plutarch's "Life of Coriolanus," is fleshed out in Shakespeare's *Coriolanus* from Plutarch's account of Alcibiades, whom Shakespeare had portrayed a year or two before in *Timon of Athens*; the debt is particularly to the account of Alcibiades in the "Comparison Between Alcibiades and Coriolanus." In light of Saldivar's perception, it might not be too much to suggest that Shakespeare's pairing of Aufidius and Coriolanus (they several times use the same imagery and are in many other ways counterparts) was inspired by Plutarch's pairing of Alcibiades with Coriolanus.

Altquellenforschung, a self-serving pedantry that works diligently at data without informing Shakespeare's plays, has justifiably been in ill repute for some decades now. It is dry precisely because it confines itself to logical connections laboriously established. *Neuquellenforschung* redeems source study by serving ends larger than itself, illuminating the work of art and watching the artist at work. It invites students to analogical perceptions and as it does so it invites them to a cast of mind not unlike Shakespeare's: associative, metaphorical, synoptic. That in itself is a justification for illative pedagogy, however short we and our students must, in the end, come of fully accepting the invitation.

THREE

THE PRESENTATION OF SHAKESPEARE

D. ALLEN CARROLL

THOSE of us who would have our students understand why *Romeo and Juliet* succeeds will acknowledge, I believe, the effectiveness of using Denis de Rougemont's insight:

> Love and death, a fatal love—in these phrases is summed up, if not the whole of poetry, at least whatever is popular, whatever is universally moving in European literature, alike as regards the oldest legends and the sweetest songs. Happy love has no history. . . . What stirs lyrical poets to their finest flights is neither the delight of the senses nor the fruitful contentment of the settled couple; not the satisfaction of love, but its *passion*. And passion means suffering.[1]

Here is a generalization large, provocative, and well put, as whatever is to engage undergraduates must be, and it is one which fascinates the young. It may not for everyone contain the whole truth about European literature or even suggest the best reading of this play. But for students it has the *necessary* kind of truth. Placed in an organized presentation it can help move students toward the deeps of the play, to the central image of the Dying Lovers, from there to the tributary verbal and visual patterns (love-death, womb-tomb, light-dark), and hopefully on beyond to a contemplation of other such fables. And yet the words are not Shakespeare's, and the mode of their utterance is not, as Shakespeare's was, the dramatic performance. The teacher is not Shakespeare—he *presents* Shakespeare. For the most part,

[1] *Love in the Western World*, trans. Montgomery Belgion (Greenwich, Conn.: Pantheon, 1956), p. 15.

48

his tasks are to use words which, while not poetry, are poetic in kind, that is, words which excite the imagination, and to give to his remarks a form which, while not drama, is dramatic, that is, a form which activates, intensifies, and resolves expectations through exploration and discovery. Ideally the classroom lecture is an art form, with its special conventions, although, like the sermon, it is a minor one.

If current experimental trends should lead to general practice, however, we shall be as far removed from this attitude as we are now from that of the last century, when Shakespeare's lines were the basis for exercises in grammar and philology and his passages were singled out for their rhetorical beauty or moral persuasion. In the future we can expect that the teaching of Shakespeare will center not on the presentation of plays but rather on their actual performance, which change will alter seriously the teacher's role. The new method will take one of two forms or some of both. First, what J. L. Styan calls the "direct method," through which in workshop form students discover Shakespeare "by playing him," and "twenty freshmen . . . become ten Lears and ten Cordelias." "God preserve us from generalizations!" Styan exclaims (quoting Chekhov); for him "even the smallest step toward conjuring the play's natural medium is better than damaging the play (and the students) by employing un-Shakespearean methods."[2] Second, through a form which exploits the vast potential of audio-visual technology, one whereby students experience in the classroom the best of recorded performances. With the flick of a switch we shall be able to offer Olivier as Hamlet and then Nicol Williamson for comparison and contrast. Here is an innovation devoutly to be wished.

None of us would reject the values implicit in this general direction, or deny its inevitability. We know the primacy of the aural and visual Shakespeare, and we know that performance, because it directly touches the senses, can

2 "Direct Method Shakespeare," *Shakespeare Quarterly* 25 (1974), 199.

hold and educate the imagination. But there are at present limitations to such a method. Many of us feel, as a matter partly of instinct and partly of experience, that for most undergraduates Shakespeare's poetry, however well performed, nonetheless requires analysis; that specific scenes need to be fitted into large, sometimes abstract, structures which students cannot see without help; that getting at Shakespeare demands to some extent an Elizabethan perspective we ought to teach; and that his wide-ranging effect on Western culture it is our duty at the least to suggest. Until performance as such provides a discernible means to satisfy these needs most of us will feel little pressure for such a radical change. There are, moreover, practical considerations. Not many universities will underwrite the cost of purchasing tapes and films (even should such be available), the cost of editing them as an individual teacher specifies for the needs of his course, or the cost of placing the appropriate equipment in his classroom. Their immense value must remain, for now, adjunctive, on the other side of the classroom door. The "direct method," as Professor Styan admits, requires large quantities of time which those of us who, like myself, have no more than twenty-five hours in which to serve up a rich and comprehensive course are reluctant to spare. We think we have too much to do. Besides, we have to do in my judgment with students indisposed by temperament and expectation to enter themselves into performance. My own experience is with earnest and intelligent juniors and seniors, primarily English majors at a large state university, whose exposure to Shakespeare has been minimal and for whom I must assume my course to be their only in-depth, formal study. By and large they expect that the teacher's role will be active, theirs passive, and they grow impatient with extensive participation by any of the other thirty-five or so members of the class. They expect to get to know Shakespeare *through* an authority in the traditional method, the lecture punctuated by questions and answers, which method, doubtless at some expense of spirit, they have adapted themselves to and learned to profit from. Not at all whining schoolboys, creeping like snails unwillingly to school, they come with great if programmed expectations. This course, they presume, will surpass others not in form but in substance, just as Shakespeare—for so they have heard and do in part believe—differs from other men. Accordingly, our problem for the future is to arrive at a congenial teaching method which combines presentation with performance as such. Our course for now is as determined as it is time-honored. We want to do well what we in fact try to do.

The following remarks, which attempt to express faith in a well-worn method, suggest something of what takes place when through it Shakespeare is taught well. Our concern is not with great teaching—which can hardly be described, let alone imitated—but with good teaching, as it is or can be carried on by teachers with modest talents, before average students, in most colleges and universities throughout the land. Should what I say appear in places to be elementary, it is because I want to be as honest and realistic as possible, and because what is elementary is often the most difficult to see. Comment as to what we actually do or should do constitutes little more than a trace in the waters which surround Shakespeare, despite the fact that most of us are teachers and only incidentally critics and scholars. We consider ourselves expert at what we do, and no expert suffers gladly the findings of another. It has been enough to make cowards of us all. Insofar as I recommend the method described, I do so in this spirit: it hath served others, it may thee.

A presentation which is to have the first chance at success must at the outset take into account whether students have read the material in question. Good students fail to complete assignments, and for reasons sufficiently human, their lives being so distracted by the varied and colorful confusions of youth. When we cannot presume half the class to be prepared, we broaden observations and consequently dissipate much of their intensity. All teachers of literature will admit to this problem. The device I am about to recommend, while it may strike many as old-fashioned or a nuisance, works admirably to solve this problem. At the beginning of the period during which, for my purposes, it is necessary that students know a play well, I give an announced, ten-minute, objective quiz. Here is a sample:

Romeo and Juliet   Fall 1974

Describes whom and what?

1.   meagre were his looks,
Sharp misery had worn him to the bones;
And in his needy shop a tortoise hung,
An alligator stuff'd, and other skins
Of ill-shap'd fishes.

                                                            Speaker?

2.   but, as I said,
When it did taste the wormwood on the nipple
Of my dug and felt it bitter, pretty fool,
To see it teachy and fall out wi' th' dug!

                                                            Speaker?

3. This, by his voice, should be a Montague.
Fetch me my rapier, boy. What dares the slave
Come hither, cover'd with an antic face,
To fleer and scorn at our solemnity?

                                                            Situation?

4.   She speaks.
O, speak again, bright angel for thou art,
As glorious to this night, being o'er my head,
As is a winged messenger of heaven
Unto the white-upturned wond'ring eyes. . . .

                                                This explains what?

5. . . . the searchers of the town,
Suspecting that we both were in a house
Where the infectious pestilence did reign,
Seal'd up the doors. . . .

THE PRESENTATION OF SHAKESPEARE

Situation?

6. It was the nightingale, and not the lark,
   That pierc'd the fearful hollow of thine ear.
   Nightly she sings on yond pomegranate tree.
   Believe me, love, it was the nightingale.

Speaker?

7. A plague a' both houses! . . .
   A plague a' both your houses! . . .
   A plague a' both your houses!
   They have made worms' meat of me.

Situation?

8. —Do you bite your thumb at us, sir? / I do bite
   my thumb, sir / Do you bite your thumb at us, sir?

Speaker?

9. Welcome, gentlemen! I have seen the day
   That I have worn a visor and could tell
   A whispering tale in a fair lady's ear,
   Such as would please; 'tis gone, 'tis gone, 'tis gone!
   You are welcome, gentlemen!

Speaker?

10.   I will kiss thy lips,
    Haply some poison yet doth hang on them,
    To make me die with a restorative.

Speaker, situation?

Bonus: O, if I wake, shall I not be distraught,
          Environed with all these hideous fears,
          And madly play with my forefathers' joints,
          And pluck the mangled Tybalt from his shroud.

Now it is a continuing surprise to me how happily students take to this device. It becomes for them a sharp stimulus to master a play (they are strongly reward-oriented); it forces them to read carefully, and to reread; and as the course is set up, it relieves them of certain special anxieties they have: they need not at a later date demonstrate so intimate a familiarity with details, and they are able through it to show some of the considerable effort they have made to grasp what to many of them is foreign and complex. In my ten years of experiment no student has objected to these quizzes, and many have declared their gratitude. While the quizzes do take some time in the making and grading (perhaps thirty minutes altogether for each quiz), and some thought, such is little and well spent when compared with their value. The questions, which usually take the form of quotations, can serve a number of functions— they can anticipate points to be made in the lecture, identify and impress upon the memory famous passages, and help indicate what is particular about a play. With *Midsummer Night's Dream*, for example, I have at times selected only passages containing images of moonlight, with *Macbeth* only those containing images of blood. With plays of great proportions, such as *Hamlet* and *King Lear*, I give two quizzes, either to render the assignment manageable (by dividing the play) or else in effect to require a second complete reading. All of us know that the true course in Shakespeare takes place not so much in our presence as outside, whenever and wherever our students read Shakespeare. We want to make sure this course takes place, as well as seek to enrich it.

The presentation itself, which we now turn to, must have a structure undergraduates can recognize, a conspicuous form, one whose parts have a clear, logical relation to one another as determined by a controlling idea. Much of teaching has to do with discovering the right form. It ought to rise out of, and therefore be capable of re-creating, our own most intense feelings about a play. At the same time it ought not to violate, indeed it may well depend upon, patterns established in the accumulated history of opinion about the play. Almost always a plan recommends itself when we follow a procedure Desmond MacCarthy has described: "I let the play pass over me, and when it is finished,

I look for the markings in the sand."[3] From such markings we select designs made up out of the basic elements of drama: theme, structure, scene, character, and to some extent image and symbol. And we look outside ourselves to others for suggestions. With *1 Henry IV*, for example, following Brooks and Heilman, we might devote the first day to theme and structure, presenting the orthodox interpretation, noting alternatives, and perhaps taking a position (it is, specifically, about The Education of a Prince, generally, about Coming of Age, and students ought not to be completely taken in by Falstaff). We might proceed on the second day to Hal and Hotspur as they dramatize aspects of the theme, and thereafter on a climactic third day to the place and nature of Falstaff. With *Antony and Cleopatra* each of the three days might take shape according to the three separate interpretations possible—that it is, first, a moving tragedy of passion and retribution (looking closely at the early scenes); second, a supreme expression of transcendent love (turning to Cleopatra's dying act); and third, a celebration of the mixed nature of love (giving attention to the middle, transitional scenes and to recurrent image patterns)—if, of course, we genuinely feel that such a plan brings about a meaningful engagement with the play. Needless to say, we never stop searching for the right plan for a play. I have never met a teacher who felt he had found a satisfactory way to teach *King Lear*, the play most alien to undergraduates.

What holds for the overall presentation of a play, that it should have a visible, effective structure, obtains as well for each day's presentation. More often than not we are inclined, as a matter of emphasis, to find *three* major points, not two or four, to make about, say, each of those great characters, Iago, Othello, Shylock, and so on, who deserves his day in the course. *Three* admits of climax (with em-

[3] Quoted in John Garrett, introduction to *Talking of Shakespeare*, ed. John Garrett (London: Hodder & Stoughton, 1954), p. 19.

phasis on the third), and of conflict (between two) and resolution (the third). We might offer, for example, the evidence from without and within the play that Shylock is meant to be mocked at, spat upon, and dismissed with vindictive laughter and contempt. We might present next the case for the noble, unduly persecuted Jew, more sinned against than sinning. And we might point finally to what, as a result, we can learn about Shakespeare's method of characterization: that he rarely accepts the simple "types" of source stories or theatrical convention, that his sympathies are deep and godlike, and that his characters are susceptible to many and therefore opposing interpretations. In the moment before the period ends we might well draw attention to one of his finest touches, Portia's query as she looks about the courtroom: "Which is the merchant here? and which the Jew?"

A plan must function primarily as a means to get at the text. With our main points, where generalization and non-textual support enter in, we have conned our parts, know precisely what we will say, when, and how. As we turn to the text, however, we freely surrender ourselves to Shakespeare, relaxed before his control, and in the moment of analysis we allow our minds to react as they will, spontaneously, to that vast reservoir of impulses that our training and sensitivity produce and over which we hold slight sway. We respond to diction, image, idea, tone, rhythm, and stage gesture and business. Thereby our students experience simultaneously a performance and a reaction to it. Selections from the text ought to be those most widely known, those we feel a special affinity for and thus do well, and those which students, left to themselves, cannot handle. A plan for teaching *Hamlet*, if it is a good one, will make a place for each of his famous soliloquies. And one for *1 Henry IV* will cover, even if briefly, the Drawer's Scene, over which students, like Francis himself, are at wit's end. They need help to visualize this apprentice running back and forth across stage in his attempt to serve two separate callings until, having collapsed, exhausted, he is caught and reprimanded by his master. They cannot see that the scene contains in miniature the large question of the play, whether Hal will hear clearly his proper vocation, and that it suggests his accomplishment as an apprentice Prince. Having earned a knowledge of common men ("Tom, Dick, and Francis"), he is prepared to be about his father's business. When on certain days we turn to scenes of exceptional power, beauty, length, and difficulty—Iago's temptation of Othello, Angelo's interview with Isabella, or the pastoral scene in *The Winter's Tale*—we ought to let the play speak and inspire, free of any formal framework, for the duration of the session.

While it may go without saying, a presentation, whatever its idea and scope, will reflect an awareness that undergraduates need simple, deliberate, and orderly introductions to material before them, to a group of plays, to a particular play, or to some aspect thereof. Our constant assumption ought to be that they have no notion at all of what they are about to consider. They must be told what a "history play" is, and a "romantic comedy," and in a cursory way what distinguishes each individual play, that it is relatively short or long, profound or shallow, puzzling or clear, that it is notable for its lyricism, atmosphere, plot, character or whatever. To give students bearings for their reading and for our own observations we must bring forward attitudes rarely conscious with us and arrange them into a few, telling generalizations which can anticipate the overall, three-day structure of a presentation. *Othello*, we might suggest in our opening comments, has always been extremely successful, first, because it is superbly constructed for theatrical effect and, second, because it gives us two extraordinary characters, Othello and Iago. In a number of ways *Coriolanus* differs from the other tragedies students have read. For one, "There is not in this great play a line of great poetry" (John Palmer). For another, it has the capacity to inspire summary praise or condemna-

57

tion. T. S. Eliot thought it Shakespeare's best. Shaw, on the other hand, called it "the greatest of Shakespeare's comedies." Students must be ready to have similarly emphatic reactions. And so on. Teaching, to a large extent, means realizing what is most obvious to oneself and saying it well.

Since the effectiveness of a presentation depends largely on our expression, on the words we choose, we do not always rely on our own powers, which are seldom sufficient to the cause of Shakespeare. Instead, drawing on the great tradition of criticism, we quote, and liberally, from the best that has been said about Shakespeare, from that which is famous for its felicitous suggestion or fascinating error. Contrary to what one might think, students at such moments are most attentive and impressionable. We quote, therefore: Rymer on *Othello*—"a Bloody Farce"; Dr. Johnson on Shakespeare's wordplay—"A quibble was to him the fatal Cleopatra for which he lost the world and was content to lose it"; Coleridge on Iago—"the motive-hunting of motiveless malignity"; Yeats on Richard II—"[that] vessel of porcelain"; and even if at some length, De Quincey's splendid prose— (which begins), "From my boyish days I had always felt a great perplexity on one point in *Macbeth*. It was this: the knocking at the gate, which succeeds to the murder of Duncan. . . ." There is almost nothing we say which cannot be produced better-said by another. We quote to make a point with precision: Eliot, on Hamlet's antic disposition, that "it is less than madness and more than feigned." We quote to demonstrate the ringing audacity of special interpretations: Charlton on Shylock, that Shakespeare was determined "to let the Jew dog have it"; Shaw on *Antony and Cleopatra*, that Shakespeare turned "hogs into heroes." And we quote simply to charm: Dumas, on the number and variety of Shakespeare's characters, that "[he] is the poet who created most after God!" We acknowledge, of course, that such finery is not our own, and when students either know or ought to know the poets, critics, or actors in the tradition, we announce our sources. Students want desperately to be educated. They are pleased to learn that others whom all admire have reacted to Shakespeare. And they have a right to this reaction as part of their heritage and course. For that matter, as Una Ellis-Fermor has put it, we want to read Shakespeare as the poets and actors read him. "These, after all, are his kinsmen and his immediate servants."[4]

As to what kinds of material and what critical approaches offer the best means to a knowledge of Shakespeare, there can be no sure rule. We assess our own strengths and weaknesses, those of our students, the time available, and the unique nature of the play before us. This procedure, in our own time, results in a presentation which in the main is formalist, but at the same time in important ways is eclectic. We freely choose any material or theoretical orientation which has potential value, though we try to exercise moderation and give balance in our selection. Our emphasis varies and shifts—"it is all a question of tact, timing, and compromise."[5]

Let me illustrate. We teach something about the Elizabethan concept of order in society and nature, but not too much, and then not apart from the plays it directly informs, such as *Richard II* and *King Lear*. Students catch it quickly and weary of insistence. By the same token, we give them a taste of the customs, words, and things of Elizabethan life, at least enough to send them to the explanatory notes. They relish antiquarian details, and on occasions have need of them. But we do not turn to a passage in class solely because it is obscure. When their grasp of an image is sufficiently clear and poetic, as is "the ravell'd sleave of care," we do not disturb them, in this instance with the Shakespearean sense of *sleave*.

We give a general priority to the formalist approach, that is, to the study of structures within a play, and we know how easily students are dazzled by its specific insights

---

[4] *The Study of Shakespeare* (London: Methuen & Co., n.d.), p. 11.
[5] To use John Garrett's words, in *Talking*, p. 19.

as to patterns, central image clusters, and key words. But we spend no more than, say, ten minutes on the intricacies of a passage of twenty lines lest we set their minds to stray. In the modern criticism of close analysis, there is little we can use. Our chief sources are critics whose views are general, highly opinionated, and who pronounce them passionately, briefly, and with style, which means, usually, those critics of the late nineteenth and early twentieth centuries.

Because the plays were intended to be acted and on a particular stage, we teach a good deal about the construction of the Elizabethan stage and about its conventions and we otherwise try to develop a consciousness in our students of the requirements of theater. Whenever area or media productions are accessible we make them part of our course, and our lectures we crowd with details from theatrical history—Burton's bodily contortion when he "shuffled off this mortal coil," the moment in Zefferelli's film when the smile on Tybalt's face becomes a grin. In all, our desire is to arouse in students an awareness of the possibilities of performance, of visual and temporal effects. How, we ask, might characters in the gulling of Malvolio scene be distributed for the greatest comic effect? What should be Cleopatra's visible response to Antony's agonized rebukes in those war scenes when she is frequently on stage but silent? Thus it is that the idea of performance, not performance as such, has place in the classroom. Though our stress here is heavy, as John Russell Brown and others have taught us that it should be, we would not overdo it.[6] Our minds tend to fix on the modern or eccentric. And there is a limit to how adequately we can represent in the classroom successful performance, even when we can imagine or have experienced such. Besides, again, part of what we want

[6] I refer in particular to two of Brown's books: *Shakespeare's Plays in Performance* (London: Edward Arnold, 1966) and *Shakespeare's Dramatic Style* (London: Heinemann, 1970).

to get at is precisely that about Shakespeare which is not of a stage but for all time.

We seek ways to render Shakespeare immediate or "relevant" to our students. Occasionally a judicious allusion to present-day issues can make meaningful that which might seem archaic and irrelevant, such as, for example, the concept of kingship which is so vital to the plays. My colleague Professor Norman Sanders, who I know is especially skilled in making the apt comparison, has had success explaining the rebels' attitude to Henry Bolingbroke and to Henry IV by reference to the man/office dichotomy as it exists in the United States. We would not, however, try to make Shakespeare our contemporary by studying problems in his plays simply because they seem appropriate to our own time. We would not, for example, design a presentation on *Richard II* in order to show how Shakespeare might have perceived the deposition of Richard Nixon, though we may in analysis of the play encourage a number of parallels to emerge. It is a matter of emphasis. To engage our students, all of us rely more or less on a low-voltage psychological approach, one which takes dramatic characters to be real people with human motives, histories, and caught up in human activities.[7] Students think this way, and qualifications waste time. I myself carry this tendency so far as to use the modern psychological terms and categories which have such an appeal to students. Richard III's malicious violence is, I say, "compensatory"; Richard II suffers through an "identity crisis"; and Hamlet's predicament is, to a large extent, "Oedipal."

Throughout, our approach is one wherein extremities are tempered and the elements mixed. We would not overteach, since students are able to take in only a part of the huge and proper life of a Shakespeare play. We do what

[7] On this attitude in teaching Shakespeare see Kester Svendsen, "Formalist Criticism and the Teaching of Shakespeare," *College English* 27 (1966), 24.

we can in the time allotted. We give two days to *The Comedy of Errors*, five to *King Lear*.

We come finally to the leading feature of the presentation, its characteristic tone, that without which all the planning and emphasis we have urged and all our dear-bought knowledge of the subject means little or nothing. That we love Shakespeare and find his poetry marvelous we must show and with every part of our being, as he himself might say, with eye, cheek, lip, and foot. When we enter the classroom fresh from reading Shakespeare our enthusiasm naturally manifests itself. But we cannot always, as we should, fully reexperience a play before the session devoted to it. What we can do, though, in a few unhurried moments beforehand, is read over our leading observations and the supporting evidence; if the form they take preserves and reflects an original, intense experience, as it should, then we shall warm to our task. We shall have honored two attitudes in the first conception of our presentation which will thereafter help us get "up" for a class and transmit our enthusiasm. First, whatever we say about Shakespeare we shall delight in saying or we shall not say it at all. And second, when we read Shakespeare, as we shall, in great swatches in every session, we shall read him well. Read with a sensitivity to tone and with the confidence which comes from practice, he has the power to renew our spirits and move our students. We can trust him.

Otherwise we are left to our own personalities and devices. I myself have found helpful an unfettered expression of bardolatry. As a teaching posture I accept without question that Shakespeare is a very great artist. So long as there are those of us, I say, who live by words and not by bread alone, we must read Shakespeare. Such bardolatry, as Professor Heilman has noticed, "on the whole serves good ends rather than questionable ones."[8] Shakespeare is so strange and confusing at first to our students that if they are to

[8] "Bardolatry," *Yale Review* 50 (1960), 265.

proceed at all, with minds susceptible to a range of new experiences, then it must be by a kind of faith. For that matter, they come to us eager to participate in the myth of his ideality, almost persuaded already. He meets some deep need they have in an era of unbelief.

The teaching of Shakespeare, I hope to have suggested, is a rigorous and exhausting, if inspiring, undertaking. We can fail, even with the best script in the world—we are therefore the more likely to fail. Any of us can get easily through a session, meandering from topic to topic, from line to line. But to teach with the kind of artistic integrity which delights as it instructs and thus befits our master, and to do so in full certainty that we can never teach him well enough—that takes commitment, time, and hard work. When Kittredge, one of the patterns of our profession, was asked just how many hours and minutes it took him to prepare his "lecture" on Shakespeare, he replied: "I refuse to answer. It's one of my trade secrets." Then he relented and said, "Just a lifetime—can't you see that?"[9]

[9] This anecdote is given in Rollo W. Brown, *Harvard in the Golden Years* (New York: Current Books, 1948), p. 101.

II. SHAKESPEARE AND THE ENGLISH CURRICULUM

FOUR

SHAKESPEARE AND THE
GRADUATE ENGLISH CURRICULUM

NORMAN RABKIN

THE question comes up repeatedly. The table of contents
of the present volume bears witness; so does the agenda for
the first annual convention of the reorganized Shakespeare
Association of America in 1973, where I was invited to
address the topic. After I had accepted the invitation, I
experienced a series of emotions ranging from apathy to
rage, and long after that occasion I am not sure I have them
all sorted out. Shakespeare's place in graduate English studies, after all, is, or should be, a less vital and controversial
issue at the moment than mother's place in the home. My
immediate question, of course, was: who is asking? If the
question is taken as an expression of curiosity on the part
of the world at large, the answer would presumably be
expected to be a simple reaffirmation of the centrality of
Shakespeare in English literature and therefore in graduate
English study. If the interlocutor is the highly publicized
first national meeting of the elders of the reborn Shakespearean church, an appropriate answer might be cast on
the model of the orations made by officials of the automo-
bile workers' union demanding jobs for their constituency.
But recent history and current fact have made me realize
that the question is neither ceremonial nor a foregone conclusion, that it has been asked by other interested parties
and may be asked with even more urgency in the near
future, and that my answers were and are less automatic
than I might have expected them to be.

As chairman of graduate studies in English at Berkeley,
I had heard the question asked by different voices in a

different tone, and I had heard embattled and defensive answers as well. Like most such programs, English at Berkeley has settled into an intense, quiet seriousness such as we scarcely remembered. In great part, I imagine, the frightening realities of the market and the economy have joined with a modest and despairing assessment, by students and their professors, of the power of English studies to affect the world, to urge what Northrop Frye called in another connection a centripetal gaze and to stifle questioning. And in Berkeley in particular things are quiet for us because we have a new graduate program in the design of which students participated vigorously. The program has turned out, after all the shouting and fear, to be very much a version of our old program, changed more in form than in substance. But the questions that led to the new program asked for justification of the place of everything; if they aren't being asked now their echoes rebound, and we shall hear them again.

I am not going to defend the study of Shakespeare. Not inconceivably the day may come—in some places it has come already, I think—when it will be possible to earn a Ph.D. in English without knowing Shakespeare well. When that time comes, when we no longer share an assumption that every professional student of English has built his learning on the foundations of Shakespeare—and Chaucer and Milton and Dr. Johnson and Wordsworth and so on —it will be time to declare traditional English studies dead and to invent something new, with a new name. That is, to say the least, an interesting prospect, but one that I am not yearning to be involved in and that I shall not address in this essay. What I want to discuss is the best way for graduate students in English to study Shakespeare. What I have to say makes me uncomfortable, and I expect that it will make others feel that way too.

For students who intend to specialize in Renaissance literature and theater and to teach Shakespeare, my proposals are anything but revolutionary: more, and better, of what we have been doing. Renaissance studies have had a renaissance of their own in the last generation, so that critics and scholars have a wealth of tools at their disposal. We know more about many matters essential to the understanding of Renaissance literature than we did before, and about how they bear on what we are interested in: iconography and the Renaissance imagination, continental literature and criticism, music and the visual arts and their entwining with literary facts and criticism, the history of ideas, anthropological study—from riddles and tales to festivals—, the dynamics of creative and responsive process, the psychology of reader and writer, theatrical history, the impact of medieval drama on that of the renaissance, rhetorical theory, textual bibliography, sixteenth- and seventeenth-century political and economic history, the subtle and all-important ways in which such history is reflected in—even can be said to be responsible for the creation of—works of art, Renaissance understandings of classical and biblical literatures, the nature of Shakespeare's audiences, the other playwrights of his theater. New texts and concordances and dictionaries have opened the way to new understandings; and the sharp eyes and questioning minds of an army of scholars (a demographer speculated recently that there are more people alive now than there are dead in the world's history; might the same be said of Shakespeareans?) keep adding to what we must know.

I cite as an instance of what learning can accomplish a small but, for those who care about such things, rather startling recent discovery such as only an informed scholar could have made. Looking freshly at the encomium Ben Jonson contributed to the First Folio, T.J.B. Spencer questions what most of us have taken for granted, the ornithological tribute Jonson paid Shakespeare by dubbing him the "sweet Swan of Avon" and thereby guaranteeing the support of a large flock of the birds in the vicinity of the Royal Shakespeare Theatre.[1] No one had bothered to think much

[1] T.J.B. Spencer, "Ben Jonson on his beloved, The Author Mr. William Shakespeare," in *The Elizabethan Theatre IV*, ed. G. R. Hibbard (Hamden, Conn.: Archon, 1974), pp. 22-40.

about the epithet except Leslie Hotson, who found a swan emblazoned in the arms of Baron Hunsdon, Lord Chamberlain and sponsor of Shakespeare's company. Hotson noted that the swan is the traditional emblem of poetry and is sacred to Apollo, and the rest of us have been content to let it go at that. But Spencer had the understanding of Jonson's classicism and the energy to find the particular precedents for Jonson's emblem, and by locating the model for the compliment in Horace's encomium to Pindar (*Odes* IV.2) as the Swan of Thebes-upon-Dirce and relating it to similar allusions in Horace, Jonson, and other poets, he has explained an image so familiar that we had forgotten it needed to be explained. (Jonson's encomium deserves still closer scrutiny. Centuries of commentators have been so ready to detect grudging patronization in some of the poem's most famous lines,

> And though thou hadst small *Latine*, and lesse *Greeke*,
> From thence to honour thee, I would not seeke
> For names; but call forth thund'ring *Aeschilus*,
> *Euripides*, and *Sophocles* to us.

that no one has troubled to ask whether Jonson is only suggesting a condition contrary to fact: even if Shakespeare had possessed, as was not the case, small Latin and less Greek, Jonson would find it more appropriate to compare him with the ancients than with the like of sporting Kyd.)

There is so much to be learned that all of us who devote our lives to our subject feel guilty and inadequate before it. For the beginning scholar in the field we must sketch out the full range, introduce the modes and implements of research, a welter of scattered bibliographies and journals and books and techniques. There is no getting around this problem: there is far more to know than there was before, and only by solipsism or by the arrogant assumption that all the energy and talent going into other people's scholarship is misdirected or worthless can one teach or write about Shakespeare without thousands of hours of hard work in all the areas I have named and others. The graduate curriculum has no choice but to build bridges into them for the future specialist. No single course will do. Recently I gave a course which, while fulfilling its departmental description as an introduction to graduate study, focused on *King Lear*, and not surprisingly I found that, with a highly motivated and intelligent class who put in a horrendous amount of work, we scarcely scratched any of the surfaces we faced. Many courses are required in which the special interests I have described can be pursued.

The proliferation of knowledge and technique in Shake-speare study is, of course, only one manifestation of what has happened to everything in English studies, and in fact to the entire academic enterprise. The exponential increase in the number of people—bright people—devoting their lives to literary study would alone have made formidable the task of the scholar, new or established. But the process has been abetted by the constantly renewed discovery that academic disciplines interlock: what happens in the other humanities, in the social sciences, even in the natural sciences, has its immediate impact on what we do, and that impact expresses itself first as a demand on our time and scope. It means, as we have all been learning, that one can no longer be a polymath in English studies. Not long ago it seemed possible to know all of English literature as a scholar, and graduate programs reflected that assumption. Now it is scarcely possible fully to know one's own area of specialization, and sometimes without consciously conceding the assumption, those of us who design graduate programs have changed their shape accordingly. Berkeley is quite typical, I believe, in arranging post-comprehensive work so that the student is expected to learn and be examined in only those areas that will be directly relevant to his dissertation; in fact we are not quite so typical in still requiring at the master's level some semblance of a comprehensive knowledge of English literature.

As I have said, for Shakespeare scholars there is no getting around the need for wide and deep knowledge, much of it acquired in courses designed for professional students. But what about the other students, those who, I have insisted, must still know Shakespeare but are going to be teaching and maybe doing research in the modern period or the middle ages? Here I think my answers become both more tentative and more radical. I want to argue against graduate courses in Shakespeare for the nonspecialist. In the *King Lear* course I taught to entering graduate students I discovered virtues I hadn't anticipated. So much more has been done in Shakespeare research than in almost anything else in English, so much criticism has been written, that one can more easily find instances of both the worst and the best kinds of scholarship on which to set students at work. One need only think of the intensity of intelligence and effort that has gone into the textual problem continuously since the eighteenth century, and of the monumental and readily available achievements of scholarship—so that, for example, one can use Professor Hinman's facsimile of the First Folio, almost inconceivable a generation ago, as an inexpensive classroom text; and in the journals and editions one can find arguments, brilliant and stupid, on virtually every square inch of Shakespearean text one wants to study. Furthermore, at least as important, bright students coming to terms with the best as well as the worst of our academic efforts learn very quickly, and rightly, that Shakespeare transcends all that we do, that there is always more, and more important, work to be done. Studying our greatest poet my students found out to their delight that what they had read on whatever critical problem they tackled was only a beginning, and a liberating one at that, and their papers renewed my faith that our discipline is in a constant state of rebirth.

But I am afraid that I discovered negative aspects that outweighed the advantage of the course for those students who were not there because they already had a commitment to the study of Shakespeare. Throughout the term I had to struggle against a kind of professional role-playing among the students that got between them and what the course was ultimately all about, *King Lear*, and in some respects I judged the course almost a disaster—a disaster created, despite what we all wanted, by the fact that we were involved in a professional enterprise devoted to a poet who is first and last beyond professional jurisdiction. By the end, I thought that my students would have been better served in some very important respects by a course designed not to make Shakespeare scholars of eager students of literature but rather to teach them, in the same way we teach undergraduates and especially those who are not English majors, to respond to Shakespeare.

Let me tell you a sad story. Several years ago, in working with the Berkeley school system, Herbert Kohl, the author of *36 Children*, set up an experimental program for junior and senior high school students who were turned off by the conventional system and were on the verge of dropping out. The program was an umbrella for a number of projects that took place outside the walls of the schools; according to their interests, students apprenticed themselves to theatrical groups or television stations or gurus of various sorts. Despite the fact that I had, and still have, considerable reservations about such programs, I tremblingly accepted Kohl's invitation to teach a group of young people who wanted to study Shakespeare. A few who showed up at the first meeting never returned, but to my surprise the majority, a half-dozen girls ranging in age from thirteen to seventeen, came faithfully to my office once a week, through rain and sometimes tear gas, and we read Shakespeare together. One member of the class was a talented actress who has since begun a professional career; another was passionately addicted to Renaissance music, costume, and history, and she wanted her school experience to serve her intellectual and spiritual needs (a naive wish, of course); the others were simply curious. Casting about desperately for a new structure to teach what was for me a new kind of student, I hit on the idea of asking them to agree on and read carefully in advance a given play, and then to devote the class to reading the play line by line, each student reading a line or two and then asking a question that had bothered her or making a comment on anything about it that seemed interesting to her or explaining her acting interpretation of what she had read. In the course of a year we read three of four plays, beginning with *Macbeth*. To my constant delight, those young people found that reading and talking about Shakespeare generated a kind of enthusiasm they had never felt before, and they asked for books to read and spent hours in preparation for our meetings.

That in itself is not at all surprising. What did astonish me, however, was that week after week, simply by attending to the text and to their own responses and by acknowledging their difficulties, they came up with perceptions that were not only right but often new: they said true and important things that no one, as far as I knew, had said before. I can no longer remember the particular questions and insights they brought, because as always happens with the best criticism and the best classroom discoveries what we did together has merged into my own total response to the plays. But I shall never forget the sheer intelligence of unaffected, unselfconscious, self-motivated response to Shakespeare that made each of those hours the intellectual experience of the week for me.

The method worked so well that I decided to use it again in my graduate course. One of our two long meetings each week was to be devoted to explorations in various sorts of methodology, and the other was to be given over to the same format I had used with the secondary students, round-robin reading and comment. What ensued passes belief. Each student felt the obligation to be brilliant and learned, to ask questions even when he didn't feel like asking questions, to put obstacles in the way of other students trying out their ideas, to argue endlessly about matters of characterization or glossarial ambiguity that sometimes did not seem to interest even the speaker. Students came in delegations to request that I censor class discussions and turn people off when they talked too much or strayed too far, but I told them individually and as a class that it was their problem, that self-discipline and judgment would have to be their responsibility, that they should aim only for the essential in their contributions, that they should not say what they did not believe. A few people withdrew into surly passivity and a few improved, but for the most part the class disability persisted like crabgrass. In fact, three weeks before the end, when I decided to throw in the towel and devote the remaining hours to critical problems students agreed to be most important, we had reached only the second act. What saved the course, and brought its message home rather startlingly, was a final meeting at my house in which, after dinner, we read the play together, without critical comment or interruption, and let ourselves be overwhelmed by its power and its ability to catch up and winnow out all the good and bad things we had said during the term.

What had made the course go wrong, I think, was its ambiance. It was a graduate course populated exclusively by students who knew that here they were learning what a professional does. They found themselves torn between the power of the play, which expressed itself in their final papers where they did grapple with its realities, in the group reading, and only sporadically in class, and their role as professionals, which demanded a performance that had to be arcane or pretentious to be valid. They wanted to read the play as the secondary students had done, and their private work and amateur acting testify that they could, but they also wanted to behave like members of the priesthood. At best the psychomachia was a standoff. In frequent moments of discomfort in class I realized that these really talented and attractive students were responding and using their minds less well than undergraduates in the senior seminar and the other Shakespeare courses of our major curriculum. And I realized that what these students needed, aside from the professional and specialized knowledge and methods the course opened up for them, was not a graduate course in Shakespeare but the kind of course we normally teach to undergraduates, nonmajor as well as major students.

In such a course the aim is, or should be, to provide a model of the intelligent reader of Shakespeare, trusting of his emotional responses, ready to use secondary knowledge when he feels it necessary but not to let it seem more important than the text, groping to understand, above all ready to make himself an active audience. We teach Shakespeare, or anything else, to graduate students as knowledge, as part of the repertoire they will employ as professionals whose commitment we take for granted in their presence among us. But we teach Shakespeare to undergraduates because we want them to see why we read him, and professional skills are a tool, as transparent as we can make them, to help us reach that goal. There is nothing that we say in undergraduate courses that we don't want our graduate students to hear; and if those courses are any good, there is very much there that can only help them find the right place for Shakespeare in their own reading and understanding as they go on to teach other literature.

If I began by arguing that graduate courses in Shakespeare will do little good for the nonspecialist, I am tempted to go further and suggest that they are unlikely to be as valuable as other kinds of professional training in preparing apprentices to make original and significant contributions. Consider again the minuscule addition to knowledge I cited earlier, Professor Spencer's demonstration of the meaning of a phrase Jonson used to characterize Shakespeare. No graduate course in Shakespeare could have taught Spencer to make the discovery, which was the product of a scholarly repertoire that includes intimacy with classical literature, an understanding of Jonson's neoclassicism, wide reading in Elizabethan and Jacobean literature, and active curiosity. One need only think of some of the best books on Shakespeare published in recent years to realize that what makes each of them uniquely valuable is the combination in its author of a sensitive understanding of Shakespeare's text with a special perspective provided by concern with an intellectual world outside the canon. The two best books on Shakespeare's comedies illustrate my point: C. L. Barber's *Shakespeare's Festive Comedy* (1959) is marked throughout by its author's superb ability to see what is in the plays, but it is his illumination of comedy by the study of "its Relation to Social Custom," to cite the subtitle, by the anthropological analysis of folk tradition rather than professional training in reading Shakespeare, that enabled him entirely to revise the accepted view of his subject; and L. G. Salingar's *Shakespeare and the Traditions of Comedy* (1974) demands another such revision by examining the comedies in the light of a number of traditions—Old and New Comedy, *commedia erudita*, romance—which we mistakenly thought we had fully understood before, and by looking at the plays in the context of the drama contemporary with them. One might cite a number of other good recent books on Shakespeare—for those who sometimes wonder why we need new books about him the number is gratifyingly large—that succeed because their authors bring other kinds of knowledge to bear on their subject than have been brought before: David Riggs's *Shakespeare's Heroical Histories* (1972), for example, which studies the rhetorical and historiographical traditions that influenced the young Shakespeare; Michael Goldman's *Shakespeare and the Energies of Drama* (1972), which asks questions about how audiences respond emotionally, intellectually, even physically to what happens in the plays and which derives some of its authenticity from its author's theatrical experience; Bernard Beckerman's *Shakespeare at the Globe, 1599-1609* (1962), which is built on a great deal of knowledge of Shakespeare's contemporaries, of Elizabethan theaters and companies, and of the problems of staging as experienced by a writer who is a director himself; and most exemplary of my argument,

77

perhaps, *Some Facets of King Lear: Essays in Prismatic Criticism*, edited by the late Rosalie L. Colie and F. T. Flahiff (1974), in which twelve essays say important new things about the play by approaching it from twelve sharply defined points outside it: the crisis of the aristocracy in the sixteenth and seventeenth centuries, the nature of pastoral, biblical lore, folklore, historiography, and the like. All of these books emerge out of intimate knowledge of Shakespeare, hard-earned learning, and innovative thinking. None of them could have been based primarily on the kind of knowledge students would acquire in a graduate course in Shakespeare. The best preparation we can offer to a graduate student who will, we hope, someday write such a book would be as thorough a grounding as we can give him in the kinds of knowledge he will need, and the kind of academic introduction to Shakespeare that we give to under-graduates.

But the graduate student will not be the only beneficiary of what I am suggesting. The English major population is shrinking now at a number of institutions. There are doubt-less many reasons for that, but I suspect that one of them is an increasing professionalization of the undergraduate curriculum such as that which has, for better or worse, afflicted the graduate program. I suggest that the renewed awareness of the humane purpose and nature of the under-graduate course, which would be required if, as I propose, graduate students must go to it for their introduction to an unprofessionalized Shakespeare, may well be as good for our undergraduates as for the graduate students themselves.

FIVE

DEROMANTICIZING THE SHREW:
NOTES ON TEACHING SHAKESPEARE IN A
"WOMEN IN LITERATURE" COURSE

WINFRIED SCHLEINER

THE NEW discipline of women's studies brings home more clearly than many others that history is part of what we are. While Renaissance literature is apparently becoming more and more remote to undergraduates—a recent poetry anthology entitled *Ancients and Moderns*[1] begins with John Donne—the relevance of Shakespeare in a "women in literature" course will go undisputed. More importantly, consideration of his plays from this perspective is, as one might expect, an undertaking that provides both intellectual and existential stimulation.

Attention to Shakespeare's female characters is of course not new. Looking through Robert C. Steemsma's (by now dated) bibliography of Shakespeare and women,[2] one might feel the despair that Virginia Woolf experienced as she consulted the British Museum's catalogue entry on women and wondered: "How shall I ever find the grains of truth embedded in this mass of paper?"[3] But most of these works have only incidentally considered the questions that will be asked by the generation of students emancipated by Germaine Greer's *Female Eunuch*.[4] The older works, if they are

[1] Ed. Stewart A. Baker (New York: Harper and Row, 1971).

[2] "Shakespeare and Women: A Bibliography," *Shakespeare Newsletter* 12 (1962), 12. The most important recent book on the subject is by Juliet Dusinberre, *Shakespeare and the Nature of Women* (London: Macmillan, 1975).

[3] *A Room of One's Own* (New York: Harcourt, 1957), p. 27.

[4] (New York: McGraw-Hill, 1970).

anything more than journalism (like Heine's *Shakespeares Mädchen und Frauen*), usually limit themselves to drawing character portraits, sometimes impressively written from a performer's point of view (such as *Shakespeare's Female Characters* by Helen Faucit, Lady Martin). But often they are marred by excessive adulation of Shakespeare the man, defensiveness about women, and facile judgments about the Elizabethan age. Thus Anna B. Jameson writes in *Shakespeare's Heroines*: "If the freedom of some of the expressions used by Rosalind or Beatrice be objected to, let it be remembered that this was not the fault of Shakespeare or of women, but generally of the age."[5] Nevertheless as T.J.B. Spencer has shown, these works provide useful information for a history of the reception of Shakespeare's female characters.[6] Germaine Greer observes that "it is still to be proved how much we owe of what is good in the ideal of exclusive love and cohabitation to Shakespeare" (p. 204).

Instead of pursuing so ambitious a topic I would like to present one way in which I have considered Shakespeare in a general course on the image of women in literature. Original stimulants for this section of the course were Greer's book, particularly the chapter "Romance," and two brilliant but seemingly perverse arguments recently advanced: that Shakespeare's Kate is a "romantic" shrew,[7] and that his romantic comedies expose romantic susceptibilities to ridicule.[8]

Although the value of theme and motif studies has been questioned[9] and some scholars believe they are "most often

5 (Philadelphia: H. Altemus, n.d.), p. 66. First ed. London, 1832.

6 "Shakespeare and the Noble Woman," *Shakespeare-Jahrbuch* (1966), 49-62.

7 Charles Brooks, "Shakespeare's Romantic Shrews," *Shakespeare Quarterly* 11 (1960), 351-56.

8 M. A. Shaaber, "The Comic View of Life in Shakespeare's Comedies," in *The Drama of the Renaissance: Essays for Leicester Bradner*, ed. E. M. Blistein (Providence: Brown Univ. Press, 1970), pp. 165-78.

9 In his chapter "Stoff und Motivgeschichte," which summarizes trends in this field of studies, Ulrich Weisstein cites the serious reser-

apprentice work of young literary historians,"[10] I organized my course according to motifs relating to the presentation of women characters. Practitioners of this method believe that a close comparison of versions of similar motifs against the background of a longitudinal cut through literary history can sharpen the observer's attention to detail in the individual work.[11] And ideally the new light generated is not shed upon the individual work alone, showing it finally in radiant isolation, but also upon the nexus between the theme and the society for which the author wrote. Furthermore, it would be a mistake to think of all motifs as conceptually "neutral," as empty receptacles to be endowed with meaning at the will of the author. There are some that are "loaded," and one of these is the motif I call "wives willfully tested."

Kate the shrew was not a favorite of the earlier admirers of Shakespeare's women—Jameson, Martin, and Heine manage to avoid discussing her altogether. But if we open our diachronic lens wide enough we can hope for some insight even from one of Shakespeare's more controversial creations.

I began my survey of women willfully tested with Enide, the heroine of Chrestien's romance *Erec and Enide*, and ended it with Rennie, the unfortunate wife in John Barth's *The End of the Road*. In between there is the best-known English elaboration of the theme, Chaucer's "Clerk's Tale" (a version of Petrarch's Griselda story) and its derivative, the Elizabethan *Patient Grissill* by Dekker, Chettle, and

---

vations of some of the ancestors of comparative literature, Baldensperger and Van Tieghem, and also of Wellek (*Einführung in die Vergleichende Literaturwissenschaft* [Stuttgart: Kohlhammer, 1968], p. 71).

[10] Reported by Manfred Beller, "Von der Stoffgeschichte zur Thematologie: ein Beitrag zur komparatistischen Methodenlehre," *Arcadia* 5 (1970), 1.

[11] See Beller, p. 8. Also Adam J. Bisanz, "Zwischen Stoffgeschichte und Themathologie: Betrachtungen zu einem literaturtheoretischen Dilemma," *Deutsche Vierteljahrsschrift für Literaturwissenschaft und Geistesgeschichte* 47 (1973), 148-66.

Houghton, and then there is Margret the lodge-keeper's daughter of Greene's *Friar Bacon and Friar Bungay*. Of course the list does not aim at completeness: if space (or in a course, time) permitted it could easily be doubled. But the examples are sufficient to point up the curious fact that these works never deal with male-female relationships in social isolation, but in the context of hierarchies of social rank.

Enide, the heroine of Chrestien's romance, is the daughter of a poor *vavassor*. Of course it is not her upbringing in poverty that causes her tribulation. But it may not be an accident that the poet thought this background fitting for his paragon of wifely obedience and love. Even at the end of the romance, after she has shown her willingness to follow every caprice of Erec's will and has been reinstated as his *dame*, her submissive love retains an element of gratitude to him for having lifted her out of poverty.[12] The disparity of wealth and rank between male tester and tested wife in Chaucer's "Clerk's Tale" is so obvious that I would hardly need to mention it except to note the interesting circumstance that Chaucer further heightened the disparity of wealth that he found in his source.[13] Splendor is Walter's attribute as much as poverty is Griselda's.

While Chaucer does not entirely condone Lord Walter's cruel treatment of his low-born wife, the Elizabethan play on the same subject forces the most out-spoken critic of the husband's actions to admit finally: "None else but Kings can know the hearts of Kings, / Hence foorth my pride shall fly with humbler wings" (*Patient Grissill*, V.ii.217-218). This may also be the message of the Margret-Lacy subplot of *Friar Bacon and Friar Bungay*, where after being wooed by Lord Lacy, the lodge-keeper's daughter receives a stunning letter from him, denouncing his affection and announcing his engagement to a high lady of the court. As she is about to

[12] For details see my "Rank and Marriage: A Study of the Motif of 'Woman Willfully Tested,'" *Comparative Literature Studies* 9 (1972), 365-75.

[13] Schleiner, pp. 365-75.

become a nun Margret learns that the letter was only a device to test her constancy. She passes the test and marries happily, and we must assume that in the eyes of Greene's audience, a lord who stooped to woo a lowly maid was justified in testing her.

I have argued elsewhere that such disparities of rank are not simply reflections of the societies for which the respective authors wrote, but that they enter very deeply into the construction of these works, affecting the sense of verisimilitude and probability, the choice of characters, and the shape of the plot. Renaissance versions of the theme of a low-born girl marrying beyond her rank can be viewed in another way as well, from another perspective, as instances of the kind of "romance" whose survival in our times has been so well documented from modern literature and subliterature by Germaine Greer. By romance she means a sex-specific and stereotyped fantasy about the marriage partner, and shows that such projection, in spite of its vicarious nature, is potent enough to distort actual behavior: "The lover in romance is a man of masterful ways, clearly superior to his beloved in at least one respect, usually in several, being older or of higher social rank and attainment or more intelligent and *au fait*." And again a few pages later, "The strength of the belief that a man should be stronger and older than his woman can hardly be exaggerated. I cannot claim to be fully emancipated from the dream that some enormous man, say six foot six, heavily shouldered and so forth to match, will crush me to his tweeds, look down into my eyes and leave the taste of heaven or the scorch of his passion on my waiting lips. For three weeks I was married to him" (pp. 170, 171).

There is no disparity of rank in *The Taming of the Shrew*; nor is there any difference of wealth between Kate and Petruchio. It may seem, then, as if the tests to which Kate is subjected are generated purely by an assumed male superiority. Many readers take the play this way. Some of them find Kate's final speech on matrimonial obedience unbearable and therefore, assuming that what should not be cannot be, go beneath the letter to interpret her disquisition ironically.[14] Actresses sometimes underscore this interpretation with smiles or flippant gestures.

But Kate's shrewishness and its cure must be taken seriously. In Germaine Greer's view, "Kate is a woman striving for her own existence in a world where she is a *stale*, a decoy to be bid for against her sister's higher market value, so she opts out by becoming unmanageable, a scold" (p. 205). This reading projects too much modern sensibility and motivation into her. A more likely meaning of the word "stale" in the context where Kate uses it (I.i.58) would be laughingstock. To see virtue in her shrewishness goes against the drift of the play. Not only is she described from the beginning as "stark mad" and "wonderful froward" (I.i.69), but the spectator witnesses her defying her father's request (I.i.102-4), torturing her sister, and maltreating her presumed music teacher. Therefore I think that in his attempt to see Kate as a "romantic shrew" Charles Brooks overemphasizes Shakespeare's "humanizing of the shrew" (giving her attractive traits that temper her shrewishness)[15] when he points to Kate's sense of shame and her pity for the servants abused by Petruchio. The shame and pity are fruits of Petruchio's "cure," and mark stages in her transformation from the shrew she was at the beginning. Her shrewishness is conceived of as a condition of dissonance or intemperance.

The medical concepts of humoral psychology are quite appropriate here. Summarizing a host of earlier views in his usual fashion, Robert Burton describes a distemper to which young women (notably virgins) are prone, listing among the

[14] Margaret Webster sees in Kate's speech a "delicious irony," and to prove her point supplies an interlinear gloss for it in *Shakespeare Without Tears* (New York: McGraw-Hill, 1942), p. 142. Although Juliet Dusinberre does not follow such a reading, she maintains in a somewhat similar vein that the very end of the play "casts a shadow of ambiguity across its conclusions" (p. 108).

[15] Brooks, p. 352.

symptoms "perverse conceits and opinions" and "preposterous judgement. They are apt to loathe, dislike, disdaine, to be weary of every object, etc., each thing is almost tedious to them."[16] Young women living at ease "in great houses" are especially likely to be afflicted by this malady, which is said to be caused by "vicious vapours" arising from excess menstrual blood in a physically and sexually inactive woman who is not bearing children. (Nuns and widows are also prone to this "feral" condition.) Again basing himself on his sources, Burton suggests that in serious cases "labour and exercise, strict diet, rigour and threats may opportunely be used, and are able of themselves to qualify and divert an ill-disposed temperament" (I,417).

Petruchio's diagnosis of Kate as choleric or distempered is clear from his description of her at their first meeting, once we read his words in their ironically intended reverse sense:

> For she's not froward, but modest as the dove;
> She is not hot, but temperate as the morn;
> For patience she will prove a second Grissel.
> (II.i.293-95)

We must also take note of Petruchio's reference to Kate's "mad and headstrong humor," especially since it occurs in a soliloquy, where he can be assumed to be speaking his mind:

> This is a way to kill a wife with kindness,
> And thus I'll curb her mad and headstrong humor.
> He that knows better how to tame a shrew,
> Now let him speak; 'tis charity to shew.
> (IV.i.208-11)

---

[16] *Anatomy of Melancholy*, 1.3.2.4 (London: Dent Everyman, 1932), I,415-16. For Burton any distemper comes to be subsumed under "melancholy" in a broad sense. John Draper, in *The Humors and Shakespeare's Characters* (Durham, N.C.: Duke Univ. Press, 1945), p. 112, briefly refers to Petruchio's treatment of his choleric "patient."

His "killing kindness" consists in pretending to take her for more seriously affected by choler than she is (he hints at this pretense in the same monologue). Thus the details of his therapy are in a sense mere show: they are intended to wear her out physically and at the same time make her aware of her eccentricity.

In the scene preceding his central monologue, Petruchio had shown a sample of his technique in throwing the food at the servants before Kate could touch it and claiming,

> I tell thee Kate, 'twas burnt and dried away,
> And I expressly am forbid to touch it;
> For it engenders choler, planteth anger,
> And better 'twere that both of us did fast,
> Since of ourselves, ourselves are choleric,
> Than feed it with such overroasted flesh.

(IV.i.170-75)

The servant Grumio's subsequent refusal to serve her certain food because "I fear it is too choleric a meat" (IV.iii.19,22) is a variation of the same idea.

The anonymous *The Taming of a Shrew* likewise has Grumio's analogue Sander refer to Kate's choler in this scene (scene xi), the only reference to Kate's "humor" in that play.[17] Thus this passage (or its antecedent in a possible common source) may have been a source of stimulation for Shakespeare. More importantly, the difference between the plays in this respect tends to support my idea about the significance of medical concepts in Shakespeare's conception of Kate.[18] The leading idea of the plot seems to be to show how a woman is changed from a shrew into a "second

[17] Theories about *The Taming of a Shrew* as possible source of *The Taming of the Shrew* are briefly summarized by Geoffrey Bullough, *Narrative and Dramatic Sources of Shakespeare*, I (New York: Columbia Univ. Press, 1964), 57-58.

[18] In her *Voices of Melancholy* (London: Routledge, 1971), p. 54, Bridget Gellert Lyons notes that according to the Induction the play proper is put on as Sly's "cure" of melancholy. There is no analogue of this idea in *A Shrew* either.

Grissel" (II.i.295). The fact that Shakespeare presents us at the outset with a singularly obnoxious shrew suggests a clear line of progression. In the anonymous *Shrew* play, Sly walks away, after partly watching the play and partly sleeping through it, thinking that he now knows how to tame his wife if she should become shrewish. I cannot imagine that Shakespeare's audience was expected to react very differently, although some of my students have objected that Sly may not be the most reliable informant.

It would seem that Shakespeare deliberately ruled out a simple "romantic" interest as Petruchio's primary motive for attempting a cure. He states programmatically that his only requirement for a prospective wife is wealth, be she "curst and shrowd / As Socrates' Xantippe" (I.ii.70-71). (Romantic habits of thinking being what they are, many readers and spectators will object that Petruchio has not yet met Kate at this point, and that he falls in love with her as soon as he sees her.) Moreover, in contrast to the other works presenting female testing that we reviewed briefly, the two protagonists are not differentiated in any scale of rank or wealth: there is none of the disparity which in later versions of the testing theme (Gerhart Hauptmann's *Griseldis* of 1909 might also be considered), and in such modern popular spectacles as *Love Story* and *Five Easy Pieces* serves as the source of "romance" in the wider sense. But there is a sense of male-female hierarchy at the center of the play. Petruchio excels Kate not only in physical strength but also in intelligence, as is evidenced by his resourcefulness in manipulating people. Whether we experience this superiority as crushing depends partly, as I have tried to show, on how seriously we take Kate's shrewishness. Of course such male-female disparity is by itself potentially a source of romance (and probably in any modern work actually its source). But the female obedience advocated by Kate in her final plea is based not on a mythic belief in male dominance but on a social conception of male-female hierarchy. As M. C. Bradbrook has rightly seen, "her grand oration does not evoke the muddled theology which winds up *The Taming of a Shrew*, but recalls man's social claims as a bread winner, protector and temporal lord."[19] In a central passage Kate says a husband is

> one that cares for thee,
> And for thy maintenance; commits his body
> To painful labor, both by sea and land;
> To watch the night in storms, the day in cold,
> Whilst thou li'st warm at home, secure and safe.
>
> (V.ii.147-51)

Surely these elements of her speech are based on a social order so natural and commonplace to the playwright and his audience that the presence of romance is ruled out. Kate's cure has enabled her to represent the old hierarchical view of marriage as a beneficial relationship in which the husband rules, protects, and "husbands," and the wife submits, supports, and produces.

Since the result of our consideration of the *Shrew* in relation to romance was essentially negative, I decided to illustrate the functioning of romance in one of the comedies usually called "romantic." I started with M. A. Shaaber's stimulating suggestion that for several of Shakespeare's *romantic comedies*, among them *As You Like It*, the stress in the term should be on the noun rather than on the adjective: "And in fact—what should be no surprise at all—the comic view of life in these plays is largely a comic view of love" (p. 172). Comparing *As You Like It* with its source, Lodge's *Rosalynde*, Shaaber found a world of difference in the dialogue of the courting situations. The difference was not merely one of euphuistic prose style versus dramatic presentation: "The truth is that Shakespeare's characters are Laodiceans in the religion of love. Not heretics: there is nothing in their conduct or their ideals which is clearly repugnant to its tenets, but they are perfunctory and indifferent worshippers at its altars" (p. 169).

[19] "Dramatic Rôle as Social Image: A Study of *The Taming of the Shrew*," *Shakespeare-Jahrbuch* 94 (1958), 145.

From a number of plays Shaaber compiles a chorus of witty disparagement of love and says:

> In *As You Like It* this gibing at love reaches a peak, for Rosalind's undertaking to cure Orlando of his infatuation, to wash his liver as clean as a sound sheep's heart, that there shall not be one spot of love in it, affords an unparalleled opportunity to canvass the affectations of lovers. She describes the marks of a lover—his lean cheek, his sunken eye, his unsociableness, his neglect of his dress —and the changeableness of women, "longing, and liking, proud, fantastical, apish, shallow, inconstant, full of tears, full of smiles." She admonishes Orlando that "Men have died from time to time, and worms have eaten them, but not for love," that love lasts not "for ever and a day" but a day without the "ever," that the wiser a woman is, the waywarder. . . . The indictment is quite comprehensive. (p. 174)

I cannot agree with this reading of Rosalind's words, although I recognize that Shakespeare added a new dimension to the plot by introducing the Touchstone-Audrey and Jacques subplots. If there is a hint of an indictment of women and romantic love in the words of Lodge's Rosalynde, there is even less in Shakespeare's Rosalind's speech; while Lodge's Rosalynde as she makes some of these remarks is playing a boy, posing as a girl, in Shakespeare's play the seriousness is one more step removed: the girl pretending to be a boy, now on a stage playing a girl, is played by a boy actor. It is curious to find even Germaine Greer taking Rosalind's false claim that she can cure love by pretense seriously: "In *As You Like It* Rosalind finds the means to wean Orlando of his futile Italianate posturing, disfiguring trees with bad poetry" (p. 204). But Shakespeare signals clearly that Rosalind is serious neither in word nor in action when she announces in an aside: "I will speak to him [Orlando] like a saucy lackey, and under that habit play the knave with him" (III.ii.295-97). The later "indictment" of women and love is likewise spoken "like a saucy lackey."

Rosalind immensely enjoys the "playing" she refers to—it allows her an even greater level of control over Orlando than a simple courting situation would. If Germaine Greer is right that at the center of the female view of romance is the dream of being "the mistress of all she surveys, the cynosure of all eyes" (p. 182) as summarized in a courting situation, then Rosalind's play represents the *ne plus ultra* of romantic fantasy.

Shakespeare's reworking of the dénouement of one strand of the main love intrigue from his source seems to confirm this emphasis. I have argued elsewhere that Lodge's technique in his romance, despite his supposedly egalitarian setting, consists in playing with certain differences in rank among his characters.[20] In terms of implied hierarchical values, the final revelation scene on the eve of the wedding day deserves attention, since it is the conclusion of the love story between Saladyne and Aliena (Shakespeare's Oliver and Celia). Rosalind has just revealed that she is the princess, and has fallen into the arms of Saladyne's brother, the noble Rosader. The shepherdess Phoebe has finally accepted the shepherd Montanus as her groom. (There is no need to regret her lack of passion for the shepherd; both she and the reader know him to be her peer in wealth and beauty, and we are to assume that they are well matched.) Along with these weddings a third is to occur: the noble Saladyne will wed the shepherdess Aliena, who has not yet made known her noble parentage. How is this love affair to be brought to an aesthetically pleasing conclusion?

> Aliena seeing Saladyne stand in a dumpe, to wake him from his dreame, began thus. Why how now my Saladyne, all a mort, what melancholy man at the day of marriage? perchaunce thou art sorrowfull to thinke on thy brothers high fortunes, and thyne owne base desires to chuse so

---

[20] " 'That virtue is not measured by birth but by action': Reality versus Intention in Lodge's Rosalynde," *Zeitschrift für Anglistik und Amerikanistik* 23 (1975), 12-15.

meane a shepheardize. Cheare vp thy hart man, for this day thou shalt bee married to the daughter of a King: for know Saladyne, I am not Aliena, but Alinda the daughter of thy mortal enemie Torismond (*AYLI*, New Variorum, p. 385).

The reader who would expect Saladyne to protest against the suggestion that "base desires" led to the choice of "so mean a shepherdess" is disappointed. Saladyne does not protest. Nor is there any reason to suppose that he is not sad about the prospect of marrying a shepherdess while his brother's fiancée has turned out to be a princess. Saladyne is "in a dump." In terms of later love theory he seriously mars the entire love experience that has gone before. Of course the idea that love can transcend social rank has since become a staple of romance. A later writer might, for example, have viewed Aliena's presumed low status as proof of the sincerity and power of Saladyne's love. For Lodge, however (if we exclude the possibility that he blundered), the aesthetic satisfaction of matching two persons of comparable rank overruled other considerations.

We cannot determine why the passage did not appeal to Shakespeare, whether because of its unromantic quality or because it did not seem dramatic enough: for whatever reason, he left it out. Led by Hymen, Celia (Lodge's Aliena) and Rosalind simply enter the stage undisguised, whereupon Hymen then pairs off the lovers. Thus our impression of Oliver's love for the lowly shepherdess ("Neither call the giddiness of it in question, the poverty of her, the small acquaintance, my sudden wooing," etc.—V.ii.5-7) remains intact. We never leave the realm of romance.

Observing the projection of male and female fantasy and its nexus with senses of social hierarchy in Shakespeare's plays can be a stimulating experience. Differences of rank at the core of most versions of female testing (potentially a source of "romance" in Greer's sense) are absent in Shakespeare's *Taming of the Shrew*. Male-female hierarchy as advocated by Kate at the end of the play can of course also be a romantic projection, but I resist this interpretation because Kate's eccentricity at the opening is extreme and her cure dominates the action, and further because her final submission appears to be couched in conceptions commonplace to the Elizabethans. While I thus find Kate not romantic, not even in Brooks's sense of good-natured shrewishness, I see Rosalind and Celia of *As You Like It*, who thrive on the courting situation which makes them "mistresses of all they survey," as truly romantic heroines. The approach requires an attention to the self and to the text, and most interestingly highlights the problem of historical perspective.

III. THE COURSE IN SHAKESPEARE:
GENRE AND CANON

SIX

ON TEACHING THE SHAKESPEARE CANON: THE CASE OF *MEASURE FOR MEASURE*

A. C. HAMILTON

THE neglected art of teaching deserves some priority over criticism, which now resembles a breeder nuclear reactor wildly out of control. Modern Shakespeare criticism breeds endlessly upon itself as each new article or book is launched from an opening footnote which catalogues the dozen or more studies on the same topic, or it spawns independently, and therefore repetitiously, by ignoring what others have often said. "The like infinite Allegories I could pike out of other Poeticall fictions," Sir John Harington boasts of his interpretation of the story of Persius:[1] how much more, then, may modern sophisticated critics pick out of Shakespeare's thirty-seven plays, each (both critic and play) being inexhaustible. Criticism proliferates in part—and I say this as one who has written a number of articles and a book on Shakespeare—because it is easy to write: for the more than has been said, the more may be said. No moratorium or temporary freeze on Shakespeare criticism would restrict its uncontrolled growth for long, even if such were desirable. However, criticism may be directed and organized by exploring the ways in which Shakespeare may be taught.

I have taught—or, more correctly, tried to teach—Shakespeare in many ways, from treating a few plays fully to treating generally a number of plays either chronologically close or in the same genre. I have used many critical ap-

[1] Sir John Harington, Preface to Ariosto, *Orlando Furioso*, trans. Sir John Harington (1591), ed. R. McNulty (Oxford: Clarendon, 1972), p. 5.

proaches, from close rhetorical analysis to an examination of historical context, from treating genre, conventions, and decorum for the comedies to reading the chronicles as background for the history plays, from problems of interpretation for the romances to a study of sources, analogues, and archetypes for any of the plays, from a study of dramatic traditions to a history of stage production and criticism. I have used whatever ways and critical approaches were needed to remedy ignorance, stock expectations, faulty response, failure to respond, or whatever seemed to stand between students and a full, informed, sensitive, and personal response to Shakespeare's plays. I was never satisfied with what I had accomplished. I found that students failed —because I failed them—to understand the plays sufficiently to be able to possess them. They understood separate scenes but not a whole play, and their knowledge of separate plays was not cumulative and progressive. Later I realized that meaning is a function of context: the meaning of any part of a play is given by its context in the play, and the meaning of the play is given by its context in the Shakespeare canon.

The turning point in teaching Shakespeare came for me when I toured with a dramatic company that was performing *Measure for Measure* in a number of small towns in the state of Washington. Since the director anticipated that rural audiences would find his interpretation of the play intellectually strenuous, he wanted an English teacher to parry questions on the evening before each performance. I expected a strong response but not such intensity and violence: the audiences found the play deeply disturbing, even distressing. The capacity of modern readers to respond deeply to the play seems to bring with it, perhaps necessarily, deep antagonism and resistance. Of course, I was worse off than the players because reading the play, and then talking about it, provided occasion to object to any scene. In parrying questions, I felt that I was confronting the play at its conception, as though the violent response of my audiences had provided the material out of which Shakespeare had written the play. I learned very quickly that my task was to explain the play without explaining it away, and to counter resistance to it without reducing its impact on the stage. In short, I had to persuade the audience to accept the play on its own terms. Any doubts that *Measure for Measure* is a problem play may be dispelled by answering questions about it from an audience in any small town in the state of Washington.

The chief problem was Isabella, in particular, her response to her brother's plea to save his life by serving Angelo's lust:

> O you beast!
> O faithless coward! O dishonest wretch!
> Wilt thou be made a man out of my vice?
> Is't not a kind of incest, to take life
> From thine own sister's shame? What should I think?
> Heaven shield my mother play'd my father fair!
> For such a warped slip of wilderness
> Ne'er issu'd from his blood. Take my defiance!
> Die, perish! Might but my bending down
> Reprieve thee from thy fate, it should proceed.
> I'll pray a thousand prayers for thy death,
> No word to save thee.
>
> (III.i.135-46)

Yet her fury toward him does not compare to the fury of my audiences toward her. They exceed Thersites' raillery against Ajax. In contrast, the response of critics is usually genteel, as in Hazlitt's finely turned scorn, "Neither are we greatly enamoured of Isabella's rigid chastity. . . . We do not feel the same confidence in the virtue that is 'sublimely good' at another's expense, as if it had been put to some less disinterested trial."[2] The response of university students is usually muted and puzzled. I wondered why this should be

[2] *Characters of Shakespear's Plays* (1817; rpt. London: G. Bell, 1884), pp. 224-25.

until an enterprising student of mine canvassed an entire woman's dorm to find out how her fellow students would respond to the terms of Angelo's ransom. Some 76 percent replied with a variation of the question: "Well, what's this Angelo like?" The rejection of Isabella by middle-aged male critics may be rejected in turn as simple chauvinism. What else would one expect of Sir Arthur Quiller-Couch than the response: "She is something rancid in her chastity; and, on top of this, not by any means such a saint as she looks," with its underlying eroticism: "One never knows where to take this paragon."[3] However, one must allow that the rejection of Isabella is too widespread to be simply prejudice. Nor is it simply a secular response. In a seminar at Toronto, a Mother Superior whom I had maneuvered into offering what I had expected to be a favorable opinion of Isabella said very firmly: "I know the type, and I would never have her in my convent." I concluded that the violent rejection of Isabella by my rural audiences was more deeply felt and openly expressed than any other I had confronted, less rationalized, blunted, or overlaid by prejudice, and that therefore it should be preserved.

Accordingly, I became uncomfortably aware that the scholarly-critical panoply that usually protects a teacher from the assaults of readers would not serve. Analogues, sources, and parallels only strengthen the case against Isabella. One major analogue, the story of the woman of Antioch who agreed upon her husband's urging to submit her body to a wealthy man if he would pay their taxes, is cited by Saint Augustine to prove that we cannot always condemn fornication.[4] What may be said then in defense of this religious novice who is so smugly assured that yielding to Angelo would be a mortal sin? In one major source, Cinthio's tale in *Hecatommithi*, the woman propositioned

[3] Preface to *Measure for Measure*, ed. Sir Arthur Quiller-Couch (Cambridge: Cambridge Univ. Press, 1922), pp. xxx-xxxi.

[4] See Geoffrey Bullough, *Narrative and Dramatic Sources of Shakespeare* (New York: Columbia Univ. Press, 1958), II, 418-19.

by the wicked judge is unwilling and tearful at first but, unlike Isabella, is persuaded to yield by her brother's appeal to "the motions of Nature in our blood and the love we have always shared."[5] Shakespeare refers to a brother's love "ever most kind and natural" but it is Frederick's for Mariana, and we learn of it only moments after Isabella has told Claudio, " 'Tis best that thou diest quickly" (III.i.150). A typical modern parallel to Cinthio's tale is the story of a Mrs. Bergmeier, a German woman imprisoned by the Russians in 1945: she asked a camp-guard to make her pregnant so that she would be sent to Berlin where she could take care of her family. The Reverend Donald Mathers concludes that even though she committed adultery, she was clearly not an immoral woman.[6] In the many versions of the story of the monstrous ransom, the terms remain essentially unchanged: a wife or sister is promised the release of a man condemned to death if she will yield herself to his judge. Being virtuous, she refuses; but finally, through bonds of family love, she is persuaded to yield.

Shakespeare follows this story to the point at which the woman goes to the prison to tell the terms of the ransom; then he makes one simple, profound change—so simple that his genius alone could make it, and so profound that it lifts a sordid tale to the level of great art: Isabella refuses to yield. There is no struggle in her mind, no agonizing dilemma over the conflicting claims of her chastity and love for her brother, and no attempt to soften her refusal; instead, there is the vehemence of her "O you beast," her loathing of his weakness, her wish that their mother had been an adulteress so that she need not accept such a brother, her unwillingness even to bend down to save him, and her willingness only to offer a thousand prayers for his death. A rare defender of her conduct, R. W. Chambers, cheats when he suggests that there is some mental anguish,

---

[5] Bullough, II, 424.

[6] Rev. Donald Mathers, *Not by Sight: Some Sermons and Occasional Talks* (Kingston, Ont.: priv. ptd., 1974), p. 26.

an agony in her soul when she denounces Claudio.[7] In her trumped-up lie to the Duke in the play's closing scene, she primly declares:

> after much debatement,
> My sisterly remorse confutes mine honor,
> And I did yield to him.
>
> (V.i.99-101)

Earlier she says unequivocally:

> Then, Isabel, live chaste, and, brother, die:
> More than our brother is our chastity.
>
> (II.iv.184-85)

Her stand for her chastity is absolute.

After the first hectic evening with my rural audience, I was tempted to invoke historical scholarship, the normal means by which a teacher seeks to disqualify modern readers, if they object to anything, by letting them know that, having been badly brought up, they are not responding as they should. For the next town I planned a short lecture, or sermon, with the defiant title, "*Measure for Measure*, or What Price Chastity?" in which I would shame my audience for its moral laxity in denouncing Isabella by citing Renaissance moralists to prove how solemnly Renaissance readers would have upheld her chastity. However, I decided not to fob them off with this academic ploy: it denied the dramatic point of Shakespeare's version of the story. Also, I couldn't trust my audience to have sufficient respect not to ask what Renaissance readers I had in mind. I doubted whether my Renaissance moralists would have read the play or, if they had, would have approved.

I was forced to recognize that one must not try to escape the shock of Isabella's refusal. The play is to be experienced rather than explained: if we accept it, we must accept that refusal and its shock to our sensibilities. For Shakespeare shaped the story to present that refusal as a simple dramatic

---

[7] *Man's Unconquerable Mind* (London: J. Cape, 1939), pp. 290-92.

act. To this end he made the brother's fault as excusable as the story allows: instead of raping a virgin, as in the sources, Claudio has consummated a *de praesenti* marriage with a willing bride. Except for Angelo, everyone excuses him, even the "enskied and sainted" Isabella who responds to the news of her brother's fornication by saying, "O, let him marry her" (I.iv.49). It is essential not to explain her refusal by taking her out of the play in order to judge her as a neurotic female with a hang-up on virginity, or by leaving her in the play to judge her as a teen-age religious novice with a hang-up on high moral standards. Shakespeare makes her a novice to indicate that she may be capable of her refusal. That refusal should come as a climactic act, as central to the play as its place in the scene and play indicates. Accordingly, I did not try to defend her before my hostile audiences or even try to explain her refusal. Instead, I claimed only that she was the kind of dramatic character Shakespeare needed for the kind of play that he decided to write.

The tour taught me, even though I may not have persuaded my audiences, that dramatic characters and their actions must be accepted without moral approval or condemnation. Since Isabella's commitment to chastity expresses her role in the play, it must be accepted as one accepts the role of any of Shakespeare's characters, whether we approve or not, as Tamora's commitment to revenge, Juliet's to love, or Othello's to jealousy. A particularly relevant comparison, because it is similar in function but contrary in its working, is the resolution of *The Two Gentlemen of Verona* in which Valentine offers his beloved Silvia to Proteus for the sake of their friendship. The act tests the protagonist's moral nature and fulfills his/her dramatic role in the play.

If Isabella's refusal is accepted as an act which fulfills her role in the play, it may be seen to test fully the virtue which fulfills her nature. At the beginning she wants to be tested by further restrictions before she enters the sisterhood. Here

A. C. HAMILTON

her virtue is hardly more than continence. When her counterpart, Angelo, who also wants to be tested before he assumes the Duke's role, tempts her, his virtue is tested against hers. He is exposed as a mere seemer while she is as she seems to be. Their confrontation is the most dramatic version in literature, for she tempts him through virtue rather than vice, and he falls through strength rather than weakness. In effect, her answer to the question, "What price chastity?" is that it is priceless: as the highest natural virtue which preserves the body and soul for union with God, it is to be preferred over the closest bonds of human love. Here the relevant contrast is with that "Roman dame," Lucrece, who chooses to submit to Tarquin rather than be killed and then slandered by him. Once her body is polluted, she is willing to suffer her "poor soul's pollution" (1.1157) by taking her own life.

In fulfilling her virtue, however, Isabella overreaches herself, for her chastity conflicts with charity toward others. Angelo perverts the relation between these virtues when he urges that charity should serve lust:

> *Ang.* Might there not be a charity in sin
> To save this brother's life?
> *Isab.* Please you to do't,
> I'll take it as a peril to my soul,
> It is no sin at all, but charity.
> *Ang.* Pleas'd you to do't at peril of your soul,
> Were equal poise of sin and charity.
> (II.iv.63-68)

Ideally, chastity leads to charity by separating love from lust. The conjunction of the two virtues is noted by the Lady in Milton's *Comus* when she addresses "pure-eyed Faith, white-handed Hope . . . And thou unblemish'd form of Chastity."[8] Their opposition is denounced by Langland: "chastite withoute charite worth [shall be] cheyned in helle."

8 Lines 212-14; *Poems*, ed. J. Carey and A. Fowler (London: Longmans, 1968).

Those who are chaste but lack charity he compares to the foolish virgins of Matthew 25:

> It is as lewed as a laumpe þat no liȝte is Inne.
> Many chapeleynes arne chaste ac charite is away . . .
> Vnkynde to her kyn and to alle cristene,
> Chewen here charite and chiden after more.
> Such chastite wiþ-outen charite worth cheyned in helle![9]

If Isabella should sacrifice her chastity in the name of charity, however, her "rank offense" would only free Claudio to keep on offending (III.i.99-100) and "Mercy . . . would prove itself a bawd" (149).

Once Chastity is tested beyond its own strength—the earlier sense of virtue—it must be assisted by some higher power. In her moment of peril, the Lady in *Comus* believes that God will send "a glistering guardian if need were / To keep my life and honour unassailed" (11.218-19), and for her that guardian appears as an attendant spirit disguised as a shepherd. For Isabella, it appears as the Duke disguised as a friar. Unlike the earlier romantic comedies, as Northrop Frye has noted, there is no "second world" into which she may flee:[10] no green world or forest, no enchanted world of fairies with magic potions to save her from others and from herself. Instead, there is only the fallen world of Vienna, marked by unrestrained concupiscence, where "corruption [will] boil and bubble, / Till it o'errun the stew" (V.i.318-19). Of necessity, then, the play breaks at this point, and the second half shows how the Duke labors to resolve the potentially tragic action as a comedy.

In discussing this second half, I found it necessary to begin by recognizing the place of the play in the canon of Shakespeare's works. Usually the larger context of a play is genre, but *Measure for Measure* stands isolated from the ro-

[9] *Piers the Plowman*, Passus i 186-92, B Text, ed. W. W. Skeat (London: Early English Text Society, 1869).

[10] Northrop Frye, *Anatomy of Criticism* (Princeton: Princeton Univ. Press, 1957), p. 183.

mantic comedies which had culminated earlier in *Twelfth Night*. To relate it to its companion play, *All's Well*, would not resolve any problems but only parallel and multiply them. While *Measure for Measure* was written during the period of the major tragedies, it stands isolated from them by its comic form. On the other hand, it seems peculiarly related to them, as though Shakespeare were shaping tragic matter into comic form. E. K. Chambers notes the special position of the play when he observes that "a narrower spiritual gulf divides *Measure for Measure* from the tragedy of *King Lear* than from the comedy of *As You Like It*."[11] It would seem that the proper context of the play is both tragedy and comedy, and specifically, the point at which the two genres clash.

The central fact about tragedy is acceptance of death. As J. V. Cunningham has shown, "the principle of its being is death, and when this is achieved the play is ended."[12] However the hero may be committed to life—by the demands of personal revenge, political ambition, or public affairs—finally he must accept death and take upon himself man's destiny as one born to die. In contrast, the central fact about comedy is acceptance of life. As Northrop Frye has shown, Shakespeare's romantic comedy has affinities with the seasonal ritual-play: "we may call it the drama of the green world, its plot being assimilated to the ritual theme of the triumph of life and love over the waste land."[13] The business of the plot is to remove all obstacles that stand in the way of this final triumph. The two genres clash in *Romeo and Juliet* in which the matter is comic and the form tragic. In the other tragedies, the hero is gradually stripped of all that commits him to life until at the end he stands alone willing his own death. Hamlet's commitment to death is marked by his sojourn in the graveyard and his resolution

[11] *Shakespeare: A Survey* (London: Sidgwick & Jackson, 1925), p. 216.
[12] *Woe or Wonder: The Emotional Effect of Shakespearean Tragedy* (Denver: Swallow, 1964), p. 12.
[13] Frye, p. 182.

that "the readiness is all." All the tragic heroes reach this point, whether it is the rejection of life in Macbeth's despairing cry, "It is a tale / Told by an idiot, full of sound and fury, / Signifying nothing" (V.v.26-28) or the acceptance of death in Lear's brave boast, "I will die bravely, like a smug bridegroom" (IV.vi.198) and Antony's "I will be / A bridegroom in my death, and run into't / As to a lover's bed" (IV.xiv.99-101).

In *Measure for Measure* this tragic point is reached in the prison scene. Isabella goes there to tell Claudio of Angelo's terms "and fit his mind to death, for his soul's rest" (II.iv.187). But his mind is fitted for death by the Duke's counsel:

> Be absolute for death: either death or life
> Shall thereby be the sweeter. Reason thus with life:
> If I do lose thee, I do lose a thing
> That none but fools would keep. A breath thou art,
> Servile to all the skyey influences,
> That dost this habitation where thou keep'st
> Hourly afflict. Merely, thou art Death's fool.
>
> (III.i.5-11)

After his lengthy counsel, Claudio is ready to die: "To sue to live, I find I seek to die, / And seeking death, find life. Let it come on" (42-43). Consequently, although Isabella fears that he may fear death, she may lead him to accept death as readily as any tragic hero:

> If I must die,
> I will encounter darkness as a bride,
> And hug it in mine arms. (82-84)

As comic characters know, however, there is "much virtue in If": Claudio's acceptance of death is conditional. Once Isabella is persuaded to reveal that he need not die if she will yield to Angelo, fear of death is stronger than contempt for life. With his plea to her, "Sweet sister, let me live" (132), the inevitable course of tragedy is suddenly stopped.

That plea echoes Falstaff's "give me life": it declares that the tragic action must be resolved as a comedy.

Until the moment when he weakens, Claudio's state manifests the life of Vienna in which unrestrained concupiscence condemns man to death. Men live under the penalty of death, which has not been paid only because the Duke has not enforced the law. Claudio says of their lives:

> Our natures do pursue,
> Like rats that ravin down their proper bane,
> A thirsty evil, and when we drink we die.
>
> (I.ii.128-30)

That same state is shared in part even by the two who do not share that life: by Angelo who enforces a law against Claudio which condemns him as soon as he is forced to "confess / A natural guiltiness such as is his" (II.ii.138-39), and by Isabella whose contempt for life leads her to accept death as a lover:

> . . . were I under the terms of death,
> Th' impression of keen whips I'ld wear as rubies,
> And strip myself to death, as to a bed
> That longing have been sick for.
>
> (II.iv.100-103)

The role of the Duke, as ruler and architect of the comic resolution, is to lead his subjects to accept life.

Since the Duke acts within Vienna, his efforts are continually balked or foiled: he is abused and discomfited by Lucio's slanders; he is deceived by Angelo's wickedness in ordering Claudio's death for a sin which he himself has committed; he is frustrated by Barnadine's unwillingness to be a substitute victim; and, at the end, he is surprised (I believe) by Isabella's willingness to kneel with Mariana to plead for Angelo's life. In all he does, he must depend on disguise, lies, and deception. In persuading Mariana to be a substitute bedmate, he resorts to an act characteristic of the fallen world of Vienna, a ready willingness to yield to fornication. He assures her " 'tis no sin" (IV.i.73) even though he has urged Juliet, who has committed the same act, to repent her sin. Lacking the "second world," he cannot expect his subjects to be converted (as Oliver and Frederick in *As You Like It*), transformed (as Demetrius in *A Midsummer Night's Dream*), or reformed (as Orsino in *Twelfth Night*); instead, he must trick, mislead, and beguile them, doing whatever he must to redeem them. In what he does, he goes some way to earn Lucio's title for him, "the old fantastical Duke of dark corners" (IV.iii.156-57).

As Isabella must be accepted in her role in the play, so must the Duke. Any explanation that he acts as Divine Providence, or excuse that his role is a stage convention,[14] is as irrelevant to our understanding the play as any denunciation of him. While my rural audiences were shocked by Isabella's refusal to save Claudio by yielding herself to Angelo, they were outraged by the Duke's subsequent actions and her willing compliance with them. Their "gut" response was the same, though less rationalized, as that given by accepted Shakespeare scholars who judge that the Duke "hardly seems to be a person to delight in" (H. C. Hart in the Old Arden edition) or that "he undergoes no inner development of character and achieves no added self-knowledge" (J. W. Lever in the New). In my baptism of fire, I learned not to defend the Duke, nor gloss over his actions, nor try to subvert a strong response by scholarly subterfuge. Instead, I tried to preserve the energy of that response without its negative judgment by pointing to the direction of the Duke's actions.

The Duke seeks to redeem his subjects by manipulating each to the point of accepting what in effect defines life in Vienna, its dedication to death. He wants to make them

14 The views, respectively, of G. Wilson Knight, *The Wheel of Fire* (London: Oxford Univ. Press, 1930), and W. W. Lawrence, *Shakespeare's Problem Comedies* (New York: Macmillan, 1931).

"absolute for death" as they were before he interceded, but now they will be under his control. Then he may invert their separate tragedies into a comic resolution by a final peripeteia. Since he must act in Vienna, his means of redeeming his subjects are parodied by Barnadine, the one character always "absolute for death" provided that it comes at a convenient time. The Provost describes him as "a man that apprehends death no more dreadfully but as a drunken sleep, careless, reakless, and fearless of what's past, present, or to come; insensible of mortality, and desperately mortal" (IV.ii.142-45). When he is called upon to die, he declares himself not ready and refuses to submit to the Duke's peremptory "O sir, you must" (IV.iii.57). Foiled of a substitute victim in him, the Duke must find another, and try again— without success as the final scene shows—to "persuade this rude wretch willingly to die" (IV.iii.81).

For Claudio, the Duke need merely take away the "if" of his "If I must die" by telling him that Angelo intends his death. Immediately, Claudio becomes "absolute for death": "I am so out of love with life that I will sue to be rid of it" (III.i.171-72). For Juliet, he need merely shrive her: knowing that Claudio must die, she regrets her own reprieve "that respites me a life whose very comfort / Is still a dying horror" (II.iii.41-42). For Angelo, he arranges the bed-trick in order to make him guilty of the crime he condemns in Claudio. Since Angelo upholds measure for measure in the law, he condemns himself by saying to Escalus: "When I, that censure him, do so offend, / Let mine own judgment pattern out my death" (II.i.29-30). Accordingly, once his crime is exposed by the Duke, he becomes "absolute for death": "Immediate sentence then, and sequent death, / Is all the grace I beg" (V.i.373-74).

For Mariana, the Duke need not make her "absolute for death": having been rejected by Angelo, she leads a melancholy, withdrawn life which Isabella judges to be not worth living: "What a merit were it in death to take this poor maid from the world" (III.i.231-32). As soon as she is married to Angelo, however, she pleads for his life and begs Isabella to plead with her. The Duke had persuaded Isabella to accept her brother's death by urging her to find comfort in his counsel: "That life is better life, past fearing death, / Than that which lives to fear" (V.i.397-98). Her response, "I do, my lord," marks the point at which she is "absolute for death." Then the example of Mariana's love persuades her to plead for Angelo's life with an argument that justifies her brother's death:

> My brother had but justice,
> In that he did the thing for which he died;
> For Angelo,
> His act did not o'ertake his bad intent,
> And must be buried but as an intent
> That perish'd by the way.

> (448-53)

The legalism of her argument fulfills the major theme of the play as announced by its title and confirmed by the Duke:

> "An Angelo for Claudio, death for death!"
> Haste still pays haste, and leisure answers leisure;
> Like doth quit like, and *Measure* still *for Measure*.

> (409-11)

Such legalism had been invoked by Angelo first to condemn Claudio and then to invite his own condemnation; fittingly, it serves now to save him. At this point Isabella's chastity leads to charity: both in the act of kneeling and in the love which her act awakens in the Duke. Earlier he had boasted to the Friar, "Believe not that the dribbling dart of love / Can pierce a complete bosom" (I.iii.2-3); now he proposes marriage. Yet first he makes Isabella and Mariana "absolute for death" by ordering them to accept Angelo's death: "Your suit's unprofitable; stand up, I say" (V.i.455). That all are "absolute for death" is confirmed by Angelo's repeated claim:

> I am sorry that such sorrow I procure,
> And so deep sticks it in my penitent heart
> That I crave death more willingly than mercy:
> 'Tis my deserving, and I do entreat it.
>
> (474-77)

At last the Duke may resolve the tragic action as a comedy by having Claudio brought in and unveiled.

Lucio provides a brief comic coda that epitomizes the action of the play. On first uncovering the Duke whom he had slandered, he fears that "this may prove worse than hanging" (V.i.360). But he escapes death by pleading: "If you will hang me for it, you may; but I had rather it would please you I might be whipt" (505-6). Finally by his wit he inveigles the Duke into punishing him only by forcing him to marry Kate Keep-down.

Further experience in teaching *Measure for Measure* has confirmed for me that negative judgments against part of the play may be deflected, and then suspended, by examining the play in all its parts. The relation of the play to tragedy and comedy suggests that its proper context is the canon of Shakespeare's plays. If this play, why not any play? Accordingly, I wrote a book on Shakespeare's early plays, armed with T. S. Eliot's insight "that the full meaning of any one of his plays is not in itself alone, but in that play in the order in which it was written, in its relation to all of Shakespeare's other plays, earlier and later: we must know all of Shakespeare's work in order to know any of it."[15] The structure of the early plays indicates that they relate to each other more directly than to other contexts, such as historical background, sources, or dramatic traditions. Each play is such a highly wrought artifact that it is difficult to relate it

---

[15] T. S. Eliot, *Selected Essays, 1917-1932* (London: Faber and Faber, 1932), p. 193. On p. 203 he observes that "the whole of Shakespeare's work is *one* poem."

to any work which is not literature. Sources prove revealing chiefly when they are no longer sources, that is, when the play departs from them. Genre studies tend to ignore a play's particularity, its unique presence. Shakespeare did not set out to write a tragedy or a comedy but rather *The Tragedy of Titus Andronicus* or *The Comedy of Errors*. To relate a play to the rest of the canon involves the danger of trying to rank the plays: to argue, for example, that *Titus Andronicus* is inferior as a play to *King Lear*. However, that danger may be avoided if one adopts the hypothesis, which careful study confirms, that each play is perfect in itself.

General critical studies of the plays do not contribute much to understanding the canon: most are flawed by an effort to trace development, evolution, or growth into maturity, wisdom, complexity, ambivalence or whatever is fashionable in current critical values. Study of the canon was not possible until the general order of the plays was established. Unfortunately, that came at the height of biographical interest in the plays and led to Edward Dowden's *Shakespere: His Mind and Art* (1875) in which he groups the plays into four periods: "In the Workshop" (the early plays of "dramatic apprenticeship and experiment"), "In the World" (the major history plays and romantic comedies), "Out of the Depths" (the problem comedies and major tragedies), and "On the Heights" (the final romances "which are at once grave and glad, serene and beautiful poems"). Modern critics, whether conservative or radical, have not gone much beyond Dowden. In his chapter on Shakespeare's development in *William Shakespeare: A Handbook*, T. M. Parrott considers the plays in terms of "a broadening, deepening, and finally a ripening of his conception of human life and his judgment of men's acts and motives."[16] In *An Approach to Shakespeare*, D. A. Traversi traces the "growing complexity" of Shakespeare's

[16] Rev. ed. (New York: Scribner's, 1955), p. 126.

verse as it reveals an increasing maturity in moral wisdom.[17] One exception is G. Wilson Knight whose spatial approach to a play is extended to all the plays, as T. S. Eliot notes in his Introduction to *The Wheel of Fire*: "To take Shakespeare's work as a whole, no longer to single out several plays as the greatest, and mark the others only as apprenticeship or decline—is I think an important and positive step in modern Shakespeare interpretation."[18] Knight's fourth principle of interpretation is that the plays from *Julius Caesar* to *The Tempest* fall into a significant sequence, and this he terms "the Shakespeare Progress."[19] Although he urges that recognition of a sequence of the plays should not be allowed to distort the view of any one play, the metaphor of progress, like those of growth, development, and maturity is limiting and betraying.

Unlike general studies of Shakespeare's plays, studies of genre have contributed much to an understanding of the canon. The central assumption behind the books on the history plays, problem plays, and final plays by E.M.W. Tillyard is that the best way to understand any play is against the background of Shakespeare's other plays. In particular, studies of the romances have related the plays to the earlier plays, as shown in Tillyard's claim that they supplement the tragedies.[20] The various groupings of the "problem plays" allow these plays to be distinguished from the other plays and so related to them. In addition to the books by G. Wilson Knight, Northrop Frye's two books, *Fools of Time* (1967) and *A Natural Perspective* (1965) offer an encompassing vision of the tragedies, comedies, and romances. There is also much incidental material in the study of separate plays, as in J. W. Lever's comment that *Measure for Measure* "prepared the way for *King Lear*"[21] and in Hallett

[17] 2d ed. (Garden City: Doubleday, 1956).
[18] Knight, p. xvii.
[19] Knight, p. 16.
[20] *Shakespeare's Last Plays* (London: Chatto and Windus, 1954).
[21] Introduction to the New Arden edition, p. xcviii.

Smith's suggestion that "the principal origin of Shakespeare's romances lies in his tragedy *King Lear*."[22]

Almost of necessity, the teacher of Shakespeare becomes a teacher of the canon because of the variety of courses he must offer. In the classroom he is uniquely placed to test modern criticism. He may separate that which merely multiplies and refines our response to a play from that which also enlarges our understanding of all the plays. In so doing, he may direct and organize its increasing proliferation. There are encouraging signs that criticism is now ready for the interpretative effort of gathering the plays and poems into a synthesis. Recent studies of themes, symbols, and archetypes have revealed what T. S. Eliot terms "the pattern in Shakespeare's carpet."[23] Yet this metaphor indicates that such studies flatten our conception of the plays as a whole, making it two-dimensional. It may be the special role of the teacher, as one required to attend to the larger dimensions of the plays, to perceive the architecture of the canon. This metaphor indicates—rightly, I believe—that the works do not consist of the thirty-seven houses in suburbia, more or less identical, fashioned by rhetorical criticism; nor the large dormitory with its comedy, history, and tragedy wings erected by generic criticism; not the one vast room imagined by visionary criticism; but form instead, in the biblical sense, a house with many mansions.

To teach the canon may not yield, as an immediate reward, a fresh interpretation of any play—as the discussion above does not present *Measure for Measure* #38—but it brings students (and teacher) a double reward: a more exact understanding of a play through awareness of its place in the canon, and a larger understanding of all the plays.

[22] *Shakespeare's Romances* (San Marino: Huntington Library, 1972), p. 55.
[23] Eliot, p. 231.

SEVEN

"THINGS CLIMB UPWARD TO WHAT THEY WERE BEFORE": THE RETEACHING AND REGREENING OF *MACBETH*

ALBERT WERTHEIM

SURELY one of the great pleasures in seeing or reading Shakespearean drama is its richness, its infinite variety, its protean quality. No two critics, no two directors, no two actors, no two viewers or readers ever quite see just the same thing in any given Shakespeare play, scene, or character. And yet, even from the beginning there has been a rage for order, a concerted attempt to make Shakespeare conform to generalizations. Caesarlike, Heming and Condell, the editors of the First Folio (1623), imperiously divide all Shakespeare into three parts: comedies, tragedies, and histories. In so doing, they impress *Cymbeline* into the ranks of the tragedies and show, moreover, no concern for the appealing finer categories—romances, Roman plays, problem comedies, and festive comedies—conceived by later critics. For a teacher who must convey the essence of Shakespeare in a semester of fifteen weeks or "cover" a single play in three or four class hours, the temptation to generalize about Shakespeare is great. And that temptation is made all the greater by the knowledge that there are few things more satisfying to a student than to write in a notebook, "Shakespeare *always* . . . ," "Shakespeare believed . . . ," or "This play conforms to the rules of Shakespearean romantic comedy." There must be few teachers of Shakespearean drama who have not sometimes been guilty of fitting Marianne Moore's description of a steamroller:

114

You crush all the particles down
into close conformity, and then walk back and forth on
them.
Sparkling chips of rock
are crushed down to the level of the parent block.

The difficult task for any teacher, of course, is to let students see Shakespeare's "sparkling chips," showing not how they flatten into empty generalizations but how they form an integrated dramatic statement, how the disparate parts of a Shakespeare play grow "to something of great constancy." Not all generalization is by definition bad. There is undoubtedly pedagogical value in considering Shakespeare's plays in groups, even according to Heming and Condell's rough division, for, after all, a single dramatic group like the tragedies will have certain things in common. At the same time, however, it is imperative to let students discover that in Shakespeare's case particularly, the ideas of the playwright freely range from one dramatic genre to another, that *Much Ado About Nothing* and *Hamlet, Macbeth*, and *The Winter's Tale* have clear thematic affinities.

The limitation created by the urge to classify and generalize is matched by another limitation likely to occur in a classroom, for Shakespeare in the classroom more often than not means Shakespeare read. The student who reads the plays is more likely to feel the power of Shakespeare the poet than of Shakespeare the dramatist. It should hardly be surprising, therefore, that a great reader of Shakespeare's poetry, John Milton, should have inappropriately characterized the prolific London playwright, a man intimately involved with the business as well as the art of play production, as "Fancy's child" warbling "his native wood-notes wild." So greatly have the readers outnumbered the viewers that Milton's image and the images of "The Bard of Avon," the natural and unworldly poet, the scop, have stuck. Shakespeare's reputation as the finest poet in the English language is surely deserved. But what of Shakespeare's equally deserved reputation as the finest English playwright? It is this reputation that a theater audience can easily acknowledge, but it is one likely to tarnish in the classroom. And the challenge for the teacher is not to replace the icon of the Bard of Avon with that of the Elizabethan Thespis but to enable students to encounter Shakespeare the poetic dramatist, the artist whose genius lies in his ability to forge dramatic statement through poetry and dramaturgy in one another's service.

Because of its brevity, uncomplicated plot, and lack of controversial subject matter, *Macbeth* is perhaps the single Shakespeare play most frequently found on school reading lists. For this reason, university students rereading *Macbeth* are usually prepared to accept it unquestioningly as a tragedy, to appreciate the poetry of the well-known set speeches like "Tomorrow and tomorrow and tomorrow," and even to discuss the recurrent imagery of fog, clothing, or children. It is, however, particularly with *Macbeth*, which seems so straightforward and clear a tragedy and to which students are likely to bring prejudices, however valid, based on reading rather than seeing the play, that the teacher has an unusually fine opportunity to enlarge his students' sense of Shakespeare's range and power. *Macbeth* lends itself well to a questioning of generic categorization as well as to a demonstration of the ways poetic and stage images can work together.

Of Shakespeare's four major tragedies, *Macbeth* stands apart in its optimistic view of life. One is tempted to say, in fact, that *Macbeth* has more in common with Shakespeare's late romances—*Pericles, Cymbeline, The Winter's Tale*, and *The Tempest*—than it does with *Hamlet, Othello*, or *King Lear*. In those tragedies most of the main characters as well as the title characters are dead or shattered when the fifth act concludes. In *Hamlet*, Horatio is left as narrator and the rule of Denmark goes from characters of depth to the brittle, martial Fortinbras, who can measure Hamlet only as a would-be soldier and who prepares for Hamlet a most inappropriately military funeral. Only a mute Iago, Cassio, and the bureaucratic Lodovico are left to conclude *Othello*. And in the concluding couplets of *Lear* we have Albany passing on rule to Kent, who foresees his own death in the near future, and to Edgar, whose final speech is partially a contemplation of his own weakness and exhaustion:

> *Alb.*   Friends of my soul, you twain
>   Rule in this realm, and the gor'd state sustain.
> *Kent.* I have a journey, sir, shortly to go:
>   My master calls me, I must not say no.
> *Edg.* The weight of this sad time we must obey,
>   Speak what we feel, not what we ought to say:
>   The oldest hath borne most; we that are young
>   Shall never see so much, nor live so long.
>
> (V.iii.320-27)

Lear and *Hamlet* both end with funeral processions and *Othello* ends with Gratiano, the new Cypriot governor, bearing off Iago and, presumably, the rest of the company bearing off the bodies of Emilia, Desdemona, and Othello. In contrast to these tragedies, *Macbeth* ends with a title character who is not mourned but rather for whose death there is general rejoicing. This being the case, one needs to ask students to perceive how Shakespeare's dramaturgy and poetry create a tragedy that concludes on a happy note. The audience is shown the severed head of Macbeth, the token of his personal and political defeat, at the same time that it hears the speech, complete with the image of a new nature, announcing the crowning at Scone of a new Scottish king, Malcolm, who will bind the wounds of Scotland and call back its exiled patriots and who initiates a new and presumably better order of nobles:

> My thanes and kinsmen,
> Henceforth be earls, the first that ever Scotland
> In such an honor nam'd. What's more to do,
> Which would be planted newly with the time,
> As calling home our exil'd friends abroad
> That fled the snares of watchful tyranny.
>
> (V.ix.28-33)

The image here of horticultural or natural time is restated in Malcolm's promise that he "will perform in measure, time and place" all the things that need to be done for his ravaged country. The closing couplet of *Macbeth*, "So thanks to all at once and to each one, / Whom we invite to see us crown'd at Scone" brings us to a coronation that restores Scotland's royal order, that restores the throne to the progeny of the murdered Duncan. Students need to see that the stage picture of the triumphant thanes acclaiming their new king, the display of Macbeth's head, and the poetic imagery of natural order together create an emphasis not on a world lost, as in Shakespeare's earlier tragedies, but on a world restored.

Probably the most important lines for understanding *Macbeth*, as well as for locating the change in Shakespeare's philosophical outlook that permits an ending on so positive a note, are delivered by Ross when he tries vainly to help Lady Macduff come to grips with her plight. Ross exclaims astutely, "Things at the worst will cease, or else climb upward / To what they were before" (IV.ii.24-25). This is a far cry from the pessimistically stoical ". . . the worst is not / So long as we can say, 'This is the worst' " (IV.i.27-28) or "Men must endure / Their going hence even as their coming hither" (V.ii.9-10) delivered by Edgar in *Lear*. Ross's statement describes the movement of *Macbeth*, and simultaneously separates *Macbeth* and the late romances from the tragedies, for in *Hamlet*, *Othello*, and *Lear* things at the worst cease; whereas in *Macbeth*, *Pericles*, *Cymbeline*, *The Winter's Tale*, and *The Tempest* things climb upward to what they were before, and are rather better for having done so. Still, we always classify *Macbeth* as a tragedy and not as a romance, because *Macbeth*, after all, *is* a tragedy. If students can, nonetheless, be made to observe Shakespeare's shifting emphasis, the way in which both visual and poetic images of new life increase in the last acts of the play, they will realize that the playwright forces us to go beyond easy classification of *Macbeth* as tragedy pure and simple. The dramatic pattern of *Macbeth* begins to beg the question of tragic form. The tragedy reaches its formal boundary, and may even be stepping over the boundary into the tragicomic realm of Shakespearean romance. The dramatic pattern of *Macbeth* as it is evinced both in action and text is the double action common in Shakespearean romance. On the one hand there are tragic destruction, blood, and chaos; but on the other hand, there is a new restoration mending the unnatural break of order. And both make their impact upon the audience with stirring, visual, dramatic force.

Since understanding the tensions between tragic disorder and romance order in *Macbeth* depends so strongly on understanding Shakespeare the dramatist collaborating with Shakespeare the poet, students need carefully to be shown how the collaborators combine their talents. Student readers are familiar with the poet. Convincing them of the power of the dramatist, however, becomes an easy matter when the play's opening scene is examined, for *Macbeth* commences with a stunning *coup de théâtre* that enabled Shakespeare's audience to feel viscerally the forces of disorder that will affect the main character. It is certainly true that Shakespeare must have meant to please James I, the great witch buff, by transforming Holinshed's weird sisters into three witches; but it is more important to remember the seemingly disparate facts that the Elizabethan playgoers very much believed in the existence of witches and that the Elizabethan playhouse had neither curtain nor houselights to signal the audience that the play was to begin. What then must have been the shock that ran through the Globe audience when, amid thunder, lightning, and probably smoke and clamor, there appeared in their midst three unearthly androgynous creatures chanting and moving with antic gesture! More than a few must have felt, at least momentarily, that they were standing face to face with the dreadful embodiments of the satanic world. Taught from the point of view of the shock value of three foul and grotesque androgynes suddenly appearing on stage, the scene and its dramatic force become clear to students. The lines about metereological disturbance and foulness take on their proper perspective as linguistic echoes of highly charged and emotionally powerful action. Further, the shocking interruption of his audience's trivial preperform-ance small talk enables Shakespeare, with great dramatic force, to have his spectators themselves experience what his characters, Banquo and Macbeth, experience two scenes later, as their small talk is likewise suddenly interrupted by the appearance of the witches:

> *Macb.* So foul and fair a day I have not seen.
> *Ban.* How far is't call'd to Forres? What are these
> So wither'd and so wild in their attire,
> That look not like th' inhabitants o' th' earth,
> And yet are on 't?
>
> (I.iii.38-42)

During the first scenes of *Macbeth*, the forces of chaos are felt personally by the audience. The croakings of Paddock and Graymalkin which italicize the first mention of Macbeth are not just mentioned but heard. The Sergeant's bleeding wounds can be seen; the breathless gasps that punctuate his narration heard. Once students realize this, they can compre-hend how, for example, the complexities of the battles the Sergeant describes are given their reality not by the Ser-geant's speech as much as by his physical presence. His reference to Golgotha is almost gratuitous when one sees him bloodstained and collapsing from his battle injuries. The sense of a world unhinging and beset by the forces of chaos is transmitted in *Macbeth*'s first scenes by physical action, physical presence, and stage effects as much as by verbiage and verse. Probably more so.

As soon as Macbeth hears the famous predictions of the witches in the third scene of the play, he seems unhesitat-ingly to enter their world, a world clearly separated by Shakespeare from the normal, natural world of the rest of the characters and of the audience. Thinking about what happens on stage as well as about what is spoken there will, as always, lead students to an understanding of the way Shakespeare makes vivid Macbeth's absorption into another world. Repeatedly, the actor portraying Macbeth must show him, with eyes glazed, to be seemingly transported, for within six lines of the witches' prognostications, Banquo can comment that Macbeth is "rapt withal" and from there on Macbeth's social encounters are dramatically marked by asides, by his nearly total concentration on what he may become, and by his psychological withdrawal from the real world and real people around him. As Banquo, Ross, and Angus discuss the old thane of Cawdor, Macbeth stands transfixed, contemplating the import of his new title. Banquo once more points out, "Look how our partner's rapt" (142). The audience hearing Banquo's discourse and being a party to Macbeth's asides must feel the counterpoint between Banquo's realistic view of the witches' prophecy:

> That, trusted home,
> Might yet enkindle you unto the crown,
> Besides the Thane of Cawdor. But 'tis strange;
> And oftentimes, to win us to our harm,
> The instruments of darkness tell us truths,
> Win us with honest trifles, to betray 's
> In deepest consequence.
>
> (I.iii.120-26)

and Macbeth's rapt leanings toward the unnatural:

> why do I yield to that suggestion
> Whose horrid image doth unfix my hair
> And make my seated heart knock at my ribs,
> Against the use of nature? Present fears
> Are less than horrible imaginings:
> My thought, whose murther yet is but fantastical,
> Shakes so my single state of man that function
> Is smother'd in surmise, and nothing is
> But what is not.
>
> (I.iii.134-42)

Regicide here more than occurs to Macbeth, for already he is nearly convinced to commit the unnatural act that will help make the prophecy come true; his body and spirit, hair and heart, react accordingly, "against the use of nature"; his human equilibrium is so shaken that he thinks neither of the present nor of the natural order of time but only of the possible future that he wishes not to let but to *make* happen.

From here on Macbeth's unnaturalness and his attempts to shape events, to wrench natural time, to "jump the life to come" are juxtaposed, often ironically, to images both metaphorical and visual of the proper order of time and of the proper rituals of life. To the stage picture of a good king surrounded by his loyal vassals, Duncan's horticultural image of himself and Macbeth, "I have begun to plant thee, and will labor / To make thee full of growing" (I.iv.28-29), to Duncan's attempt to secure the natural royal succession through the investiture of Malcolm as Prince of Cumberland, and to Macbeth's own hollow acknowledgement of the relation between subject and ruler

> Your Highness' part
> Is to receive our duties; and our duties
> Are to your throne and state children and servants;
> Which do but what they should, by doing every thing
> Safe toward your love and honor.

$$\text{(I.iv.23-27)}$$

is juxtaposed Macbeth's aside wherein he sees, contrary to Duncan's image of natural process, the future as a staircase that he cannot climb step by step; wherein he asks for the abrogation of light, God's first achievement in the ritual of Creation; and wherein he sees the dissolution of the "single state of man" so that eye and hand act separately:[1]

---

[1] The closing couplet may likely be meant as a contrast to God who, in Genesis, looked at his deeds and saw that they were good.

The Prince of Cumberland! that is a step
On which I must fall down, or else o'erleap,
For in my way it lies. Stars, hide your fires,
Let not light see my black and deep desires;
The eye wink at the hand; yet let that be
Which the eye fears, when it is done, to see.

(I.iv.48-53)

For students who are used to being readers rather than
viewers of Shakespeare, this aside, what precedes and what
follows it, should display the importance of timing as well
as of the interplay of poetic and visual effects. Macbeth bids
Duncan adieu so that he may travel to Inverness and help
his wife prepare the formal festivities befitting the king's
intended visit. However, before he makes the exit that
should follow directly upon his formal leave-taking, Macbeth once more stops short and glazedly withdraws to the
dark world growing inside him, speaking his aside. The
aside and Macbeth's delayed exit are, ironically, followed by
Duncan's comparison of Macbeth's valorous achievements
to a banquet, a ritual of life that, as most readers of *Macbeth*
have recognized, represents an essential part of a social
process that Macbeth is shown to violate. Since Elizabethan
plays moved at a fast pace and with uninterrupted action,
the entrance of Lady Macbeth reading Macbeth's letter and
stating that her "fell purpose" cannot be shaken by "com-
punctious visitings of nature" (I.v.45-46) follows Duncan's
speech without pause. The total effect then is of a repeated
staccato alternation between Duncan and the Macbeths, between images of natural orders and images of violence to
those orders. That same effect is again achieved at the end
of the sixth and the beginning of the seventh scenes. Here
Duncan tells Lady Macbeth that he loves her husband,
"And shall continue our graces towards him." The stage
directions—directions students are likely to forget—then
call for considerable stage business, for "a Sewer *and divers*

Servants *with dishes and service"* to make an appearance.
The large number of servants and the plate they carry,
presumably to an adjoining banquet room, must make an
impact even upon a modern audience of the play, for the
retinue are an impressive reminder of the order and the
harmonious social microcosm a state dinner represents. The
stage direction is quite precise in withholding Macbeth's
entrance until the servants have passed; for Macbeth then
enters with his preassassination "If it were done, when 'tis
done" soliloquy (I.vii.1-28). Again social organization and
proposed social disorganization are dramatically juxtaposed.
Shakespeare achieves his effect both as a poet and as a playwright, using in harmony language, action, and knowledge
of theater.

As in answer to Macbeth's "Stars, hide your fires" and
Lady Macbeth's "Come, thick night," Macbeth's resolve, at
the close of Act I, to murder his liege is followed by total
darkness in Act II. Banquo and Fleance, illuminated only
by a torch, make clear what the audience is meant to imagine, that "the moon is down" and that the stars, heaven's
candles, "are all out." Moreover, the action and dialogue
between Banquo and his son, that occupy the first dozen
lines of Act II, are a fine example of the way Shakespeare,
with great dramatic economy, italicizes at once a tense
atmosphere, Macbeth's already disintegrating situation, and
the brutality of the bloody deed that will be carried out
between the first and second scenes of this act. In the middle
of night we see Banquo divesting himself of his armor, his
sword, and his shield. He acknowledges that he is already
half asleep, "A heavy summons lies like lead upon me," and
that he, who like Macbeth has had a prophecy, also has
"cursed thoughts that nature / Gives way to in repose," but
calls upon heaven, the "merciful powers," to restrain his
evil thoughts. As Banquo is about to drop off to sleep,
Macbeth enters, by contrast, still armor-clad. Banquo suddenly lunges for his weapon exclaiming, "Give me my
sword. / Who's there?" Supposedly safe in his friend's castle,

Banquo should not instinctively jump for protection. Reminiscent of the opening of *Hamlet*, the stage business of this scene combines with the poetry to create a highly charged atmosphere filled with nervous tension and the sense that something is rotten in the state of Scotland. With Macbeth's armed entrance, with Banquo's tenseness, and with Banquo's remark, "What, sir, not yet at rest?" the audience is moved to shudder at the reason for Macbeth's insomniac perambulations, to see in Macbeth the man who has called upon the wicked spirits to aid his cursed thoughts instead of the merciful ones to restrain them, and to feel already the wakefulness of the man who will sleep no more. It should be no difficult task for a teacher to show how the actions as well as the speeches in a mere twelve lines foreshadow impending chaos and that the effect achieved is then intensified by the vision of the bloody air-drawn dagger and the vivid description of the unnatural, demonic world it heralds:

> It is the bloody business which informs
> Thus to mine eyes. Now o'er the one half world
> Nature seems dead, and wicked dreams abuse
> The curtain'd sleep; withcraft celebrates
> Pale Hecat's off'rings.
>
> (II.i.48-52)

So often, and with good reason, students have their attention drawn to Macbeth's famous soliloquy before the murder and to the equally famous dialogue between Lady Macbeth and her husband immediately following the murder. The speeches are, after all, rich in rhetoric, imagery, and poetry. Attention should, however, also be drawn to Macbeth's aloneness before he goes to Duncan's chamber as well as to Shakespeare's use of the ringing bell to punctuate Macbeth's soliloquy and serve as a cue for Macbeth's exit from innocence and entrance to murder. Nature seems dead and the demonic thrives. After the murder takes place, Macbeth returns from Duncan's chamber and his bloodstained hands speak more eloquently to an audience than his verbal recounting of regicide. As the well-known knocking at the gate begins to be heard, Macbeth first realizes the consequences of what he has done:

> Will all great Neptune's ocean wash this blood
> Clean from my hand? No; this my hand will rather
> The multitudinous seas incarnadine,
> Making the green one red.

(II.ii.57-60)

Holding forth to the audience his own red hands, Macbeth invokes his separation from the greenness of nature, a separation that becomes increasingly wide as the play continues. Significantly and central to the meaning of *Macbeth*, however, Shakespeare will show green nature not permitting itself to be permanently incarnadined and polluted but fighting back to destroy Macbeth and to restore itself.

The murder of Duncan, the completed act that brands Macbeth as a criminal and marks his irrevocable enthrallment by the powers of evil, is climaxed by the infernal Porter's scene, which conjures up the image of St. Peter's opposite number at the gates of hell admitting sinners to an eternity in Beelzebub's "everlasting bonfire." The vision is of hell and corresponds to the hell on earth that Macbeth has wrought. Yet, most significantly, the knocking at the gate which the Porter answers is the knocking of Macduff, the man who will eventually lead Scotland back to normalcy. And Macduff is, strikingly, a character never before seen in the play or even hitherto mentioned in passing. It is as though Macbeth's deed grants a victory to Satan, but at that same moment engenders the force that will quell the chaos of the satanic world. This counterpoint is reiterated in the heavily symbolic scene with the Old Man that follows. The power of the scene depends almost exclusively on the symbolic imagery of its poetry, but it is worth noting to students, nonetheless, that the Old Man, who enters the play from nowhere at this point, lets the audience keep in mind the other old man, Duncan, who has just been killed. The violence to an individual human life is thus felt at the same time that Ross and the Old Man recount the ominous acts that record that night's more general violence-in-nature. Day has turned into night and the world is in its pre-Creation state once more, for "darkness does the face of earth entomb" (II.iv.9). " 'Tis unnatural, / Even like the deed that's done" (II.iv.10-11) comments the Old Man comparing the preeminence of darkness to the regicide. The equilibrium of the natural world is likewise askew, for "A falcon, tow'ring in her pride of place, / Was by a mousing owl hawk'd at, and kill'd" and Duncan's horses "turn'd wild in nature" have broken loose "contending 'gainst obedience" to devour each other (II.iv.12-13,16,18).

Macduff enters this conversation to tell how the things that must be done after the regicide ought to be executed in orderly fashion. The scene which begins with harrowing descriptions of nature gone berserk ends, therefore, with attention to order, and, importantly, with the Old Man's couplet to Ross and Macduff:

> God's benison go with you, and with those
> That would make good of bad, and friends of foes!
> (II.iv.40-41)

The rapid blank verse stichomythia that precedes gives special weight to this rhyming couplet spoken as the characters make their exit. In short, the descriptions of nature in disorder are met by the physical entrance of the characters "that would make good of bad." As in Shakespeare's last plays, the climax of evil is met by the birth of the powers that will bring restoration to society and nature. *Macbeth* heralds Shakespeare's new point of view which sees violence done to nature as a barren winter's tale but sees at the same time that while winter covers the earth, the seeds of the springtime are germinating under ground. This archetypal seasonal pattern is no news to readers of Northrop Frye or of the Shakespearean romances, but it is important for students to see that this is the very pattern that informs a great Shakespearean tragedy as well.

It is a pattern that Macbeth himself begins to sense after his sin. He sees that the witches have "plac'd a fruitless crown" upon his head and "a barren sceptre" in his hand:

> For Banquo's issue have I fil'd my mind,
> For them the gracious Duncan have I murther'd,
> Put rancors in the vessel of my peace
> Only for them, and mine eternal jewel
> Given to the common enemy of man,
> To make them kings—the seeds of Banquo kings!
> Rather than so, come fate into the list,
> And champion me to th' utterance!
>
> (III.i.64-71)

Macbeth has placed his soul, his "eternal jewel," into the hands of "the common enemy of man." And Shakespeare makes a consequent horticultural contrast between Macbeth's "fruitless crown" and the kingship of the fruitful "seeds of Banquo." It is worth pointing out to students that the metaphor of fate coming into the lists fighting with Macbeth in single combat will later be actualized in the fifth act by Macbeth's man-to-man battle with Macduff. Macduff, fate, the future, the force that stands in opposition to Macbeth, increasingly become identical.

The murder of Banquo intensifies Macbeth's violation of nature and his own separation from the natural processes of society and the human body. This is nowhere as tellingly made as in the scene that directly follows Banquo's death. Students, like many readers of plays, tend to gloss over stage directions. However, in the case of Shakespeare's plays, for which the playwright usually provides little more in the way of stage directions than exits and entrances, it is imperative not to let a stage direction like "*A banquet prepared*" go unnoticed. As in the earlier scene showing the dishes carried across the stage (I.vii), the banquet scene of Act III provides a potent stage picture of a central social ritual that should be the mirror of social order. At his feast, however, Macbeth

cannot himself partake of food and his seemingly mad rav-
ings create a feast broken. What should be an orderly adieu
made according to social rank becomes rather an impressive
visual image of societal dissolution as Lady Macbeth cries,
"Stand not upon the order of your going, / But go at once"
(III.iv.118-19) and as the company of thanes make an un-
gracious, disorderly exit. As they leave, Macbeth again
invokes the bloodiness in which he is steeped, saying, "It
will have blood, they say; blood will have blood" (III.iv.121)
and

> I am in blood
> Stepp'd in so far that, should I wade no more,
> Returning were as tedious as go o'er.
>
> (III.iv.135-37)

And Lady Macbeth reminds us once more of her husband's
insomnia and its unnaturalness: "You lack the season of all
natures, sleep" (III.iv.140). To this we have directly juxtaposed, if we dismiss the intervening spurious witch scene,
the exchange between Lennox and the nameless Lord, who
tells us that Macduff has gone to Edward the Confessor,
"the holy king," in England,

> To wake Northumberland and warlike Siward,
> That by the help of these (with Him above
> To ratify the work) we may again
> Give to our tables meat, sleep to our nights;
> Free from our feasts and banquets bloody knives;
> Do faithful homage and receive free honors.
>
> (III.vi.31-36)

Macduff, Edward, Northumberland, and Siward, blessed by
God, become the forces that are to restore the breaches of
nature; to mend the feasts, bring back sleep, banish blood,
and reinstate societal order.

The only feast of which Macbeth may partake is the
witches' feast, the vivid unnaturalness of which should not
be allowed to escape the notice of any student. The ingredients, held up for exhibition, exclusively consist of the

disembodied parts of organisms: eye and toe, tongue and leg, wing and liver. With *Macbeth's* recurrent irony, however, an irony stemming from the tragedy meshing with romance, it is at this feast, where the parts of dead things are brewed, that Macbeth is shown the four apparitions, which he interprets narrowly, but whose wider interpretation outlines the vitality of natural time and bespeaks the structure of the play more generally. For Macbeth the first three apparitions seem harmless; the fourth provokes his wrath because Banquo's, and not his, descendants are shown in Scotland's future. For the audience, however, who can see as well as hear about the apparitions, they are a tableau of violence-in-nature overturned. A disembodied part of an organism, the armed head, and a bloody child are followed by another child, this time crowned and bearing Nature's symbol, a tree, and by a show of kings reflecting an orderly, unbroken chain that stretches from Banquo's offspring to James I and beyond.

The difference between Macbeth's point of view and the point of view outlined by the successive apparitions is the difference between the clock time of individual life and the eternal time of Nature. It is precisely the difference between tragic time and and romance time. Appropriately, Macbeth reacts to the line of kings by saying, "Let this pernicious hour / Stand aye accursed in the calendar!" (IV.i.133-34). Macbeth having jumped the life to come, having *made* the future happen, has shaped only the immediate future of his own life but has failed to mold the future that cannot be measured by chronometers and calendars, the future of Life in general that is measured by the eternal seasonal cycle and by the progress from generation to generation unto eternity. Clock time like tragedy ends with death. As generations of students have assumed, *Macbeth*, then, is, from the point of view of the title character, a tragedy, and one much akin to *Doctor Faustus* and *Tamburlaine*. Yet, at the same time, in its affirmation of the supremacy of Nature's greenness over human destruction, of the crowned child with the tree over the bloody child, *Macbeth* calls into question its sup-

posedly secure place within the confines of the tragic genre
and demands to be viewed as well in the tradition of romance in general and of Shakespearean romance more particularly. It is no accident that Macbeth's calendar reference
is followed only forty lines later with Ross's characterization
of Macduff as a man who "best knows / The fits o' th' season." Likewise it is also no accident that Macbeth's renewed
resolution to control clock time,

> Time, thou anticipat'st my dread exploits:
> The flighty purpose never is o'ertook
> Unless the deed go with it,
>
> (IV.i.144-46)

causing him to commit the futile murder of Macduff's family should be followed less than forty lines later by the central affirmation of romance time: "Things at the worst will
cease, or else climb upward / To what they were before."

Acts IV and V of *Macbeth* present the intensification of
the two disparate times or rhythms, tragic and romance,
that define the play, its characters, and action. Increasingly,
Macbeth's destructive bloodiness is associated with disease
and Hell, whereas the camp of Macduff and the regreening
of Scotland are associated with health and heaven. King
Edward, who aids Macduff's forces, brings divine cure to his
diseased subjects:

> How he solicits heaven,
> Himself best knows; but strangely-visited people,
> All swoll'n and ulcerous, pitiful to the eye,
> The mere despair of surgery, he cures,
> Hanging a golden stamp about their necks,
> Put on with holy prayers, and 'tis spoken,
> To the succeeding royalty he leaves
> The healing benediction. With this strange virtue,
> He hath a heavenly gift of prophecy,
> And sundry blessings hang about his throne
> That speak him full of grace.
>
> (IV.iii.149-59)

To this is contrasted the general picture, drawn by Ross, of Scotland as beset by what no one in Shakespeare's audience would fail to recognize as the worse ravages of the plague:

> Alas, poor country,
> Almost afraid to know itself! It cannot
> Be call'd our mother, but our grave; where nothing,
> But who knows nothing, is once seen to smile;
> Where sighs, and groans, and shrieks that rent the air
> Are made, not mark'd; where violent sorrow seems
> A modern ecstasy. The dead man's knell
> Is there scarce ask'd for who, and good men's lives
> Expire before the flowers in their caps,
> Dying or ere they sicken
>
> (IV.iii.164-73)

Of course, if the teachers have done their jobs, students will, by Act IV, recognize that Ross's description merely echoes and lends eloquence to what Shakespeare has already, through action, made his audience feel viscerally, for they have witnessed the wanton and unclearly motivated murder of Macduff's young son and wife. The slaying of an innocent child was pretty strong stuff even for an Elizabethan audience inured to bizarre homicides in the theater. The "sighs and shrieks that rend the air" is not empty rhetoric for viewers who have shortly before seen and heard Lady Macduff as she exits pursued by her murderers.

In the last lines of Act III, Lennox hopes that "some holy angel / Fly to the court of England," and in the first scene of Act IV Lennox reports to Macbeth that "Macduff is fled to England." Shortly thereafter, comparing Macduff with Macbeth, Malcolm recollects for the audience another angel reminding them of the disjunction between angelic and satanic, between Macduff and Macbeth: "Angels are bright still, though the brightest fell" (IV.iii.22). And finally, Shakespeare, through a highly effective oral trick—one that readers are likely to miss—shows how far Macbeth has entered the thralldom of Lucifer, for Macbeth punctuates his tragic isolation with cries to his servant Seyton, pronounced *Satan*:[2]

> Seyton!—I am sick at heart
> When I behold—Seyton, I say!—This push
> Will cheer me ever, or disseat me now.
>
> (V.iii.19-21)

Macbeth has a curious double momentum, once again related to the rhythms of tragedy and romance. The flights of Malcolm and Donalbain and of Fleance are followed by the unruly exit of the thanes after the appearance of Banquo's ghost. During the play more and more noblemen depart for England. Macbeth is king of a crumbling, dying, diminishing realm:

> Now does he feel
> His secret murthers sticking on his hands;
> Now minutely revolts upbraid his faith-breach;
> Those he commands move only in command,
> Nothing in love. Now does he feel his title
> Hang loose about him, like a giants robe
> Upon a dwarfish thief.
>
> (V.ii.16-22)

The description is affirmed by our seeing Macbeth in Act V surrounded by illness and those who tend the sick. He is seen, too, increasingly keeping his own counsel in comparison to the community of opinion and the increase in new faces—Menteth, Cathness, Old and Young Siward—we see among the forces that oppose Macbeth. Lady Macbeth with "mind diseas'd" already having withdrawn into the private world of her madness, dies. And Macbeth stands, at the end of the play, old and alone. The tragic momentum is one whereby people and power with increasing rapidity drift away from Macbeth leaving him starkly alone to meet his

---

[2] See Helge Kökeritz, *Shakespeare's Pronunciation* (New Haven: Yale Univ. Press, 1953), pp. 177-80, and Helge Kökeritz, *Shakespeare's Names* (New Haven: Yale Univ. Press, 1959), p. 89.

tragic doom. At the same time, with increasing momentum of their own, the forces that seek to drive out Macbeth, "To dew the sovereign flower and drown the weeds" (V.ii.30), to aid those that would be "the med'cine of the sickly weal" (V.ii.27) rapidly increase. And the new forces that are marshaled to drive out the old and worn tragic main character are, appropriately, "many unrough youths that even now / Protest their first of manhood" (V.ii.10-11). Nature asserts its everlasting cyclical momentum and a new generation supplants the old and wasted one, the crowned tree-bearing child supplants the bleeding one, an image made literal by "a moving grove."

Macbeth in his anagnorisis recognizes his tragedy in terms of his exclusion from nature's regeneration and from nature's eternal time. "My way of life / Is fall'n into the sear, the yellow leaf" (V.ii.22-23), he says, seeing it as the autumn leaf whose life is ending and which has, moreover, been cut off from the larger on-going life of the tree and its boughs. Likewise he is cut off from cyclical, eternal time and left only with the time of his own making, the clock time of human mortality:

> To-morrow, and to-morrow, and to-morrow,
> Creeps in this petty pace from day to day,
> To the last syllable of recorded time;
> And all our yesterdays have lighted fools
> The way to dusty death. Out, out, brief candle!
> Life's but a walking shadow, a poor player,
> That struts and frets his hour upon the stage,
> And then is heard no more. It is a tale
> Told by an idiot, full of sound and fury,
> Signifying nothing.
>
> (V.v.19-28)

Certainly for those who measure past, present, and future only in terms of mortality, yesterdays and tomorrows mark a petty pace, become way stations on the road to inevitable annihilation. Seen without a connection to some larger on-

134

going Life, individual human existence is a walking shadow, a tale told by an idiot, and insignificant. The tragedy of Macbeth is that he has made both his life and his death meaningless by severing them from Nature's eternal rhythm and time. Macbeth's tragic appraisal of life uttered to himself, perhaps to the attending Seyton, is followed by the announcement of "a moving grove" and then by the dazzling, unforgettable entrance of an entire army camouflaged with green boughs. This moment, a student must realize, is the crowning moment of Shakespeare's dramatic power, the one in which there is unblemished fusion of the play's poetic images of greenness with the visual effects of stage action. It is also the moment of the triumph of the play's romance rhythms over its tragic ones. For the audience watching *Macbeth* there is the overwhelming sense that Nature herself, decked in all her greenness, is marching across the stage to drive out the bloody tyrant and reassert her power. And indeed, Nature achieves her victory but not without two deaths, Macbeth's and Young Siward's. These deaths, however, are radically different from each other. They are meant to show two disparate attitudes toward human existence. For Macbeth death is an end to a life that has become meaningless. His death, unlike Hamlet's or Lear's, occasions no eulogy and not even a comment. Young Siward's death, on the other hand, is part of a meaningful struggle to create the rebirth of Scotland. Old Siward can then see the loss of his son as something significant and can say:

> Why then, God's soldier be he!
> Had I as many sons as I have hairs,
> I would not wish them to a fairer death.
> And so his knell is knoll'd.
>
> (V.ix.13-16)[3]

The play ends not with Macbeth's tragic defeat so much as with Nature's victory and the restoration of natural order.

---

[3] The untragic tone of Siward's speech is underscored by his pun on hairs-heirs (see Kökeritz, *Shakespeare's Pronunciation*, p. 111).

The Malcolm whom Duncan had pronounced his heir rides off to Scone to be crowned. The march of Birnam Wood to Dunsinane and the ensuing triumph of the young men under Macduff and Malcolm's command must convince even the dullest member of a class of the impossibility of calling *Macbeth* pure tragedy or of limiting one's esteem of Shakespeare merely to his genius as a poet.

The example of *Macbeth* is a useful one for teachers. It is a play rich in language and poetry and it is a play likewise well endowed with actions, sounds, and stage effects. The poetry and rhetoric of Macbeth's contemplations are italicized by his bloody hands, his physical and psychological separation from other men, the sickness and death that surround him. The incantations of the witches and the disorder they describe are made vivid by the thunder, lightning, and croakings in the background; by the witches' costuming and make-up; and by the objects, such as the disembodied pilot's thumb, they display to the audience. Scotland as a charnel house is repeatedly described and the descriptions are made believable and immediate through the devices of the playwright: the ghost of Banquo with its "gory locks," the banquet terminated in confusion, the brutal murder of an innocent wife and child by professional killers, and the mad sleepwalking of Macbeth's partner in crime. There is hardly a page of *Macbeth* on which the teacher cannot show the ways in which the language and its imagery are attuned to what is happening on stage. It provides, moreover, an excellent opportunity for teachers not to convert their literature students into theater students but rather to have them glimpse Shakespeare the poetic dramatist and to apprehend the meaning of poetic drama. From *Macbeth* it is a short step to the rest of the Shakespeare canon.

If Shakespeare asks to be judged beyond the standards of mere poetry or mere drama, he asks as well to be seen as more than a writer of comedies, tragedies, and histories. Shakespeare's works are appealing for a variety of reasons.

Not the least of these is that they reflect a relentlessly probing mind. And if teachers can convey this to their students, they have done a great deal. Regardless of the way we try to fit him into categories and classifications, Shakespeare tends to elude us, for he seems to fit the play to his ideas rather than pouring his ideas into some preconceived dramatic mold. It is for this reason that *All's Well, Measure for Measure,* and *Troilus and Cressida,* the so-called problem plays, *are* problem plays; that the Folio editors placed *Cymbeline* among the tragedies; or that students can profitably argue whether Antony and Cleopatra died tragically or whether, as Dryden would have it, they did well to lose the world. *Macbeth,* especially if students come to it after *Hamlet, Othello,* and *King Lear* and before Shakespeare's last plays, can be a stimulating illustration of Shakespeare's probing mind, for it brings the darkness and bloodiness of tragedy to the brighter and green confines of romance. It is as though Shakespeare poses the question of whether wrongdoing must necessarily lead to death and destruction, to the limits of man's existence, to the edge of his territory, the Dover cliffs facing the sea, and end there. Is the misanthropy of *Timon* the proper response to the bitter-ending *Lear*? In *Macbeth* there is tragedy as powerful as in Shakespeare's previous plays, but there is also the triumph of Nature and order over Macbeth and the disorder he has wrought. It is important that students see Shakespeare going beyond the standard tragic form, but it is more important that they be able to recognize that Shakespeare's push beyond the frontiers of tragedy is indicative of his changing concept of man's fate, man's capabilities, and beneficent workings of higher powers. *Macbeth* proves so fine a play in the classroom because it has the ability to provide such strong reasons for admiring Shakespeare as poetic dramatist and Shakespeare as thinker.

EIGHT

LEAR'S COMIC VISION:
"COME, LET'S AWAY TO PRISON"

PAUL M. CUBETA

ONE OF the great joys in preparing to teach a course in Shakespeare is the recognition that there is no way in which our planning strategies can fail. This happy thought may not be fully consoling when we also acknowledge that the material we confront must inevitably defeat the intention, no matter what the design, the length of time, the inventiveness of the teacher, whatever his scholarly, literary, and professional competence. The challenge is at least to fail in a responsible but imaginative way.

Organizing a course by the chronology of the plays would have difficulties enough for teaching even if we were fully confident of the dates of completion. To follow the traditional editorial device from 1623 to the present of dividing Shakespeare's plays into Comedies, Histories, and Tragedies is obviously arbitrary and blurs Shakespeare's art for cutting across these genres, for amalgamating one inside the other, for parodying his tragedy by creating a comic perspective within it, or for suggesting by what small a turn comedy could become tragedy or tragedy, comedy. Juxtaposing plays by genre as a teaching strategy may at least deny us the dubious generalizations of compartmentalized definitions of genre. Shakespeare seems to have viewed dramatic type so casually as to suggest that he might have paraphrased Frost's definition of poetry: "Plays are something I wrote some of." Since Shakespeare's protean imagination seems neither easily to repeat achievements nor completely to forget them, his art partakes of the magical and natural metamorphosis that Ariel sings of:

Nothing of him that doth fade,
But doth suffer a sea-change
Into something rich and strange.
(I.ii.400-402)

To follow the teaching of *As You Like It* with *King Lear*
is one way to reveal how Shakespeare constantly returns to
comic subjects and strategies for transmutation into tragedy.
Maynard Mack has illustrated how *King Lear* echoes those
earlier pastoral devices and comic patterns and conventions
so that the tragedy becomes "the greatest anti-pastoral ever
penned."[1] I propose here to attempt to demonstrate how,
by studying comedy and tragedy back to back, *As You Like
It* can enrich the context of students' perceptions of *King
Lear*. As a beginning for one class on the last scene of
King Lear, set against the background of *As You Like It*,
I select the famous speech in which Lear joyfully accepts
future prison life with Cordelia so that I can explore how
and why Shakespeare distorts the literary forms of comedy
and pastoral to illuminate tragic meaning:

> No, no, no, no! Come let's away to prison:
> We two alone will sing like birds i' th' cage;
> When thou dost ask me blessing, I'll kneel down
> And ask of thee forgiveness. So we'll live,
> And pray, and sing, and tell old tales, and laugh
> At gilded butterflies, and hear poor rogues
> Talk of court news; and we'll talk with them too—
> Who loses and who wins; who's in, who's out—
> And take upon's the mystery of things
> As if we were God's spies; and we'll wear out,
> In a wall'd prison, packs and sects of great ones,
> That ebb and flow by th' moon.
> (V.iii.8-19)

Shakespeare here manipulates his pastoral devices of *As
You Like It* to show how Lear forgets all he has learned in

---

[1] Maynard Mack, *King Lear in Our Time* (Berkeley: Univ. of California Press, 1965), pp. 64-66.

suffering his night of malignant nature when "the wrathful skies / Gallow the very wanderers of the dark, / And make them keep their caves" (III.ii.43-45). Shakespeare, I suggest, turns into serious parody the traditional genres of pastoral and comedy to illuminate Lear's deceptive understanding of his experience in nature, red in tooth and claw, and thus reveal to us a profounder tragic intuition than even Shakespeare's greatest character can comprehend. The assumptions of Shakespearean comic art are misperceived by his tragic hero so that the playwright can achieve a more complex literary statement about the human necessity for Lear to assent to some kind of illusion if he is to maintain his precarious sanity.

Lear has already learned that the Dover heath is far less hospitable for "Grace and a codpiece," as the Fool describes his master, than Arden, itself a frail home for grace and felicity. Orlando, the archetypal Abel, has fled into Arden with old Adam to escape murder in a society where familial bonds and political responsibility are violated, a society where "wealth, office, power are at auction," as Henry Adams would perceive it. Orlando Non-Furioso discovers that he does not have to enforce his charity like Edgar, disguised as poor Tom, but only because the usurped Duke has before Lear told painted pomp to take physic and has allegedly exposed himself to feel what wretches feel and so "by the art of known and feeling sorrows, / [is] pregnant to good pity" (IV.vi.222-23). In his pastoral setting we believe on faith, not by sharing Lear's bitter anguish, that Duke Senior has accepted the "churlish chiding of the winter's wind," which has taught him to smile and say " 'this is no flattery: these are counsellors / That feelingly persuade me what I am.' / Sweet are the uses of adversity" (II.i.7, 10-12). Because, despite his fool, Lear will not weep and cannot smile, he will instead go mad. When Lear asks, "Who is it that can tell me who I am?" (I.iv.230), there is only the Fool to respond, "Lear's shadow" (I.iv.231), and he does not have Amiens' easy complacency to flatter his lord for so happily translating "the stubbornness of fortune / Into so quiet and so sweet a style" (II.i.19-20).

Shakespeare always enjoys playfully complicating his literary genres so that we should encourage our students to expect double perspectives, long before they encounter Lear seeking a romantic escape into a deadly walled garden. In *As You Like It* every perspective reflects its alter image. Every literary mode has a balanced counterform—harsh realism or sentimental romanticism. Every response, its rejoinder: creative laughter or contemplative melancholy. The comic rhythm of antinomies—court and country, youth and age, nature and fortune—makes all things in art and life reconcilable with no necessity of choice. It is the forest's gift. The pastoral contest is mocked and advocated. The love-eclogue of assaulting the impenetrable Phoebe is burlesqued in the casual making of Audrey, the goat girl. A Shakespearean boy actor plays a pastoral romantic magician princess disguised as a shepherd boy acting as the haughty mistress of a wretched Petrarchan sonneteer. It is folly to go to Arden and folly to stay home.

By Rosalind's and Touchstone's mockery through such traditional devices as the pastoral débat and the folk ballad, one's recognition of the limitations of love, time, and freedom is humorously reinforced. Laughter achieves a balanced proportion of judgment and emotion about experiences powerfully realized.[2] Everything is sport and spectacle, folk play and courtly ritual: the wrestling match—to the winner goes the girl; the procession of the deer hunt—to the winner goes the cuckold's horns. Court jester is married to country wench—not by the puritan Martext, but by Hymen, the God of Marriage, a *deus ex machina* who echoes the New Testament. As Shakespeare's craft blends classical and English literary forms, so his characters can control time and fortune either by an act of the mind or by poetry which is most feigning: in the Forest of Arden merry

2 C. L. Barber, *Shakespeare's Festive Comedy* (Princeton: Princeton Univ. Press, 1959), pp. 237-38.

men like old Robin Hood of England "fleet the time care-
lessly, as they did in the golden world" (I.i.118-19). Time
travels like the Arden journeyers "in divers paces with divers
persons" (III.ii.308-9). Time is springtime, kept time, and
ring time—vernal season, music, and wedding. The present
day is every day is holiday. There may be no clocks in the
forest, but time does not stop:

> And so from hour to hour, we ripe and ripe,
> And then from hour to hour, we rot and rot;
> And thereby hangs a tale.
>
> (II.vii.26-28)

Touchstone can turn time into a rake's progress just by
corrupting language with an Elizabethan homonymic pun
on *hour* and *whore*. Decaying time is promiscuous sex because a motley fool in the forest enjoys railing on Lady
Fortune, the strumpet. Look more darkly beyond verbal
ingenuity and the lines become dying Gloucester's last
words to Edgar in the shadow of a tree: "A man may rot
even here" and his son's stoic response:

> Men must endure
> Their going hence even as their coming hither,
> Ripeness is all. Come on.
>
> (V.ii.8-11)

Act I of *As You Like It* defines a corrupt court of grace
banished and order destroyed. The Senior Duke's fortunes
as well as Orlando's have been overthrown in a fallen world.
The dialogue insists on terms which point the way to tragedy: "O Hamlet, what a falling-off was there" (I.v.47). Celia
warns that Nature may make a fair creature but she may
"by Fortune fall into the fire" (I.ii.44). The ghost of Hamlet's father could not have advised better. Yet the pastoral
comedy continually holds its ambiguous posture as the mask
of comedy looks into the mask of tragedy and sees that there
but for the grace of Shakespeare it could go otherwise. The
wrestling match—"you shall try but one fall" (I.ii.204)—is

a sport with fratricidal intent, but there are no illegal holds or poisoned rapiers and the good guy comes out on top. Language then sportingly converts the wrestling match into match-making and love-duel, as Rosalind hints that Orlando's victory has overthrown "more than your enemies" (I.ii.255) and Orlando declares that his "better parts / Are all thrown down" (249-50). That bawdy possibility is not lost on Celia, who urges Rosalind to "wrastle with thy affections" (I.iii.21) in hopes of a fall. Physical combat is transformed into verbal repartee. In the last act Touchstone can instruct us how to duel by the book of good manners, a social sport in which words replace rapiers and weapon is never drawn. But Edmund would never listen to Rosalind's fool or Lear's: "Your If is the only peacemaker; much virtue in If" (V.iv.102-3). Virtue enough to mold reality into the "If" of comic art, for violence can be transmuted by the artistry of the pastoral engagement. Values of life and love tested in Arden as a game are to be lived in a "better world than this" (I.ii.284), one that Le Beau in Act I could only poignantly mock, but one finally made possible by the transforming power of "our returned fortune" (V.iv.174), by the beneficence of a regenerating nature, by the intellectual grace of comic heroine and wittily aphoristic fool. It will be lived in the unwritten Act VI, after music, dance, and marriage when the characters, atoned and attuned, securely poised between license and limit, begin again. Even old language can be translated into new meaning, as the Duke proclaims in his first act of regained power:

> Mean time, forget this new-*fall'n* dignity,
> And *fall* into our rustic revelry.
> Play, music, and you brides and bridegrooms all,
> With measure heap'd in joy to th' measures *fall*.
> (V.iv.176-79)

Except for Jaques, the dissenter from the pastoral covenant who is at odds with the theatrical forms of comedy and pastoral in which he plays, and at odds with the Globe

Theatre, in which he acts but can only use as trite meta-phor—"All the world's a stage"—and who can describe no Shakespearean character in any play I have taught, for he perceives life reduced to a simplistic series of preordained social roles caricatured by his language and repudiated by the play. The black and melancholy Jaques' approach to the seven ages of man is as absurd as Touchstone's seven stages for approaching a duel. Touchstone will never fight nor will Jaques ever live. Jaques' name may be a French pun on "privy," but he brings no fertilizer to this garden. Jaques is at odds with the pastoral Arden in which he rails delight-fully, at odds with the romantic society which he repudiates, at odds with himself as the mocking satirist who proposes to cleanse the foul body of the infected world, yet retreats to the solitary confinement of a dark abandon'd cave, uncrea-tive, unfulfilled, and sterile. Jaques believes "there is much matter to be heard and learn'd" (V.iv.185) in that retreat from life. As Helen Gardner reminds us, even Francis Bacon could have warned him of his folly: "In this theatre of man's life, it is reserved only for God and angels to be lookers on." Jaques claims the role of the divine as his own.[3] Unlike Adam, who at fourscore sets out to seek his fortune, Jaques abandons "this wide and universal theatre" which "Presents more woeful pageants than the scene / Wherein we play in" (II.vii.137-39).

Shakespearean pastoral artifice reflects almost endless kaleidoscopic patterns, strange capers always offering varied perspectives, but we should ask our students to make no final moral choices, only to witness that the inevitable outcome is to reward all choices, even whimsical ones. The form of the play and its creation make it so. But these games of Shakespearean comedy have also their anti-selves in *King Lear*, where moral judgments are always to be confronted,

[3] Helen Gardner, "*As You Like It*," in *More Talking of Shakespeare*, ed. John Garrett (London: Longmans, Green, 1959), pp. 17-32. Reprinted in and quoted here from *Shakespeare: The Comedies*, ed. Kenneth Muir (Englewood Cliffs: Prentice-Hall, 1965).

and there are no assured consequences of easy reward even for right choices. All is changed, as Yeats has it in "Easter 1916," changed utterly and "a terrible beauty is born."

Like the characters in Act V of *As You Like It* and all Shakespearean comedy, Lear too in Act V plans for his future, although his options are more circumscribed than he understands. He would not, like Duke Senior, return to his kingdom if he could. He vehemently repudiates Cordelia's admittedly hopeless efforts at reconciliation with "these daughters and these sisters," who have undergone no Oliver-like transformation. As a prisoner of Edmund, Goneril, and Regan, therefore, he accepts prison and converts it as do Rosalind and her father: "Sweet are the uses of adversity." He will "translate the stubbornness of fortune / Into so quiet and so sweet a style" (*AYLI* II.i.12,19-20). What if the prison would seem as ominous as Jaques' cave, Cordelia and he can transform it from what it rightly is. "There is nothing either good or bad but thinking makes it so" (*Hamlet* II.ii.249-50). To Hamlet, it would be a prison, but for Lear it will be the best of all possible worlds of comedy, pastoral, romance, even satire. Let us, he thinks, just forget that "nature's above art in that respect" (IV.vi.86). He will say to Cordelia as Kent did when exiled: "Freedom lives hence, and banishment is here" (I.i.181). If students recall Celia's affirmation on leaving her father's court—"Now go we in content / To liberty, and not to banishment" (I.iii.137-38) —they will begin to sense how Shakespearean comic strategies shape Lear's dream of freedom.

Lear's readiness to forget his experience of that night before is beyond comprehending even as an effort to cheer and bolster Cordelia or as an attempt proudly to prevent his enemies from seeing him downhearted in the face of danger. After all he has suffered on a heath as mad as he, after outfacing "with presented nakedness" "the winds and persecutions of the sky" (II.iii.11-12), he survives beyond man's nature which, Kent says, "cannot carry / Th' affliction nor the fear" (III.ii.48-49). He has contended with the fretful element within his tormented brain, his wits crazed with grief; he has confronted nature's eyeless rage greater than his own. Now he has been unbound from fortune's wheel of fire where his own tears scald like molten lead. He has been taken out of the grave, he believes, by a lady whom he thinks to be his child Cordelia. In a comic recognition scene like the ending of *As You Like It*, he is reunited in his own kingdom with his daughter, revealed and restored, and prays that she will forget and forgive. The comedy has ended. "Louder the music there" (IV.vii.24).

Act V, the last hour of Lear's life and Cordelia's, moves to the act beyond any comedy where hero and heroine return home, exhilarated by recollections of happy springtime, "the only pretty ring time" (*AYLI* V.iii.19). Lear knows he has been defeated by Edmund's armies, but that is no matter because, as Cordelia acknowledges, "We are not the first / Who with best meaning have incurr'd the worst" (V.iii.3-4). Lear does what other romantic writers, not just Shakespeare, have done: he converts unpleasing reality into an act of the imagination, but then he tries to move into that pleasurable world of his comic art which ignores the tragic possibility of evil intent and death. "Come, let's away to prison," he invites Cordelia. The desire to create an ideal vision out of our impossible fantasies is the creative impulse of the final moments of comedy. The invitation to the dance of future life ends all Shakespearean comedies: Orsino's "Cesario, come" in *Twelfth Night* and Benedick's "Come, come, we are friends; let's have a dance ere we are married" in *Much Ado About Nothing* are echoed in Duke Senior's "Play, music . . . . Proceed, proceed. We'll begin these rites, / As we do trust they'll end, in true delights" (V.iv.178,197-98). "Prison" for Lear will become the salubrious community of comedy and romance: the way to a long and prosperous life. "We two alone will sing like birds i' the cage." The irony of that impossible "alone" or of imprisoned birds is lost on Lear as he sings with a lyricism never before heard from those vocal cords of four-score years and upward. But this is not the palace of "Sailing to Byzantium," where golden nightingales will sing to eternal emperors in art of what is past or passing or to come.

Shakespeare, who also had *The Faerie Queene* much in mind as he wrote the subplot of *King Lear*, trusts his audience's recognition implicit in all Renaissance garden myths that Lear's prison is as deceptive as Acrasia's Bower of Bliss, a false Eden of self-indulgent spirit, if not body. In a fallen world Lear cannot be Adonis in his garden living above change in "eternal bliss," "joying his goddesse and of her enjoy'd" (*F.Q.*III.vi.48). It is as false as Jaques' cave of splenic contemplation. No learned Theban, no Athenian philosopher nor sweet and bitter fool has urged this vision upon the old man. Lear falls into the temptation Despair offers the Red Cross Knight, and who but a pompously pious teacher of Shakespeare would not sympathize with the desire to rest, to succumb to security, or domination:

> Sleepe after toyle, port after stormie seas,
> Ease after warre, death after life does greatly please.
> (*F.Q.*I.ix.40)

Lear's understandable illusion, hopeless in its optimism, is that he can return to his retirement plan in Act I when it was rudely shattered by Cordelia's "Nothing" and now at last "shake all cares and business from our age . . . while we unburthen'd crawl toward death" (I.i.39-41). This is not a joyous peace born of the scandal and mystery of his sufferings; it is a quixotic alienation, a parody of pastoral, an escape into unknowledge and into a corrupt and sentimentally romantic story-telling and pointless political gossip. He will endlessly replay the end of Act IV, the tragedy's only illusory moment of reconciliation and restoration, of Cordelia's kiss and tears, of her prayer for paternal benediction, of comfort, music, and fair daylight. Lear willingly pledges a moral reordering of the social structure: in humility he will kneel before a daughter, and it will not be an unsightly trick like his earlier kneeling before Regan in a lurid burlesque of contrition. It will be an acknowledgment of moral manhood, not preemptory kingship, a right order of compassion and companionship. In one exultant sentence of celebration, Lear's Ode to Joy is sung as he is manacled to Cordelia and under guard. He dreams that they will tell old tales of courtly romance—"once upon a time there was a king who had three daughters and the oldest two daughters were more wicked than the oldest son of a knight named Sir Rowland de Boys who had three sons." Their sport will be to "sit and mock the good huswife Fortune from her wheel" (*AYLI* I.ii.31-32) as Rosalind and Celia did: "In good set terms" they will laugh at gilded butterflies named Le Beau. They will play Shakespearean comic heroine and wise fool, for like Rosalind and Touchstone, they too will go in content "To liberty, and not to banishment" (*AYLI* I.iii.138) to the prison of Dover. They will attain the detached perspective of social and political satire as they hear "poor rogues / Talk of court news; and we'll talk with them too— / Who loses and who wins; who's in, who's out." The story of King Lear will no longer be one of tragic involvement, for were the play to begin again, Lear would again arrogate to himself another divine role—this time that of Jaques the looker-on, who would repeat the opening lines of the play: "I thought the King had more affected the Duke of Albany than Cornwall." It might be diverting to cope with a Jaques in his sullen fits as he "pierceth through / The body of the country, city, court" (II.i.58-59), for he is no poor fool and knave that might again show Lear the way that madness lies. In Lear's visionary world where no action is demanded, one can move to a transcendent state and "take upon's the mystery of things," more as prophet and poet, than as poor, bare, forked animal or as man "more sinn'd against than sinning" (III.ii.60). Never has pastoral bower or utopian court been so effortlessly created and out of the torment of a poor, infirm, weak, and despised old man.

Lear, who had come to such a lowness because as king he

failed in his responsibilities as God's vice-regent, now readily accepts the task of providing God with a perspective on
man's affairs. Indeed in a role more curious than that of
Jaques, the looker-on, Lear, that "ruined piece of nature,"
might better keep a paranoidal eye on God. How should
Lear and Cordelia serve as security agents of a god so in-
secure about cosmic security? Shakespeare's comedies may
have no need of God, but the tragedies have great trouble
finding Him. Nevertheless, Lear, despite the pelting of that
pitiless storm, is now convinced of the immortality bliss-
fully awaiting him in this world, for he can outlast all parti-
san politicians and their schemings, all sectaries astronomi-
cal and theological, all the sequent effects of these late
eclipses in the sun and moon which portend no good
(I.ii.103-6). Lear will even survive King Lear. Time now
ebbs and flows by the moon, not turned by the wheel of
fortune, and Lear yields to that inconstant rhythm. He and
Cordelia would in eternal paradise triumph over prison
stone and iron bars in the liberation of their own spirits.
For that worldly repudiation, Lear tells Cordelia, the en-
vious gods themselves would throw incense and would now
kneel before their own creations to worship these mortals
in admiration for having taken upon themselves godhead,
the mystery of things. The gods would imitate Lear's sin
against nature; they would reverse the cosmic order of
being as he once did. This ritual of divine love surpasses
any Spenserian Venus' adoration of Adonis; it may parody
the romantic rituals of pastoral, but it makes a travesty of
Lear's tragedy. How feeble and fragile is that precious little
he has learned through all that agony. Lear fondly dreams
that to shape a fantasy from the materials, rituals, and
gestures of comedy is to be able to live them; but his creator
Shakespeare has designed a tragic form where man cannot
transcend time, obliterate memory, or watch the kind gods
worship sinful mortals, perhaps to ask forgiveness for killing
man for their sport as wanton boys do flies.

But there is no time for such divine sport, for this is

Edmund's human hour. The comic, almost epic, vision of
Lear is mocked and destroyed in evil's instant moment.
From Act I Lear has always dreamed of an impossible future
without consequence. Edmund always seizes the instant—
carpe diem is ever the motto of the Shakespearean villain—
for he knows that "men / Are as the time is" (V.iii.30-31).
Edmund knows his loyal lieutenant. And his man knows the
difference between man and animal: "I cannot draw a cart,
nor eat dried oats, / If it be man's work, I'll do't" (V.iii.38-
39). There is no pastoral idealism in that commitment
which cynically scorns all in *King Lear* who serve but do not
seek for gain. Man's work is murder when rewarded by those
whose "power / Shall do a court'sy to [their] wrath, which
men / May blame, but not control" (III.vii.25-27). No animal kills its own kind in such devotion to another. Against
such bonds of fidelity, the gods do not or cannot or will not
defend Cordelia. Lear's poor fool is hanged in that cage of
singing birds. Lear's only deed there is not to talk nor kneel
nor pray nor sing nor laugh but rather to revenge in instant
wrath. His good biting falchion slashes the slave in a deadly
blood bath. Lear's most violent act in the play precipitates
the cracking of his heart and the real release from the rack
of this rough world at the end of a tragedy in which Shakespeare, if not the defending gods, denies his hero the privilege of spending his last years in the good, set terms of pastoral comedy.

Telling tales is an inevitable ritual in any dramatic
denouement; in *As You Like It*, Rosalind's revelation of her
true self and pastoral sport, Orlando's other brother's report
of land restored and society repentant, Hymen's hymns of
redeeming wedlock fulfill the comic design of benediction.
In *King Lear* final tales of court news are sung to no music
of caged bird, freed at last; instead Edgar narrates Kent's
most piteous tale of Lear. As Kent "bellowed out / As he'd
burst heaven" (V.iii.213-14) his account of Shakespeare's
tragedy, his strings of life begin to crack. Telling old tales
like the Lear story leads not to comic restoration, but only

to deeper despair, then death. Indeed, Kent's tale of his part in Shakespeare's play is told in "puissant grief" as he flings himself across the body of Gloucester already dead, for the flaw'd heart of that old man could not support the hearing of the Shakespearean subplot of Edgar's pilgrimage. A moment earlier, the father had collapsed as he gave his son his paternal blessing, and his heart " 'Twixt two extremes of passion, joy and grief, / Burst smilingly" (V.iii.199-200). Moments later, Lear reenacts this scene in reverse paradigm by telling us of Cordelia's dying. If, as this father kneels over the body of his daughter, her lips move—"Look on her! Look her lips" (V.iii.311)—they speak only to Lear of the "mystery of things" and then Lear's heart too bursts smilingly. "When thou dost ask me blessing, I'll kneel down / And ask of thee forgiveness" (V.iii.10-11). Shakespearean pastoral comedy honors the wishes of its characters with public celebration in the green world, rustic revelry, marriage vows, and divine blessing. This Shakespearean tragedy honors the wishes of its characters with an irony closer to the secret "mystery of things" than their comprehending— or ours—can encompass, for we smell no incense thrown by the gods. And no bird sings.

The final reconciliations in *King Lear* grotesquely parody the marriages of comedy as Edmund, dying, learns that Regan is poisoned by Goneril, who commits suicide: "all three," he mockingly declares, "Now marry in an instant" (V.iii.229-30). For love of him. The recognitions and reunions of parent and child are not Duke Senior's: "I do remember in this shepherd boy / Some lively touches of my daughter's favor" (V.iv.26-27). Comedy and pastoral here are reversed in tragic design, which transmutes and perhaps transcends them. Lear longs to attain the idealizing possibilities of the conventions of those genres after having endured their alternate reality in pastoral gone mad and in comedy travestied. Lear wishes to live in his own artistic comic form, to share its celebrating free spirit, to declare its limits on his terms without regard to physical or moral consequence. But his life, in the tragic mode Shakespeare designs for him, forces him instead to endure the lost vision of Cordelia's patience and sorrow, "those happy smilets / That play'd on her ripe lip" (IV.iii.19-20) but which offer us at least no epilogue like Rosalind's to conjure us "to like as much of this play as please" us. In tragedy, for character, actor, audience, there is only the complex unity of these forms suggested by Yeats's tragic gaiety in "Lapis Lazuli":

> Yet they, should the last scene be there . . . ,
> Do not break up their lines to weep.
> They know that Hamlet and Lear are gay;
> Gaiety transfiguring all that dread
> All men have aimed at, found and lost;
> Black out; Heaven blazing into the head:
> Tragedy wrought to its uttermost.

Perhaps through such an exploration balanced between pastoral comedy and tragedy, a class in Shakespeare may gain a new perspective into Shakespeare's art and some new discovering of self and others as we face our mirror selves in comedy and tragedy. Our best hope is for a comic rhythm which after the experience of such a course returns us like Rosalind to the "full stream of life," from a promised end to a better beginning. Like Duke Senior, a teacher of Shakespeare can only try to translate the stubbornness of fortune into benefit, social and educational, so that we can attain for ourselves and our students Frost's "momentary stay against confusion," and so that we can hold our precarious balance—like that between the tensions of pastoral comedy and tragedy. If that is not a fantasy as great as Lear's, perhaps then we may come closer to the mystery of things only hinted at in the joyful mystery of literary art, no matter what teaching strategies we devise to encounter both in Shakespeare.

NINE

PLAYS WITHIN PLAYS IN
SHAKESPEARE'S EARLY COMEDIES

DAVID M. BERGERON

IF ONE teaches a year-long course in Shakespeare, the chances are good that the study will be divided chronologically between early and late—the middle sometimes has to fend for itself—or apportioned according to genres, with the histories and comedies often grouped together. In any event, for the purpose of this paper my concern is with the early comedies. Unless one teaches play by play with no reference to issues of artistic development or links between plays, one may seek some dramatic problem or theme as a point of reference in order to provide coherence to the course. I suppose the basic problem is that which, according to Madeleine Doran, faced Renaissance writers: how to bring unity out of multiplicity, a unity that provides integrity without smothering the diverse parts. As every sensible teacher knows, one must be careful not to become obsessed with some single issue and thus make every play resemble all the others; under such circumstances students will soon find the "key" to success in the course, if not to a greater and richer understanding of the dramatist.

Is there any student who has not at least heard Jaques' much celebrated comment, "All the world's a stage, / And all the men and women merely players" (*AYLI* II.vii.139-40)? The student, knowing nothing of the context, may even casually use the quotation in conversation. Macbeth's statement is often etched indelibly in students' minds: "Life's but a walking shadow, a poor player, / That struts and frets his hour upon the stage, / And then is heard no more" (V.v.24-26). A few students may know Prospero's

DAVID M. BERGERON

"Our revels now are ended. These our actors / (As I fore-
told you) were all spirits, and / Are melted into air, into
thin air" (*Tempest* IV.i.148-50). The common denominator
of all these comments is the awareness of the metaphor of
life and stage, the *theatrum mundi* image. While fully
acknowledging the presence and validity of the play metaphor throughout Shakespeare's drama, I intend to focus on
the dramatic device of the play-within-the-play. Through
this analysis I avoid merely rehashing what has already been
skillfully done in Anne Righter's important book,[1] and I
offer an approach to teaching Shakespeare's early plays;
clearly one could also pursue the problem in the later plays,
Hamlet being the most obvious example.

We are often cautioned that as teachers of Shakespeare
we must not forget the stage and theatrical practice as we
discuss the drama, that we should help students visualize
the stage action and production problems.[2] The admonition
is no doubt warranted as it is easy to slip into habits of
teaching that so concentrate on other approaches that we
may overlook the significance of theatrical devices; surely
we often have students who have seen few, if any, Shakespeare productions. My guess is that a majority of teachers
basically take some variation of the "new critical" approach
to the text, to which I must plead with Berowne, "Guilty,
my lord, guilty! I confess, I confess" (*LLL* IV.iii.201).
Image-hunting, analysis of characters, language study, and
summing up of themes may occupy a large measure of our

---

[1] Anne Righter, *Shakespeare and the Idea of the Play* (Baltimore:
Penguin, 1967). For other studies explicitly of the play-within-the-play
device see: Dieter Mehl, "Forms and Functions of the Play within a
Play," *Renaissance Drama* 8 (1965), 41-61; Arthur Brown, "The Play
within a Play: An Elizabethan Dramatic Device," *Essays and Studies*
(1960), pp. 36-48; Robert J. Nelson, *Play within a Play: The Dramatist's Conception of His Art: Shakespeare to Anouilh* (New Haven:
Yale Univ. Press, 1958).

[2] Recently by Jackson G. Barry, "Shakespeare with Words," *Shakespeare Quarterly* 25 (1974), 161-71; and Edward Partridge, "Re-presenting Shakespeare," *Shakespeare Quarterly* 25 (1974), 201-8.

teaching; and certainly each has its place, as I believe that we should expose students to different critical methods, including at least some awareness of textual problems. But the play is the thing in which, if we do not catch the conscience of our students, we should catch their attention and interest. As a dramatic device, the play-within-the-play represents a possibility for a happy combination of concern for theatrical practice as well as the more literary aspect of drama.

In many ways this theatrical convention calls attention to the play as a play and thereby links several centuries of drama, ranging from medieval to modern. One of the things we learn about medieval cycle drama is that the process of anglicizing or "Englishing" the biblical stories helped fuse the contemporary moment with the historical past. Even though the audience may have shrunk back in fright at the presence of a raging Herod, there was little effort to disguise the fact that these were plays. Modern dramatists like Pirandello, Tennessee Williams, and Thornton Wilder have consciously broken down dramatic illusion with certain characters sharing the perspective of the audience. In Shakespeare's time George Peele in *The Old Wives' Tale* and Francis Beaumont in *The Knight of the Burning Pestle* offer artful, convoluted plays within their plays, it being sometimes difficult to determine very precisely the main play. In the Induction to *Bartholomew Fair* Jonson goes so far as to draw up an official covenant between audience and dramatist. Though one of the qualities always discussed about Jonson's play is its "realism," there can be little doubt of its artifice. Similarly, the device of the play-within-the-play allows us to witness the machinery of drama while at the same time deepening the sense of dramatic illusion.

The many examples of dumb shows in Renaissance drama suggest another manifestation of plays within plays. Their tableau form surely bears a relationship to the civic pageants of the period, which with their several pageant devices form part of a larger play offered in honor of the sovereign or magistrate. One recalls, for example, that in the royal entry entertainment in honor of Elizabeth's passage through London in January 1559, the author of the descriptive pamphlet suggests: "So that if a man should say well, he could not better tearme the citie of London that time, than a stage wherin was shewed the wonderfull spectacle, of a noble hearted princesse toward her most louing people."[3] Metaphor and actuality combine as Elizabeth's responses to the dramatic scenes constitute the larger drama with the tableaux being plays within that spectacle. Thus, almost anywhere we look, whether in the regular drama or in street pageants, we gain an appreciation of the concept of the play-within-the-play.

In using this stage convention as an approach to teaching certain plays, I believe that we should not too narrowly define what necessary ingredients are involved. Indeed, one of the pedagogical values of this critical method is, with the students' help, to expand and alter initial concepts of the play-within on the basis of the study of individual plays. Absolutely essential, of course, is some sense of an audience or spectators; typically we see the audience watching the action, but I think it is also possible for the audience to be imagined. Certainly in the most extended and elaborate plays within plays the acting is conscious and deliberate, often carefully prepared beforehand. But there are instances in which the character may be unaware that he is acting out a role within a role. Something of the diversity of the uses of this device will become apparent in the discussion below of representative comedies. We should not, I think, try to trace some sort of evolution in Shakespeare's use of this device—a problem apparent in Robert Nelson's book—but rather focus on the experimentation and variety so represented. This may enable us to raise with our students larger issues of critical method, such as the problem of seeking evolutionary development in Shakespeare's art. But primarily an examination of the play-within-the-play helps us

[3] *The Quenes Maiesties Passage through the Citie of London*, ed. James M. Osborn (New Haven: Yale Univ. Press, 1960), p. 28.

as teachers to pose and examine questions of dramatic construction and dramatic illusion, problems to which our undergraduate students will have given little prior thought.

Four of the early comedies, *The Taming of the Shrew*, *Love's Labor's Lost*, *A Midsummer Night's Dream*, and *Twelfth Night*, illustrate different techniques and purposes of the play-within-the-play, which in each instance corresponds in some way to the larger drama. Obviously in *Shrew* the whole story of Petruchio, Katherine, Bianca, and others functions as a play within the frame of the Induction's presentation of Christopher Sly, initially stage-managed by the "Lord." Nowhere else does Shakespeare so establish a frame, a sign here of experimentation. It is thus especially interesting to note Sly's early quotation, "Go by, Saint Jeronimy" (Ind.i.9), an obvious reference to Kyd's *The Spanish Tragedy*, a play often cited as one of the first to have a substantial play-within-the-play. In the tragedy, Kyd frames the main action with the presence of the Ghost of Andrea and Revenge, who watch and respond to the unfolding tragedy. But in Shakespeare's play the frame is incomplete because, after the brief conversation at I.i.249-54, we hear no more from Sly. Critics are still divided on whether there might have been some conclusion or epilogue, now lost, which would have offered final comments from Sly.[4] We have only the stage direction, *"They sit and mark."* This whole point would surely be worth debating with students as to why Shakespeare would let the frame evaporate, as it also raises staging problems of what the director should do with Sly and the others who are presumably watching the main play. Thelma Greenfield has correctly observed, "Although ostensibly the main play is incidental to the frame, actually, of course, the frame is usually incidental in meaning and interest to the play it embraces."[5]

It is somewhat surprising to note how many critical essays

[4] See Richard Hosley, "Was There a 'Dramatic Epilogue' to *The Taming of the Shrew?*" *Studies in English Literature* 1 (1961), 17-34.

[5] Thelma N. Greenfield, "The Transformation of Christopher Sly," *Philological Quarterly* 33 (1954), 37.

on the *Shrew* do not discuss the Sly business at all; we need to consider, then, what, if anything, the Induction contributes to the total play. (Many productions do not bother with the Induction at all.) Here students can stretch their critical wings by analyzing the relationships of the frame to the main action. I suggest a few points that come to mind. The drunken Sly is transformed and given a new sense of identity and importance, corresponding nicely to the change which comes in Katherine, who is also acted on by other agents. An important distinction can be made, namely, that Sly's transformation is at best temporary, while Katherine's seems stable and permanent. The emphasis on giving Sly a "costly suit" and wrapping him in "sweet clothes" finds its counterpart in Petruchio's telling comments on the insignificance of clothes as a measure of the true person—witness his wretched appearance at the wedding. Obviously both frame and main play pose the almost inevitable questions of appearance and reality. The Lord says that he "will practice on this drunken man" (Ind.i.36), and surely no one is better at "practices" than Petruchio as he tames the shrew. The young Page who plays Sly's supposed wife greets him with "My husband and my lord, my lord and husband, / I am your wife in all obedience" (Ind.ii.106-7), a theme echoed in the Petruchio-Katherine action and a statement especially appropriate for the Katherine of Act V, scene ii. When the increasingly appreciative Sly asks his "wife" to undress and come to bed (Ind.ii.117), the Page understandably refuses, arguing that the physicians have ordered continence for Sly lest his malady return. With the situation reversed, Petruchio rushes his bride away from the wedding festivities and immediately sets forth on a journey to his country estate, foregoing wedding night pleasures (III.ii). Just as the Lord sports with the unsuspecting Sly, so Petruchio does with Katherine. The play-within-the-play and the main play thus share themes and incidents both through parallels and contrasts.

Unlike the rather straightforward action in Kyd's play of Andrea and Revenge simply sitting on the stage watching, a closer analysis of the Induction of *Shrew* suggests that we in fact have a play-within-a-play-within-a-play. By this I mean that we first watch the Lord and others watching the duping of Sly, which for all we know at the moment may be the main action. Then we settle back with Sly to watch the action of Petruchio-Katherine. Perhaps Shakespeare challenges our smugness as audience by this double action, as he plays freely with the matter of dramatic illusion. For me, that is part of the art of the Induction, a point which our students can come to appreciate. As the Lord gives out orders on how to dress and treat Sly, he is truly instructing in drama. Appropriate, then, that the first Huntsman should respond, "My lord, I warrant you we will play our part" (Ind.i.69). The Lord offers very practical stage advice for the page who must play Sly's wife: use an onion to produce tears (124-28). In the midst of all this the real actors appear. The Lord offers instructions to them also, and the Player assures him that they can sustain the necessary illusion— "we can contain ourselves" (100). The Messenger brings in the main play in the second scene of the Induction, a "pleasant comedy" to bring "mirth and merriment" to Sly. Like many theater-goers, Sly asks, "Is not a comonty [comedy] a Christmas gambold, or a tumbling-trick?" (ii.137-38). Questions of staging technique, dramatic form, and thematic relevance are all raised in the Induction, and the whole of *The Taming of the Shrew* would be the poorer without it.

Turning to *Love's Labor's Lost*, students will have little difficulty in recognizing the Pageant of the Nine Worthies in Act V as a play-within-the-play, and immediately they should perceive the radical difference between this and the Induction of the *Shrew*. But I believe there is a case to be made for other, earlier episodes as also qualifying as plays-within. The dramatic construction of the first 215 lines of IV.iii suggests just such an occasion. Here each of the men of Navarre exposes himself as a lover, not knowing that he is overheard by others.[6] As we recall, Berowne enters first and then hides when he hears the King coming. In turn Longaville and Dumaine enter and read their love poems. Each man withdraws as he hears the next arriving. Through it all we share Berowne's perspective for this "performance." Having skillfully set up this structure, Shakespeare then unwinds it as each comes forth to expose the other with Berowne momentarily triumphant over all, he alone having observed the guilt of each lover. The men cannot know, until all is revealed, that they are part of a "scene"; they only know that they are spectators. But our interest as audience is in watching them watching one another as we wait for the whole thing to explode.

Berowne documents his superior position, shared with us, in his comment, "Like a demigod here sit I in the sky" (IV.iii.77). His remarks, especially those made in response to Dumaine, are almost identical in tone to the reaction of the audience at the later Pageant, as if Shakespeare is testing it out here. Dumaine's exclamation, "O most divine Kate!" (81), is undercut by Berowne's, "O most profane coxcomb!" (82). There is even something of a plot with the climax coming at the moment each man steps forward to expose the other (125-52). The denouement may be Berowne's stepping "forth to whip hypocrisy" (149). But the conclusion (catastrophe) comes when Jaquenetta and Costard identify Berowne also as a lover. There is nothing for him to do but admit his guilt. All illusions, dramatic and otherwise, receive a severe blow by the earthy reality embodied in Jaquenetta and Costard. Each man had come with a carefully rehearsed part—his love poem. But finally there are no soliloquies because others on stage hear them as we in the theater observe the whole spectacle. I would argue that

[6] The levels of discrepant awareness are skillfully pointed out by Bertrand Evans in *Shakespeare's Comedies* (Oxford: Clarendon, 1960), pp. 20-22, though Evans does not explore the possibility of a play-within-the-play.

this event has sufficient dramatic integrity to warrant designating it as a play-within-the-play.

Students are sometimes perplexed by the appearance of the men of Navarre disguised as Muscovites in V.ii.158-265. What are the form and function of this episode? One answer, though not the only one, is that we witness again a play-within-the-play. In this instance the women form the audience, though they are surely not mere spectators. They have switched the favors that they wear in order to confuse the men and have some sport with them. And of course the theater audience shares the perspective of the women. In many ways this event may be seen as a logical sequel to the action discussed above; that is, the men have been shown for what they are—desperate lovers—and now they come to try their skills, but the women are the "demi-gods" in the sky. The conscious masks, costume, dance, and music all suggest a play of some sort.

Ironically, though naturally, given the confidence of the Navarre men, the men believe that they are in charge; but of course Boyet had heard their plans and disclosed them to the ladies. Unsuspecting, the men come with Moth, who has been given a speaking part as if he were the Prologue to this encounter. His performance, though brief, is a total failure as the combination of his own ineptitude and Boyet's mocking drives him out of character (V.ii.158-74). Moth complains: "They do not mark me, and that brings me out" (173). Surely, this must consciously anticipate the Nine Worthies Pageant. It is also a microcosmic reflection of the men's failure as they are, by Berowne's own admission, "all dry-beaten with pure scoff!" (263). I would invite students to comment further on how this play-within-the-play corresponds to the larger play of *Love's Labor's Lost*. In form it may in some manner foreshadow the Pageant, and in function it perhaps predicts the ultimate failure of the men to gain commitment of love from the women in this strange comic world in which "Jack hath not Gill" (V.ii.875). Here in the masquerade the women mock the seriousness of the men, as at the end of the play they are not convinced that the love pursuits have been much more than games.

Contrary to some critical opinion, if what I have argued is valid, then the Pageant of the Nine Worthies is prepared for, if explicitly in only one place, V.i.95-155. The entertainment value of the show (V.ii.486ff) is apparent, but again students may inquire as to whether it has any other purpose. One cannot fail to observe the irony that in an action so devoid of success the Nine Worthies should be deemed a fit subject for dramatic representation, an irony further intensified by a most unlikely, *un*worthy cast—Armado, Holofernes, Nathaniel, and Costard. (It is worth pointing out also the practical theatrical device of doubling the parts —V.ii.538-39.) The "play" has no plot, but instead is a set of narratively unrelated speeches, resembling many of the outdoor entertainments of the Elizabethan period (and perhaps also paralleling the larger play as well).

This play-within-the-play would hold little fascination without the reaction of the stage audience, a common situation for most plays-within. Practically speaking, the audience drives the actors out of character; for example, Holofernes (alias Judas Maccabaeus) admits, "You have put me out of countenance" (621). When he concedes this, the necessary dramatic illusion disintegrates, and we end up with a parody of a play. It is equally interesting to observe that it is the men, with the exception of the King, who battle with their wits against the actors. Boyet joins in the mocking and "helps" just as he had against Moth in the masque of the Muscovites. But for the perjured lovers, I wonder if their zest here is not something of a compensation for their failure elsewhere. Certainly they weren't so keen, witty, or successful against the women in the Muscovite episode. The contrast between the men's caustic wit and the silence of the women is striking. The men continue to thrash about, while the women sit quiet and secure in their ironclad hold on reality. Only the Princess interrupts occasionally but without fail out of pity and gentleness.

Just as Jaquenetta and Costard provided the dispelling reality to Berowne's superior illusion back in IV.iii, so here Costard reveals that Jaquenetta is allegedly "quick" with child, presumably by Armado. And poor Armado can't quite get over the fact that he is not Hector, whom he represents. But when threatened with battle, he must own up to the "naked truth" (710). There is, however, a much harsher reality that finally cuts through the dramatic illusion of the play-within, and that is the message of death brought by Marcade, the death of the Princess' father. The entertainment ends just as the larger play world must fade: the audience at the play-within disperses and goes about its necessary business just as the theater audience must. As is often the case with the device of the play-within-the-play, the stage audience imitates a real audience.

Yet another variation of the play-within is the presentation by Bottom and his companions of the Pyramus and Thisby drama in *A Midsummer Night's Dream*, though it resembles of course the Pageant of the Nine Worthies. Some critics would argue that the dramatic interlude in Act V is another sign of the superiority of *A Midsummer Night's Dream*.[7] Certainly no other play-within in the comedies has attracted more critical attention. A natural subject for discussion with our students might be a comparison of the handling of the Pyramus and Thisby show and the Worthies Pageant. As with the other examples, we must again consider how this business relates to the larger play.

The preparation for the Pyramus and Thisby entertainment is extensive, beginning with assigning parts in I.ii. Through this process Shakespeare offers much insight into practical matters of staging, a point worth emphasizing to students. Something of the difficulty of simply assigning roles is apparent in I.ii, which may also suggest that just as the course of love never did run smooth, so also the course of staging is fraught with perils. Nelson observes that "they

---

[7] For example, Peter G. Phialas, *Shakespeare's Romantic Comedies* (Chapel Hill: Univ. of North Carolina Press, 1966), p. 116.

[the actors] are no more committed to creating an illusion than the spectators are prepared to accept one."[8] This is a bit harsh, for the characters seem to want to create dramatic illusion, but honestly don't know how. It is doubtful that the concept is ever consciously in their minds. By the close of I.ii, Bottom urges them to gather in the woods outside Athens, "and there we may rehearse most obscenely and courageously" (107-8). There being, so far as I know, no very good explanation for the word *obscenely* in this context, I always suggest to my students, often to their dismay, that there are *scenes* and *ob-scenes*—a nice way of retaining the play metaphor. Bottom's malapropism—and he is justifiably famous for many of them—may carry a sense of profaning, an appropriate analysis of what ultimately happens in the dramatic rendering of Pyramus and Thisby. Unwittingly, Bottom may be speaking more than he can know. In any event, the men are to gather in the woods to rehearse and thus avoid the likely disturbance in the city, a movement which parallels the destination of Hermia and Lysander, who seek refuge without "the sharp Athenian law" (I.i.162). From early moments in the play Shakespeare invites us, perhaps compels us, to become interested in the mechanicals-cum-actors, a focus not apparent in the two previously discussed comedies and a certain indication of the expansion of the form of the play-within-the-play. It has its own momentum and development.

Using the green plot as a stage and the hawthorn brake as a tiring house, the mechanicals rehearse the play in the woods in III.i. Additional problems occur about the planned production, such as the necessity for moonlight and a wall; these are resolved practically and realistically, betraying a dangerous literal-mindedness. Bottom requests a prologue to assure the audience that no harm is intended: "and for the more better assurance, tell them that I Pyramus am not Pyramus, but Bottom the weaver. This will put them out

[8] Nelson, p. 14.

of fear" (19-22). It may indeed put the audience out of fear, but in the process it will eliminate the possibility of dramatic illusion.

Shakespeare is not content to let the rehearsal go forward, however shakily, but imposes Puck into the action. Puck's first reaction to the "hempen homespuns" is significant: "What, a play toward? I'll be an auditor, / An actor too perhaps, if I see cause" (79-80). Long before the actual presentation of the interlude to Theseus, the actors have an audience at their rehearsal; and we in the theater audience are interested in Puck's reaction to their performance. Puck intervenes, not content to be only an auditor. His response to the Pyramus and Thisby show may anticipate the reaction of the audience to the actual performance in V.i. Certainly throughout the play Puck, and Oberon too, functions as spectator and participant. Through Puck's mischief Bottom is "translated," given an ass's head. Such a transformation parallels Lysander's sudden, irrational doting on Helena in II.ii, as again the play-within bumps up against the larger play world. With a bravado worthy of a Falstaff, Bottom carries on, wonderfully unaware of what has happened to him and welcoming the devotion of Titania and the services of the fairies. In a sense, he becomes a kind of Pyramus, at least for the moment a romantic lover, a role unanticipated in his mundane life as actual weaver.

After the final brief gathering in IV.ii, in which Bottom returns to their number, the rustic actors go to the court of Theseus for their production. Anne Righter notes three "medieval" qualities that Bottom and his fellows have: "they have extraordinarily literal minds; they are profoundly in earnest; and they cannot tear their attention away from the audience."[9] These attitudes lead to disaster so that the interlude becomes, in Righter's words, "an essay on the art of destroying a play." The tragic impact of the Pyramus and Thisby story is vitiated, and thereby the per-

[9] Righter, p. 97.

165

formance becomes a fit one for so festive an occasion. I have concluded after several years of teaching this play that if a student cannot respond to the irresistible delight of this play-within-the-play, then that student is truly beyond hope. Hippolyta may argue, "This is the silliest stuff that ever I heard" (V.i.210), but Theseus has already instructed us that most activities of love and poetry will seem that way when scrutinized with absolute objectivity. Fortunately, imagination can amend such events and thus provide the proper perspective.

The reaction of the stage audience is as fascinating as the actors are inept. This audience destroys dramatic illusion even as the larger play raises problems of illusion, shadows, and dreams. The play-within collapses, corresponding to the world of the romantic lovers which has been broken down and then restored with a right vision that dispels confusion. Larger issues of the real play world are constantly colliding with the events of this "palpable-gross play" which beguiles "the heavy gait of night" (367-68). The mocking by the stage audience is intense, and Shakespeare with his doggerel verse seems to mock other dramatic styles. The ineptitude of the actors is thus matched by a verse style that renders serious tragedy impossible.

Several practical matters occur as one examines the interlude. Students are often confused, justifiably so, by the time sequence of the whole play, and editors of the play are frustratingly silent on this point. For example, the mechanicals seem to have assumed all along that they are to perform for Theseus, and Bottom states it as a certainty in IV.ii.39: "our play is preferr'd." But in the opening of V.i, Theseus is trying to decide which dramatic event to see (32-60). Philostrate further compounds the problem by assuring us that he has seen the rehearsal of Pyramus and Thisby (68) —a comment seldom glossed. I don't know of any absolute answers to these problems, though one could suggest that IV.ii. and the opening of V.i. may be viewed as more or less simultaneous actions. We can take some refuge in the well-documented fact that Shakespeare often paid little attention to such niceties of plot sequence; and of course in a world of dreams, who can insist on precise time? At 192-93, Bottom as Pyramus says: "I see a voice! Now will I to the chink, / To spy and I can hear my Thisby's face." This sounds more like the real Bottom who gets the senses confused in IV.i.211-14. Rather subtly Shakespeare sends a signal to us in the theater, a point which the stage audience could not have known. However superior the stage audience may seem, we in the theater are the true demi-gods. Also, if Bottom can become a Pyramuslike lover, as suggested above, why not a Pyramus who has Bottom's characteristics? After Pyramus and Thisby have both died, Lion, Moonshine, and Wall enter "to bury the dead" (348-49), in Theseus' words. This represents in fact a common solution to such a problem on a curtainless Elizabethan stage, much as Falstaff at the end of *1 Henry IV* carries off the dead Hotspur, a gesture full of emblematic irony as well as being a practical solution.

Romantic love is the subject of *A Midsummer Night's Dream*; it is also the subject of the play-within. But in the first instance the thwarting parental will is overcome and the lovers are properly paired off, thanks to the intervention of the supernatural, while the latter becomes a parody of that happy success. The Pyramus and Thisby show reminds us of the potential for tragedy implicit in the play's initial conflict. We can breathe a sigh of relief and laugh at the mechanicals' rendition only because the play's main problems have been resolved. In that sense we can understand the designation "very tragical mirth." If rustics can be transformed into actors and Bottom himself be especially "translated," then lovers can also have their conflict transmuted by love's alchemy.

If students survive up to this point in the typical course and have begun to grasp the techniques and meanings of the play-within, I would send them scouting on their own— perhaps to do papers—in the other early comedies for examples that can be set alongside the more obvious ones. Clearly, investigation into *Much Ado, As You Like It,* and *Merry Wives* should produce results. I examine here briefly *Twelfth Night* for just such an incidental use of the play-within. For some reason I am usually dissatisfied with my teaching of this play. (How anyone could fail with such material is almost incomprehensible.) But perhaps a way out can be found in focusing on the play-within and working out from it. Since the narrative action and stage business of the play hinge on the success of Viola's disguise and the illusion that she creates, one might join that issue to the nature of stage illusion that surrounds Malvolio: he seems to have dramatic illusion thrust upon him, and at moments he achieves it himself.

Because there is nothing in the play resembling very closely the frame device of *Shrew,* or the Worthies Pageant, or the Pyramus and Thisby entertainment, we can lead students to appreciate another variation of the play-within. Part of the business of the larger play in *Twelfth Night* is the deception of Malvolio, which is ably assisted by his own brand of self-deception. Righter comments on the theatricality of the plot against Malvolio: "it is essentially a little play which Malvolio alone fails to understand; its chief actor Feste is in disguise; it is observed from a distance by its creators, and it is really, if regarded seriously, quite far-fetched."[10] The whole process of duping Malvolio, found in II.v, III.iv, and IV.ii, may be considered a play-within, for it certainly contains a semblance of its own plot—the climax coming in III.iv—and generally has a stage audience. Just as the Lord "practices" on Christopher Sly, so Maria and her group do on Malvolio; in fact, Olivia remarks to Malvolio at the end of the play, "This practice hath most shrewdly pass'd upon thee . . ." (V.i.352).

As with other examples of the play-within, we hang on every word of the stage audience, who in this instance (rather like the men of Navarre in IV.iii of *Love's Labor's*

[10] Righter, pp. 136-37.

Lost) hide in the box tree in II.v, unknown to Malvolio. Their anticipation of the coming "performance" of Malvolio is epitomized in Fabian's comment: "If I lose a scruple of this sport, let me be boil'd to death with melancholy" (2-3). In an observation that says more than it at first seems, Maria notes that Malvolio "has been yonder i' the sun practicing behavior to his own shadow this half hour" (16-18). The word *practicing* conveys both the sense of his rehearsal and his playing a trick on himself—his self-deception.

Malvolio's speeches, which he has every reason to assume are soliloquies (again like the Navarre men), constitute a virtuoso performance and demonstration of self-love. His comments are counterpointed by the unseen onlookers. But before he picks up the stage prop of the forged letter and thus completes the action of the playlet, he engages in a reverie, which may constitute a play within this play-within. His imagination, in Fabian's words, "blows him" (43), as he sees himself as having been married to Olivia for three months. In his mind's eye he comes from his day-bed, where he left Olivia sleeping, in a "branch'd velvet gown" (47-48)—shades of the benighted Christopher Sly! He continues: "I frown the while, and perchance wind up my watch, or play with my—some rich jewel" (59-60)—a pregnant pause perhaps. He even begins to quote himself from this imagined scene. Thus within the scene artfully set up by Maria, Malvolio has his own very personal moment of delight, envisioning himself beloved of Olivia and head of the household, attended by obedient servants, all those things that are not possible in his real world. From his description we are able to imagine another stage audience, as it were, watching him and indeed fawning over him even as we hear the actual stage audience respond to his inflated vision of himself. I believe that Malvolio's brief dramatic role within the larger one being set up here accomplishes for the dramatist at least two things: it gives us an exquisite self-portrait and illustrates how vulnerable Malvolio is to illusion (little wonder that he falls for the ruse of the letter), and it attenuates dramatic anticipation.

Malvolio lives up to the expectation of both stage audience and theater audience when he finds the letter and concludes that he has been especially favored by Jove with a propitious message. In III.iv, we witness the fruition of the plot, for Malvolio follows the letter's instructions perfectly, much to the puzzlement of Olivia. It would strain the point to call this scene a play-within, primarily because an essential figure, Olivia, does not know what is going on, though surely Malvolio is acting out a role. Olivia believes that he simply suffers from some variety of midsummer madness. In one of Shakespeare's most self-conscious remarks, Fabian says, "If this were play'd upon a stage now, I could condemn it as an improbable fiction" (III.iv.127-28). Fabian momentarily breaks his own dramatic illusion in order to share the theater audience's perspective as Shakespeare gives the whole issue of illusion yet another twist. The final "practice" comes in IV.ii, when Malvolio, now imprisoned in a dark room, is visited by the Clown. But even the onlookers, Maria and Toby, leave about halfway through the episode. While the scene is part of the overall plot against Malvolio, only marginally might it be considered a play-within; more accurately it is a scene of deception, largely one person against another.

The play-within-the-play in *Twelfth Night* underscores the issue in the whole play of illusion, beginning with Viola's disguise. As Bertrand Evans observes: *"we are not to be allowed to forget . . . that Malvolio's outrageous performance before his lady is set within the frame of Viola's masquerade."*[11] The cross-gartered yellow stockings and attitude that Malvolio puts on serve as a parody of Viola. Orsino and Olivia have their own versions of illusion, all tied to the problem of love. The burden of the play is to expose these illusions and correct them, just as in the play-within Malvolio's self-love is mercilessly revealed. (Admittedly

[11] Evans, pp. 133-34.

Malvolio's illusions are not altogether "corrected.") Malvolio demonstrates the vulnerability of illusion when in battle with reality. What the play seeks finally is, in the Duke's phrase, "a natural perspective" (V.i.217).

I believe that a classroom study, as sketched here, of the device of the play-within-the-play opens up many possibilities for our students' better understanding drama itself. Examining the survey of this dramatic convention in the comedies leads one to see that the play-within touches at least three broad areas: practical, aesthetic, and thematic. On the simplest level it gives rise to production problems: roles must be assigned, props taken care of, and rehearsal arranged, all pointing to the performance. Students may gain some appreciation of the particular kinds of staging problems inherent in the Elizabethan theater. Even in the less formal manifestations of the play-within, literally setting up the scene involves similar problems—the box tree must be provided in *Twelfth Night*, II.v, the place to hide in *Love's Labor's Lost*, IV.iii.

The construction and artistry of drama are apparent in the play-within; by this I mean that we get a glimpse into how a dramatist proceeds to develop a play. Though Shakespeare sets up the Worthies Pageant and the Pyramus and Thisby interlude in order to tear them down, we nevertheless can learn something of the nature of drama through this procedure. We certainly come to understand what artistic necessities are being violated in these episodes as we also perceive the various dramaturgical devices that the writer uses. The dramatist gains through the play-within a unique opportunity to examine his craft in the midst of the art work itself; he can, as Shakespeare does in the comedies, turn the whole thing on its head. It lets him mock himself as well as others. One cannot, of course, successfully parody if one does not have the necessary artistic understanding and control. The range of variation of the play-within in the comedies studied here suggests a dramatist trying out many things to see which work and how well—a frame device, formal plays-within, a convoluted layer within the device, and varying levels of awareness.

These variations invite one to explore the thematic relationships of the play-within to the total context of the play; namely, why is it included and what does it do for the larger play? Through such a critical practice students may sharpen their skills of looking at other dramatic events and analyzing their revelance also; at least students may learn to ask the right questions. With the representation of a stage audience Shakespeare may be raising questions of the function of any audience. I do not think that he means that we should react as directly and immediately as the audiences do at the Worthies Pageant and Pyramus and Thisby show, but surely he means to imply that we should not be merely passive. This issue opens into the very large matter of the concern for audience—the dramatist's involvement of the audience in his artistry, the reaction of an audience, and the perspective of the audience, which may be shared with groups on stage. Unavoidable is the matter of illusion, which has both its dramatic and thematic dimensions. The deliberate breakdown of dramatic illusion in some of the plays-within spells their certain failure. But the creation of the necessary illusion in the first place suggests the inevitable question of illusion and reality in drama, a problem that drama seems uniquely equipped to deal with by virtue of the stage presentation itself. If one can have a play-within-the-play, ostensibly not the "real" world, then all kinds of other possibilities are available. By the nature of assuming roles actors provoke the question of the distinction between illusion and reality. In each of the comedies examined here reality triumphs over illusion as confusions are sorted out, identities made known, and correct pairings made. Drama can cut through, expose, and reveal, whether in the play-within or in the larger play.

Not only is all the world a stage, but all the stage is a world. The play-within device calls attention to this truth as we get to watch an audience watching a drama, thus resembling our experience. As the stage audience may at times have to respond, as Fabian would have it, to improbable fictions, so do we in the theater, as we must accept shipwrecks, fairies, lightning-fast romances and equally swift love reversals, and a host of other such events. Through a sympathetic and intelligently sensitive understanding of what the play-within-the-play is and how it works, we may be better equipped to appreciate Shakespeare's infinite variety and dramatic artistry. If somehow through the foolishness of teaching we bring our students close to that appreciation, we shall indeed have been successful.

IV. EXEMPLARY APPROACHES TO
PARTICULAR PLAYS

TEN

HUNTING FOR CLUES IN
MUCH ADO ABOUT NOTHING

RAY L. HEFFNER, JR.

In addition to other superhuman qualities, the teacher of Shakespeare should possess some of the attributes of that great folk-hero, the fictional detective. He should have the intuitions of Lord Peter Wimsey, and the little grey cells of Hercule Poirot. In confronting any play, he should be properly skeptical of the established view of the case, and alert to suggestions from the most improbable sources, including students. Above all, he must not be satisfied with his own preliminary hypotheses, no matter how neatly the pieces seem to fit together. Some unexpected turn of events may cause him to rearrange the clues he has, and to search for others in a place no other detective would have thought of.

Some years ago Josephine Tey utilized the parallel between the detection of crime and literary and historical scholarship in her fine novel about Richard III, *The Daughter of Time*,[1] and numerous indeed are the scholars, critics, and playwrights who have published detective fiction under pseudonyms. Ultimately, of course, the parallel breaks down in a way that may account in large measure for the popularity of the genre as diversion. In the last chapter of the detective story there is always a solution to the puzzle, a final hypothesis which is confirmed by confession or other overt act of the criminal. A teacher of Shakespeare must be content with proximate truth, with an endless series of tentative and exploratory readings, knowing that his view of the

[1] Josephine Tey (pseud. for Elizabeth Mackintosh), *The Daughter of Time* (New York: Macmillan, 1951).

177

case will again be modified and extended the next time he teaches the course.

With this important *caveat*, I propose to treat *Much Ado About Nothing* as a case for detection, running through a few solutions proposed by editors, critics, and directors, and reserving my own "solution" for the end. Of course, as in many detective novels, there is a view firmly held by the police and other members of the establishment that no crime has been committed—that the play is a delightful comedy adequately and unambiguously described by its title, without any pattern of underlying significance to be ferreted out. But the true devotee of critical detection will look for a thematic pattern which can be related to the two plots and most if not all the characters, but which is best explicated by focusing attention on a single clue—preferably a chance remark or a bit of offhand philosophizing offered in a suspiciously innocent context by a minor character. Shakespearean detective work thus has its equivalent of the criminal as well as of the incriminating clue; I have organized this paper around several candidates for this role of thematic spokesman or symbolic center, including some who have been proposed by others, and some who might be.

To represent the Establishment, I have chosen Professor Josephine Waters Bennett. The choice is in some ways unfair, since Professor Bennett exhibits few of the characteristics of the stolid policeman who is the usual foil for the brilliant detective. The introduction and notes to her Pelican edition are admirably succinct and helpful to students; I have used the edition for several years in teaching the play and expect to continue to use it. Nevertheless, her insistence that the tone throughout remains light, and especially that Shakespeare's deliberate art prevents the audience from taking very seriously the issues raised by the Hero-Claudio plot, does seem to me open to question. She writes:

> Shakespeare carefully keeps us from entering into the emotions of either Hero or Claudio. This he does by the

title he gives the play, by the selection of a familiar story whose happy outcome was familiar to his audience, by his handling of the characters of Hero and Claudio, and finally by his manipulation of the plot so that we know even before Hero is denounced that the Watch have all the evidence necessary to clear her.[2]

Later she adds:

Shakespeare by keeping the audience informed of the truth (while his characters deceive each other) flatters us into a mood for laughter and effectively insulates our emotions from the distresses of his deluded characters.[3]

The evidence of the title is at best ambiguous. As Paul Jorgenson says, most editors have seen it "as a symptom of genial carelessness or as a clue that all will turn out happily."[4] Mrs. Bennett is of the latter variety, saying:

The title of the play is not, as is sometimes claimed, evidence of Shakespeare's indifference, but is his careful reassurance that the gravest events of the play will have no serious consequence.[5]

But that we must choose between readings of the title which make the play seem either trivial or comforting is by no means self-evident. Throw-away titles with potentially ambiguous meanings are the general rule for the "comedies" in the First Folio. If we believe that *All's Well that Ends Well* does not have an unequivocally happy ending, and that *A Winter's Tale* is not just a moldy tale by which to while away a winter evening, we need not see such a simplistic reduction in the title of *Much Ado About Nothing*. As both

[2] Josephine Waters Bennett, "Introduction: *Much Ado About Nothing*," in *William Shakespeare: The Complete Works*, ed. Alfred Harbage (Baltimore: Penguin, 1969), pp. 274-75.

[3] Bennett, p. 276.

[4] Paul Jorgenson, "Much Ado About *Nothing*," *Shakespeare Quarterly* 5 (1954), 287.

[5] Bennett, p. 275.

Paul Jorgenson and Rosalie Colie have shown, there was an extensive tradition of Renaissance paradox about "nothing," with meanings ranging from the obscene ("nothing" or "naught" as the female genitalia) to profound philosophical speculation about the nature of Being.[6] We have only to recall the opening scene of *King Lear* to be reminded how very complex a word "nothing" can be. He who says confidently, "Nothing will come of nothing," had better be wary. The score in the fencing match about the title seems to be, in Osric's words, "nothing, neither way"—or rather, "nothing, either way"—since it opens up so many possibilities but forecloses few.

Nor is Mrs. Bennett's argument from the supposed familiarity of the source story really convincing. After all, *King Lear* was based in part on an old play in which Cordelia did not die; but no familiarity with the main line of the story in Holinshed and Spenser can serve to minimize the shock, for a reader or for a member of the audience, of Lear's entry with the dead Cordelia in his arms. Bottom and his fellow actors amply demonstrate that the greatest familiarity of an audience with a story cannot fully determine the genre of a play, which may indeed be "very tragical mirth." And Joyce Hengerer Sexton has recently argued that Shakespeare in adapting his Italian sources moved in the direction of Spenser and the Tudor moral interlude as he deepened the consideration of Slander as a truly formidable enemy of Love and Virtue.[7] Certainly the way in which Hero's pretended death and resurrection are treated seems to anticipate similar scenes which evoke awe and wonder in Shakespeare's late romances. As Professor Bullough says, this

[6] Jorgenson, 287-95; Rosalie Colie, *Paradoxia Epidemica: The Renaissance Tradition of Paradox* (Princeton: Princeton Univ. Press, 1966), pp. 219ff; see also Thomas Pyles, "Ophelia's Nothing," *Modern Language Notes* 44 (1949), 322-23.

[7] Joyce Hengerer Sexton, "The Theme of Slander in *Much Ado About Nothing* and Garter's *Susanna*," *Philological Quarterly* 54 (1975), 419-33.

oft-told tale "had many moral meanings"—Ariosto's editors and his translator, Sir John Harington, Bandello, Belleforest, Beverley, and Spenser could all see different ethical ideas implicit in the story.[8] Shakespeare was at perfect liberty to choose, or to find his own moral meaning. What would be surprising would be if he chose to dramatize the tale without any concern for serious ethical questions.

Finally, the argument from Shakespeare's careful manipulation of the plot is not clear-cut, either. During the denunciation of Hero in the church scene (IV.i), we may know that the Watch "have all the evidence necessary to clear her," but that this evidence will ever be understood and presented to the right people in usable form is much in doubt. Not until after the church scene, in IV.ii, does the Sexton intervene to get a straight story from the Watch, and by this time Beatrice's command to Benedick, "Kill Claudio," has introduced a new reason why the revelation of Hero's innocence may come too late to produce a happy ending. Only after Borachio's direct confession to Claudio and Don Pedro in V.i is the outcome really assured. Far from minimizing the suspense in the Hero-Claudio plot, Shakespeare seems to have been at pains to complicate it, to draw it out ironically through the intervention of Dogberry's comic cunning and the romantic passion of Beatrice and Benedick, but still to emphasize it.

For all this, I accept Mrs. Bennett's point that Shakespeare allows the audience little direct access to the mind of Hero or of Claudio. But this matter is related also to the contrast between the taciturnity of this pair of lovers and the loquacity of Beatrice and Benedick, and to the theme of effective expression of emotion. It does not of itself imply any direction of attention away from the problems of Hero and Claudio, nor the imposition of a consistently comic rather than a tragicomic or melodramatic expectation. As I read

[8] Geoffrey Bullough, *Narrative and Dramatic Sources of Shakespeare*, II (New York: Columbia Univ. Press, 1958), 73.

the play, the balance between festive comedy and pathetic melodrama is quite precarious; the meaning of the double plot lies in the ironic interplay between these dramatic modes, not in the complete or at least not in the early victory of the comic spirit. Certainly for a modern audience, even that "merry war" between the sexes which is illuminated in the Beatrice-Benedick plot seems more like a global conflict whose end is not yet in sight than like a trivial skirmish, easily concluded by a matrimonial truce. I believe we must go on to consider thematic patterns in the play identified by other sleuths.

First Suspect: Balthasar

In II.iii, before the benevolent deception is practiced on the concealed Benedick, Balthasar sings a song; he pretends reluctance, however, and must be wooed at some length to sing by Don Pedro.

> *D. Pedro.*   Nay, pray thee come,
> Or if thou wilt hold longer argument,
> Do it in notes.
> *Balth.*   Note this before my notes:
> There's not a note of mine that's worth the noting.
> *D. Pedro.* Why, these are very crotchets that he
>   speaks—
> Note notes, forsooth, and nothing.
>   (II.iii.52-57)

Since Richard Grant White more than a century ago,[9] critics have pounced with delight on this series of puns, taking it as the clue to the play's major themes. There is indeed much warrant for reading the entire play as about "noting," in the sense of "observing" or "perceiving," and this apparently aimless passage seems even more pregnant with meaning when we observe that in it Balthasar plays also with the

---

[9] *The Works of William Shakespeare*, ed. Richard Grant White (Boston, 1857), III, 226-27; cited by Jorgenson, p. 287.

ideas of slander (44-45) and of wooing an unworthy mistress (49-52). Moreover, the further pun, on "noting" as "producing musical notes, singing," directs attention to the theme of effective expression, particularly of emotion, which is also important in the play. The difficulty with the passage as a thematic nugget is that it seems merely to underline or to "note" themes which are developed elsewhere in the action and the dialogue; in itself, it adds little to our apprehension of these matters. What does it mean to understand that a "nothing" can be also a "noting" (observing), or that "noting" (singing) can be "nothing"? Intellectually and thematically, this particular expression of the double pun is not very functional.

Whether or not it serves as a capsule summary of the action, the scene is replete with ironies, not the least amusing of which is that, as W. H. Auden has pointed out, despite the long introduction, none of the listeners seems to pay the slightest attention to the words of Balthasar's song; they may "note" the "notes" but they hear only the sentiment they expect to hear.

> Claudio, for his part, wishes to hear music because he is in a dreamy, lovesick state, and one can guess that his *petit roman* as he listens will be of himself as the ever-faithful swain, so that he will not notice that the mood and words of the song are in complete contrast to his daydream. For the song is actually about the irresponsibility of men and the folly of women taking them seriously, and recommends as an antidote good humour and common sense. If one imagines these sentiments being the expression of a character, the only character they suit is Beatrice . . . I do not think it too farfetched to imagine that the song arouses in Benedick's mind an image of Beatrice, the tenderness of which alarms him. The violence of his comment when the song is over is suspicious.[10]

10 W. H. Auden, "Music in Shakespeare," *The Dyer's Hand and Other Essays* (1962; rpt. New York: Vintage, 1968), p. 517.

I think Auden is a little overingenious in the chain of associations he expects the audience to make. But there is no question that there is irony here—an irony directed not just against a conventionally lovesick Claudio but even more against Benedick, whose comments both before and after the song treat it as the mushy sentimentalism which it very evidently is not. The song itself, then, as well as the staged conversation which Benedick overhears directly after it, is another example of the ease with which deception may be accomplished, when the one deceived cooperates so completely in his own deception.

SECOND SUSPECT: THE THIEF "DEFORMED"

The most ingenious of the detectives who have considered *Much Ado About Nothing* is probably James A. S. McPeek, who accepts the suggestion of the Watch and follows the trail of "Deformed," who has been "a vile thief this seven year" and who "goes up and down like a gentleman" (III.iii.125-27). Mr. McPeek connects this figure—apparently the pure creation of the watchman's misunderstanding of Borachio's rhetorical question, "Seest thou not what a deformed thief this fashion is?"—with the targets of a number of contemporary satirists:

> It seems certain that no one of these several authors would have been mystified by Shakespeare's Deformed. Greene would have recognized him as an agile cony-catcher ready to prey on the unwary. Lodge would have seen in him an allusion to a creature of demonic provenance and powers, a crystal in which to read the signs of a large social menace. Guilpin and other satirists who may actually have witnessed Deformed's activity in *Much Ado* would manifestly recognize in him their own knave of fashion, the fashion-monger, a symbol of dissimulation and detraction. And even if the resemblances of *Cynthia's*

Revels and *Much Ado* be discounted as adventitious, the result of the common currency of the ideas, it is still clear that the creator of "AMORPHUS, or the *deformed*" would have identified Dogberry's Deformed with fair accuracy.[11]

Of course Mr. McPeek does not read the play as centered only in Borachio's excursus on Fashion, and its misunderstanding by the Watch; as the title of his article indicates, he considers Balthasar an accomplice, and joins those who read the play as "Much Ado about *Noting*." For me, Ben Jonson's character Amorphus, in *Cynthia's Revels*, is the most convincing of the parallels Mr. McPeek cites for Shakespeare's Deformed, and the others do not seem entirely off the mark. Nevertheless, to read *Much Ado* primarily in the context of these dramatic and nondramatic satires is quite misleading. The main thrust of Shakespeare's play is not toward social satire, not toward the exposure of the pernicious effects on polite society of the worship of a monstrous Fashion; the focus is on love and other passions of the heart, and on an immense variety of forms of deception and self-deception, only some of which are related to fashion and its deformations. Borachio's digression on fashion should be allowed to remain tangential and not taken as central; it can suggest, rather to our surprise, some additional issues to which the pattern of analysis in the play is not entirely irrelevant, but it does not define the major theme.

THIRD SUSPECT: DON PEDRO

Rather a different kind of relocation of the center of the play occurred in the very popular 1972 production by Joseph Papp and the New York Shakespeare Festival, di-

[11] James A. S. McPeek, "The Thief 'Deformed' and Much Ado About 'Noting,'" *Boston University Studies in English* 4 (1960), 65-84.

rected by A. J. Antoon, which was seen first in Central Park, then on Broadway, and then adapted for a very large television audience. I have asked several classes to watch a videotape of this production, and then to write a paper on some aspect of the interpretation of the text by the director and the cast. For many students, the most surprising element is not setting the play in small-town America in about 1910, with all the accompanying visual jokes about Teddy Roosevelt and the Keystone Kops and ladies sneaking cigarettes, but the prominence given to the role of Don Pedro, played by Douglass Watson, later renowned as a very virile Father Nature in a televised tobacco commercial, who was given star billing alongside Kathleen Widdoes as Beatrice and Sam Waterston as Benedick. What Antoon and Watson did with Don Pedro is well summarized by Henry Hewes in his review of the Broadway production for *Saturday Review*:

> The tone of this production is set and continuously sustained by Douglass Watson, who plays Don Pedro, the middle-aged commander of the visiting military contingent. Watson makes Don Pedro a kind of godfather, who helps his young captains, Claudio and Benedick, to prosperous marriages with the wealthy and beautiful heiresses, Hero and Beatrice. But Watson goes way beyond being just a plot mover. His Don Pedro becomes the quietly tragic example of a man who put off marriage until too late, and the play's most deeply felt moment occurs when, after Beatrice has said she would like to marry someone just like Don Pedro, the older man risks pain and humiliation by proposing to her. Beatrice's embarrassed rejection pushes Don Pedro to a sad awareness of his inevitable alienation from youthful joys, and Watson expresses this awareness so beautifully that it colors the rest of the play.[12]

[12] Henry Hewes, "Frothy Shakespeare; Obsessed O'Neill," *Saturday Review*, 16 Dec. 1972, p. 72.

The performance of this scene by Widdoes and Watson is touching, as Don Pedro wipes a tear from his eye and heaves a sigh before returning to his destined role as matchmaker, not bridegroom. But it has, I think, very little to do with the major themes of the play as Shakespeare develops them. This is not a play about the wistful regrets of middle age, and Shakespeare's Don Pedro is not a tragic figure. Let us look at the dialogue which accompanies the moment which Mr. Hewes describes so poignantly:

> *Beat.* Good Lord, for alliance! Thus goes every one to the world but I, and I am sunburnt. I may sit in a corner and cry "Heigh-ho for a husband!"
>
> *D. Pedro.* Lady Beatrice, I will get you one.
>
> *Beat.* I would rather have one of your father's getting. Hath your Grace ne'er a brother like you? Your father got excellent husbands, if a maid could come by them.
>
> *D. Pedro.* Will you have me, lady?
>
> *Beat.* No, my lord, unless I might have another for working-days. Your Grace is too costly to wear every day. But I beseech your Grace pardon me, I was born to speak all mirth and no matter.
>
> *D. Pedro.* Your silence most offends me, and to be merry best becomes you, for out a' question, you were born in a merry hour.
>
> *Beat.* No, sure, my lord, my mother cried, but then there was a star danc'd, and under that was I born.
>
> (II.i.318-35)

In its context, this exchange has a light tone and demonstrates primarily Beatrice's mental agility and sense of balance, as well as her merry disposition and unwillingness to take marriage seriously. As the repeated "your Grace" shows, it is conditioned by Beatrice's complete awareness of the class difference between them, a difference necessarily obscured by Antoon's American setting. Don Pedro is Prince of Arragon and Beatrice's sovereign lord; Leonato is but

Governor of Messina, and his niece Beatrice, though well born, knows her place. In this as in so many things she is contrasted with her cousin Hero and indeed with all her relatives, who were quite ready to accept as plausible the rumor that Don Pedro sought to marry Hero himself. But it seems to me clear that Don Pedro is joking here, just as he was when he spoke love to Hero at the masqued ball. Beatrice is the one who would be embarrassed if she were so foolish as to take him seriously. She responds in the proper merry tone, and receives Don Pedro's deserved applause. But she has also, in her mirthful way, thrown down the gauntlet to Don Pedro now and aroused his matchmaking zeal. The scene thus leads directly and naturally to his plot to match Beatrice with Benedick.

How Director Antoon came to his interpretation of this scene and of its importance for the play can be surmised. In some ways, what he is doing here is like those many places in which he takes a glancing and figurative reference in the text literally, translates it to visual imagery, and causes it to dominate a scene. For example, Claudio says, "Bait the hook well, this fish will bite" (II.iii.108), and Antoon puts Benedick into a canoe, with a fishing pole. Beatrice says, "I am stuff'd, cousin, I cannot smell" (III.iv. 64), and we know that her cold is a disguise, like Benedick's toothache; but Antoon not only makes her sneeze but shows us how she caught cold, when Hero and Ursula turned a sprinkler on her, as she hid in the conservatory. Here also he takes Don Pedro's remark, "Will you have me, lady?" (II.i.326), reads it literally, changes its tone, and magnifies it beyond all proportion. Antoon's motive for this particular overreading I conjecture to be a desire for a "serious" interest, to balance the slapstick of Dogberry and Verges and the light comedy of Beatrice and Benedick. Having trivialized the plot of Hero and Claudio (Don John is an ineffectual villain, who shoots *at* ducks on a pond but always misses; Hero has a childish voice, and goes to bed with a Teddy bear; Claudio's callow youthfulness is also exaggerated), he is forced to invent the frustrated love of Don Pedro for Beatrice. But why not leave, as the balancing "serious" plot, the one Shakespeare wrote into the play?

FOURTH SUSPECT: LEONATO

If we were to invent an interpretation of the play along the lines of Leslie Fiedler or some psychoanalytic critic, our attention would perforce be directed to Leonato. He and Hero must take their places in the long line of fathers and daughters plagued by conflict and misunderstanding which includes Egeus and Hermia, Shylock and Jessica, Old Capulet and Juliet, Brabantio and Desdemona, and Lear and Cordelia, with a few others like the Duke of Milan and Sylvia, the old shepherd and Joan of Arc, Duke Frederick and Celia, Polonius and Ophelia, and Baptista and his two daughters Katherine and Bianca dimly perceived in the background. Of this list, only Juliet has a living mother, and almost all the pairs are involved in a conflict of some sort concerning the daughter's marriage. An outstanding characteristic of almost all the fathers is the excessive emotion with which they react to their daughters' defections. Egeus, Shylock, and Old Capulet, in addition to Leonato, all wish their daughters dead; the old shepherd cries out concerning his daughter Joan, "O, burn her, burn her! hanging is too good" (*1 Henry VI*, V.iv.33). Surely Leslie Fiedler is right in suggesting that some powerful private myth is here at work on Shakespeare, in addition to the primitive archetypes buried in us all. And surely Fiedler is also right in adding to this list Portia's dead father, with the casket riddle which attempts to extend his control beyond the grave, and the incestuous Antiochus, whose riddle Pericles guesses, to his deadly peril.[13] Some sort of incest riddle seems to be hidden in all these caskets.

13 Leslie A. Fiedler, *The Stranger in Shakespeare* (New York: Stein and Day, 1972), pp. 101ff. Fiedler's complex argument is interconnected, and his provocative book should be read in its entirety.

Of these angry fathers, Leonato is not the least emotional in his unwarranted denunciation of his daughter:

> But mine, and mine I lov'd, and mine I prais'd,
> And mine that I was proud on, mine so much
> That I myself was to myself not mine,
> Valuing of her—why, she, O she is fall'n
> Into a pit of ink, that the wide sea
> Hath drops too few to wash her clean again,
> And salt too little which may season give
> To her foul tainted flesh!
>
> (IV.i.136-43)

The sentiment here may recall Old Capulet:

> Wife, we scarce thought us blest
> That God had lent us but this only child,
> But now I see this one is one too much,
> And that we have a curse in having her.
> (*Romeo and Juliet* III.v.164-67)

But, despite the artful rhetoric, Leonato here also anticipates the passion of Othello:

> But there, where I have garner'd up my heart,
> Where either I must live or bear no life;
> The fountain from the which my current runs
> Or else dries up: to be discarded thence!
> Or keep it as a cestern for foul toads
> To knot and gender in!
>
> (*Othello* IV.ii.57-62)

Leonato's reiterated "mine, mine, mine" emphasizes the extreme egotism of his narrow concern for his honor. Though Claudio has cruelly denounced Hero in public and rejected her, and Don Pedro has supported him, on the apparent evidence of their senses, it is left to her father to wish her dead and to threaten to "tear her," with no such evidence, and with the quite different reactions of Beatrice, the Friar, and even Benedick to underline his own strange, immediate conviction of her perfidy. Moreover, Hero has never defied his authority; to the contrary, she has meekly accepted his instructions to welcome the suit of Don Pedro, despite the urging of Beatrice that she consider her own preference, and then just as meekly and silently acquiesced when the intended bridegroom turned out to be Claudio instead of Don Pedro—again a match apparently arranged by her father without the slightest thought of consulting her wishes. Of all the fathers, Leonato seems to have the least obvious personal motivation for the violence of his language. Joan of Arc has denied her parentage, Desdemona has married without her father's consent, Jessica has eloped with a hated Christian and stolen Shylock's ducats, even Juliet and Cordelia have defied their fathers. But Hero, to Leonato's direct knowledge, has simply accepted and suffered.

The strange excess in Leonato's behavior stands out if we compare him with his counterparts in the versions of Ariosto and Bandello, which are among Shakespeare's probable sources. Ariosto's heroine, Genevra, is the daughter of the King of Scotland. When she is accused of fornication, her father, though he thinks her innocent, is forced by the hard Scottish law to condemn her to death unless she can find a champion to clear her name in ritual combat with her accuser:

> The King (of crime that thinkes *Genevra* cleare)
> Offers to marrie her to anie knight
> That will in armes defend his daughter deare,
> And prove her innocent in open fight.
>
> (V.68)[14]

Bandello's Lionato attributes the repudiation of his daughter Fenicia by Sir Timbreo to social snobbery, and says to the messenger who has conveyed Sir Timbreo's "bitter and contemptuous message":

[14] *Orlando Furioso*, trans. Sir John Harington (1591); rpt. Bullough, II, 98.

Surely if he repented of his promise to make her his wife it would have been sufficient for him to declare that he did not want her, and not to have laid against her this injurious accusation of whoredom. It is indeed true that all things are possible, but I know how my daughter has been reared and what her habits are. God who is our just Judge will one day, I believe, make known the truth.[15]

When Fenicia faints, for several hours everyone believes her dead; when she recovers, it is Fenicia herself who says, "O how much better it would be, if I were dead and free of my afflictions." But her mother praises God that she is still alive, and as for Lionato, "there is no need to ask if he was glad to see his daughter restored to herself."[16]

By V.i, Shakespeare's Leonato has come round to the side of those who believe in his daughter's innocence, but he is still remarkably passionate. His brother Antonio tries to restrain his suicidal grief with philosophy:

> If you go on thus, you will kill yourself,
> And 'tis not wisdom thus to second grief
> Against yourself.
>
> (V.i.1-3)

When Leonato will not be consoled, Antonio advises him to direct his anger against those who make him suffer; and this advice Leonato ironically considers reasonable:

> *Leon.* I pray thee peace. I will be flesh and blood,
> For there was never yet philosopher
> That could endure the toothache patiently,
> However they have writ the style of gods,
> And make a push at chance and sufferance.
> *Ant.* Yet bend not all the harm upon yourself;
> Make those that do offend you suffer too.

[15] Novella XXII from *La Prima Parte de le Novelle del Bandello* (1554); trans. Geoffrey Bullough, Bullough, II, 118.
[16] Bullough, II, 121.

Leon. There thou speak'st reason; nay, I will do so.
My soul doth tell me Hero is belied,
And that shall Claudio know; so shall the Prince,
And all of them that thus dishonor her.

(V.i.34-44)

I have cited this scene at some length in order to point out that the germ of it is in Ariosto; but there it is the lover Ariodante, the counterpart of Claudio, who is so overwhelmed by the supposed treachery of Genevra that he is close to despair and must be restrained by his brother Lurcanio, or "else him selfe for griefe had surely slaine." Lurcanio advises "just revenge," saying:

For of my counsell this is the conclusion,
Put up your sword against your selfe prepared,
And let her sinne be to the king declared.

(V.54)[17]

Likewise, Bandello's lover Sir Timbreo, after hearing Fenicia accused of treachery, is so "blinded with the veil of jealousy" that he seems "more dead than alive"; when he sees the man climb the ladder to her chamber, he swoons, "overcome with the keenest suffering," until righteous anger banishes every feeling of jealousy and converts love to cruel hate.[18]

Shakespeare's Claudio, while not entirely dispassionate, seems much more restrained; certainly by V.i both he and Don Pedro are surprisingly calm, even callous, in dealing with the seriocomic anger of the two old men. Shakespeare, while toning down the reaction of Claudio, has given to Leonato passions of jealousy, grief, and anger which might be considered more appropriate to the bridegroom than to the father.

The situation in the church scene seems much like that of

17 Bullough, II, 95.
18 Bullough, II, 117.

Othello as described by Leslie Fiedler:[19] not all Desdemona's purity can save her from the insinuations and ostensible evidence of Iago, because Othello so deeply fears that she will—indeed, she must—make him a cuckold. Here Leonato takes on some of the function of Othello. Not all Hero's acquiescence, nor the maiden blushes which the Friar observes so closely, can save her from her father's anger, for he seems to have an irrational but total conviction that his daughter must be a whore. I am not suggesting that Shakespeare wants us to see Leonato as dominated by incestuous passion, but rather that we are in this play as in *Othello* exploring the kind of situation which can be pushed toward the cuckold joke or toward tragic rage. Here as in *Othello* we have a comparison of the jealous lover and the jealous father as figures who may be either comic or tragic, but who cannot for long be either wisely calm or completely trusting in their relationships with the females who must submit to their domination. The same kind of male "bad conscience" is at the root of the trouble, whether the man be husband, father, or assertive, match-making prince.

FIFTH SUSPECT: BENEDICK

Leslie Fiedler observes in both Chaucer and Shakespeare an awareness of "the ironic link between the sentimental melodrama of the abused wife and the pornographic farce of the betrayed husband."[20] Elizabethan cuckold jokes always seem tedious and in bad taste to a modern audience, but for a moment at the start of this play we seem to have an ally in Benedick. When Leonato is greeting Don Pedro, he replies to the Prince's polite remark, "I think this is your daughter," with the embarrassing cliché, "Her mother hath many times told me so" (I.i.104-5). At this point Benedick intrudes with a sally that makes us cheer, "Were you in doubt,

19 Fiedler, pp. 139 ff.
20 Fiedler, p. 149.

sir, that you ask'd her?" Leonato rather lamely tries to turn the joke back on Benedick with, "Signior Benedick, no, for then were you a child," but Benedick has exposed the skull of fear and cruelty beneath the light jokes of male chauvinist society. The conversation is disturbingly like that between Kent and Gloucester at the opening of *King Lear*, with Edmund standing by: "Do you smell a fault? . . . the whoreson must be acknowledg'd" (I.i.16-24).

One might hope that Benedick's true wit would put an end to cuckold jokes, at least for this play, in which especially they seem out of place, since a false accusation of female unfaithfulness will come close to destroying the festive mood. But they go on and on, with Benedick often enough the one who starts the joke, or the one against whom it is directed. At the end he says:

> Prince, thou art sad, get thee a wife, get thee a wife. There is no staff more reverent than one tipp'd with horn.
> (V.iv.122-24)

These jokes assume that a married man is synonymous with a cuckold; the only choice is to be a bachelor and a cuckold-maker, as Benedick is reputed to be at the beginning of the play. The jokes thus provide the soil—male fears of inadequacy after marriage mingled with a male assumption of irresistibility to all females before marriage—in which an immediate belief in Hero's unchastity can take root. That no one seems to question why or whether Hero should find Borachio attractive, let alone ask when she would have found opportunity for those thousand lascivious acts, is to a modern audience most amusing, as it was to Lewis Carroll.[21] But the lack of opportunity for the acts of which the maligned lady is accused is of course one of Thomas Rymer's objections to *Othello*, and a rational analysis of opportunity never stopped the jealous Moor, any more than it stops

[21] Lewis Carroll, "A Letter to Ellen Terry," from Ellen Terry, *The Story of My Life* (New York: McClure, 1908), pp. 385-86.

Claudio, or Don Pedro, or Leonato.[22] As shown in Shake-spearean comedy as well as tragedy, the Elizabethan husband, bridegroom, or father is usually more than ready to be convinced that his females have played him false.

We might expect Benedick to be cured of his propensity for cuckold jokes when he discovers and admits his love for Beatrice; he trims his beard,[23] tries his hand at poetry, is

[22] Thomas Rymer, *A Short View of Tragedy* (London, 1693); rpt. J. E. Spingarn, *Critical Essays of the Seventeenth Century* (Bloomington: Indiana Univ. Press, 1957), II, 240. It is interesting that in one of Shakespeare's probable sources for *Much Ado* the issue of lack of opportunity *is* raised. Bandello's Sir Timbreo, "reflecting more on what he had seen, and his anger having cooled, and reason lending him new vision, he thought to himself that maybe the man who had entered the house might have been doing so for another woman than Fenicia, or even to commit a theft. He recalled to himself that Messer Lionati's house was very big, and that nobody dwelt in the part of it where the man had climbed up, and that it was impossible that Fenicia, who slept with her sisters in a room leading off that of her parents, could have come out to that wing of the house since she would have to pass through her father's room—and so on, till assailed and afflicted with his thoughts he could not find repose" (Bullough, II, 123). The chain of reasoning would be a little different but, as Lewis Carroll pointed out, a similar argument for the defense would clear Hero easily.

[23] The remarks of Claudio, "the barber's man hath been seen with him, and the old ornament of his cheek hath already stuff'd tennis balls," and of Leonato, "Indeed he looks younger than he did, by the loss of a beard" (III.ii.45-49), seem to imply that Benedick's beard has been shaved rather than neatly trimmed. But in V.i, Benedick can still refer contemptuously to Claudio as "my Lord Lackbeard" (192). And Beatrice, in II.i, was very definite in seeing a smooth face as an indication of sexual insufficiency, not of a lover's attractiveness. Of course Beatrice's remark is part of a witty and paradoxical demonstration that she cannot marry at all "till God make men of some other metal than earth":

> *Leon.* You may light on a husband that hath no beard.
> *Beat.* What should I do with him? dress him in my apparel and make him my waiting-gentlewoman? He that hath a beard is more than a youth, and he that hath no beard is less than a man; and he that is more than a youth is not for me, and he that is less than a man, I am not for him. (II.i.32-39)

willing to endure the jokes of his friends, and shows other signs of conversion. And he remains with Beatrice and Hero when Claudio and Don Pedro leave the church, committing himself to the bride's side in this not-so-merry war. Immediately his loyalty and newfound romantic devotion are tested with the command, "Kill Claudio!" I would agree with Mrs. Bennett that this moment is not only melodramatic but also richly comic. Immediately after Benedick declares his independence of the male fraternity, with its cuckold jokes gone sour, he is forced into an equally stereotyped role as his mistress's unquestioning avenger. Must he be either a snickerer at bachelors' dirty jokes, or a character in a romantic novel written for females? Is there no middle ground on which he can be merely or completely human?

The search for a middle ground between farce and melodrama, or for an attitude which may comprehend and transcend both, may be seen as the "action" of both Beatrice and Benedick, and perhaps as the action of the entire play. But it would be wrong to assume that either of them has already achieved the requisite balance at the beginning of the play, or that they find it easily when they discover their love for each other. Both continue to make mistakes of excess in both directions until very late in the play. And their development is not synchronized, so that at any moment the greater comic coolness of one can be played against the more ardent romanticism of the other.

To see Benedick as in quest of the spirit of comic balance rather than one who embodies it from the beginning or on whom it is miraculously conferred by Cupid's arrow may help to explain some of his odd behavior. For example, in

---

Faced with this dilemma, Benedick might well seek a compromise; one would think he might prefer to err on the side of being "more than a youth" rather than on that of being "less than a man." A. J. Antoon, in setting III.ii in a barbershop in which Benedick loses a luxuriant moustache instead of a beard, seems to make the point even more obscure, since one can hardly assume that a lover c. 1910 would shave a moustache in order to be more attractive to his lady.

RAY L. HEFFNER, JR.

contrast to Don Pedro, he seems strangely unsympathetic
when Claudio reveals his growing love for Hero (I.i.161-96);
despite the obvious sincerity of Claudio's questions, Benedick refuses to believe that he is not "in sport," and persists
in a series of jokes that are quite out of keeping with Claudio's mood. Professor Charles T. Prouty and others have
emphasized that Claudio is not really a romantic lover but
a proper young man trying to arrange a marriage of convenience.[24] Professor Prouty thus sees Benedick in this scene
and elsewhere as providing a needed dose of realism, to
counteract Claudio's foolish and improper attempts at ro-
manticizing an essentially unromantic situation. But I
think the irony implicit in the incongruity of attitudes is
also directed at Benedick, and not just because of his comic
hubris in defying the love god. In her repartee with the
messenger at the beginning of this scene, Beatrice suggests
several deficiencies in Benedick, besides his foolish pride in
challenging Cupid at the flight: that he lacks courage on the
field of battle, that he is inferior to her in wit, and finally
that he lacks the virtue of constancy to his friends and
"wears his faith but as the fashion of his hat" (I.i.75-77).
This is, of course, primarily ironic preparation for Beatrice's
reversal in the scene in which she commands Benedick to
"kill Claudio." But it also helps us to see, in Benedick's
conduct later in the same scene, a lack of the sympathy one
might expect to find in a true friend.

Certainly Benedick's behavior in II.i, when he as much as
Claudio believes that Don Pedro has betrayed his friendly
office by wooing Hero for himself, seems culpably callous.
He may see Claudio as a "poor hurt fowl," but he does
nothing to comfort his friend; he seems rather to gloat on
Claudio's misery, and to relish his own role as "lady Fame"
in bringing the bad news. Benedick sums up the cynicism
of his view of life at this early stage in the play by the re-

[24] Charles T. Prouty, *The Sources of Much Ado About Nothing*
(1950; rpt. Freeport, N.Y.: Books for Libraries, 1970), pp. 39ff.

mark that Claudio is "worthy to be whipt" for his misplaced trust in Don Pedro, and Don Pedro underlines the paradox: "Wilt thou make trust a transgression? The transgression is in the stealer" (II.i.225-26). In contrast to Claudio, who believes that "Friendship is constant in all other things / Save in the office and affairs of love" (II.i.175-76), Benedick at this stage has no faith in either love or friendship, and takes a perverse delight when his view of the way the world wags seems to be borne out by events.

Even at the beginning of the church scene (IV.i), Benedick seems still the unreformed cynic. It is difficult to assess the tone of his remark, "This looks not like a nuptial" (IV.i.68), spoken after Claudio, the Prince, and Don John have all denounced Hero in no uncertain terms but before they have described the tryst with her supposed lover they think they have observed. If Benedick's remark does not have at least a trace of the earlier cynicism with which he greeted the news of Don Pedro's theft of Claudio's "bird's nest," it seems almost incredibly inane. Benedick's only other comment during the exposure of Hero, made as Claudio begins to reveal his anger, is less open to varying interpretation:

> *Friar.* If either of you know any inward impediment why you should not be conjoin'd, I charge you on your souls to utter it.
> *Claud.* Know you any, Hero?
> *Hero.* None, my lord.
> *Friar.* Know you any, Count?
> *Leon.* I dare make his answer, none.
> *Claud.* O, what men dare do! What men may do! What men daily do, not knowing what they do!
> *Bene.* How now? interjections? Why then, some be of laughing, as, ah, ha, he!   (IV.i.12-22)

Even without Benedick's odd remark, the ironic contrasts are severe among the formality of the Friar's ritual question,

the simple dignity of Hero's response, the foolhardy jovial-
ity of Leonato's "daring," and the bitter cunning with which
Claudio moves to entrap them. But certainly Benedick, in
his comment on this developing discord, is himself most out
of key. Of course, his laughter may be simply expressive of
astonishment, a way of saying what he later puts in more
straightforward language: "For my part I am so attir'd in
wonder, / I know not what to say" (IV.i.144-45). But it is
revealing that Benedick, who resented being called by
Beatrice "the Prince's jester," almost instinctively tries to
break the tension with what Prince Hal might have termed
a "fool-born jest."

Though he has said in III.ii, "I am not as I have been,"
the conversion of Benedick the cynical jester into Benedick
the man of sober purpose is centered in the church scene.
The stage is thus set for the reversal of V.i, in which it is in
the turn of Claudio and Don Pedro to attempt tedious and
inappropriate jokes, while Benedick is "in earnest" and can
say to them:

> I will leave you now to your gossip-like humor. You
> break jests as braggards do their blades, which, God be
> thank'd, hurt not.
>
> (V.i.185-88)

Benedick, of course, is never completely cured of his jesting,
for the which God be thanked, despite the embarrassment
of his return to the stale horn joke at the end of the play.
But eventually he is cured, I think, of the cynicism which
provided the cover from which he shot his early bolts.

In the delightful scene of witty wooing between Benedick
and Beatrice in V.ii, we have references back to much earlier
material. Thus when Benedick asks her, "for which of my
bad parts didst thou first fall in love with me?" and she
replies, "For them all together" (V.ii.60-62), we know she
speaks truth, for we have heard her anatomize those bad
parts in the very first scene of the play. And in some of the

following exchange, we might think we hear the old, cynical Benedick:

> *Bene.* Thou and I are too wise to woo peaceably.
> *Beat.* It appears not in this confession; there's not one wise man among twenty that will praise himself.
> *Bene.* An old, an old instance, Beatrice, that liv'd in the time of good neighbors. If a man do not erect in this age his own tomb ere he dies, he shall live no longer in monument than the bell rings and the widow weeps.
> *Beat.* And how long is that, think you?
> *Bene.* Question: why, an hour in clamor and a quarter in rheum; therefore it is most expedient for the wise, if Don Worm (his conscience) find no impediment to the contrary, to be the trumpet of his own virtues, as I am to myself. So much for praising myself, who I myself will bear witness is praiseworthy.
>
> (V.ii.72-88)

This sounds a little like the smug self-satisfaction Benedick expressed in II.iii, just before he heard that Beatrice was in love with him. And certainly the contrast between an ancient, golden "time of good neighbors," and this harsh present age, in which it is "expedient" for a man to be "the trumpet of his own virtues," because even a widow can be expected to mourn no longer than a quarter of an hour, sounds like cynicism.

That Benedick in this passage does not emerge as either smug or cynical depends in part on a very complex manipulation of tone. The exchange is structured as a rather formal combat of wits; Benedick accepts Beatrice's challenge that he try to defend the paradoxical proposition that "a man should praise himself." Such rhetorical exercises, of course, were designed to demonstrate dexterity in arguing for a bad cause, not to establish truth. Benedick's "argument" has something in common with the last part of Falstaff's familiar catechism on "Honor": "But will't not live with the living?

No. Why? Detraction will not suffer it. Therefore I'll none of it" (*1 Henry IV*, V.i.138-40). But imbedded in Benedick's paradox is another standard form of the genre, a paradoxical encomium, or praise of that which is not considered praiseworthy—in this case, Benedick himself. All of this indicates that Benedick is from the start turning the joke against himself and is offering no target for the kind of deflating wit Beatrice trained on him in the early acts.

As important as the paradoxical structure for establishing the tone of the passage is the context in which it occurs. Though it contains references to the facts that Benedick is awaiting Claudio's reply to his challenge and that Hero in her grief is "very ill," the dialogue occurs after Borachio has revealed the full truth to Claudio and Don Pedro in V.i. In this case, then, I can accept Mrs. Bennett's argument that the audience knows, even if the characters on stage do not, that a happy ending is assured. Thus Benedick's levity seems much less inappropriate than it did in IV.i, and Ursula's arrival with the joyful news seems only a fitting conclusion to the gay scene, not a sudden turn from sadness to joy.

If Benedick proceeds to develop paradoxical arguments which are little more than exuberant display of his wit, he nevertheless begins with a paradox which he intends "seriously"—that he and Beatrice are "too wise to woo peaceably." He does believe that in wooing wittily and by combat rather than conventionally they are exhibiting wisdom rather than folly. And he proceeds, by indirection, to demonstrate the truth of this proposition, even if he does not show that all wise men must sing their own praises in this decayed age, nor that he himself is a fully praiseworthy subject. And so, in the annoying way that good paradoxes do, this one turns round and bites its tail. Benedick *has* earned the right to praise himself without impediment from Don Worm (his conscience) because he has humbled himself to Beatrice and to Love. Thus he can playfully reassert his masculine supremacy—"Sweet Beatrice, wouldst thou come when I call'd thee?" (V.ii.42-43) and "Serve God, love me, and mend" (V.ii.93)—knowing that Beatrice would never accept, and he would never require, any simple and conventional subservience.

SIXTH SUSPECT: BEATRICE

I do see Benedick, then, as having achieved by the end of the play some considerable success in his quest for a comic attitude which transcends his earlier cynicism and which combines, through paradox, the sharp observance of true wit with the leap of sentimental faith. If he ends this scene with a declaration of his own worth, he begins it with a poetic confession to the "god of love," who knows "how pitiful I deserve." But what of Beatrice? She has sinned against the comic love god of *this* play as much by her fierce command, "Kill Claudio," as by her initial defiance of his power. Whereas in the beginning she expressed an assumed contempt for Benedick's fidelity to his friends as well as for his courage and skill at arms, she now commands him to kill his friend without any recognition that this might produce heartache for her lover—or even that he himself might be killed in the duel.

Beyond question, Beatrice suffers a conversion to love in the scene in which she is deceived by Hero and Ursula; in rapturous lyric, she bids farewell to "contempt" and "maiden pride" and vows to tame her wild heart to Benedick's loving hand (III.i.109-12). When we next see her, in III.iv, she must undergo penance by enduring Margaret's taunts, parallel to Benedick's penance at the hands of Claudio and Don Pedro in III.ii. In the church scene (IV.i), her usual loquacity is much subdued; she has only five lines of the first 252, and two of these are but exclamations of concern and dismay (113-14). When she and Benedick are alone, we learn that she has "wept all this while" (255). In the dialogue which follows, Benedick declares his love simply and directly, but Beatrice cannot yet bring her-

self to direct statement, and must cover her confusion with
the "nothing" quibble:

> *Bene.* I do love nothing in the world so well as you—
> is not that strange?
> *Beat.* As strange as the thing I know not. It were as
> possible for me to say I lov'd nothing so well as you, but
> believe me not; and yet I lie not! I confess nothing, nor
> I deny nothing. I am sorry for my cousin.
>
> (IV.i.267-73)

A few lines later, praying for God's forgiveness, she does
make open confession—"I love you with so much of my
heart that none is left to protest" (IV.i.286-87)—but since
this is followed immediately by "Kill Claudio" and has
been preceded by references to "a man's office" in fighting
a duel and reminiscences of her old taunts about Benedick's
valor, we are entitled to at least a suspicion that there may
be an element of calculation in her declaration of love.
When she recovers her power of extended speech, it is
only to pour out her anger against Claudio, her frustration
at not being a man, and her contempt for the low estate
into which male valor is fallen in these late times:

> O that I were a man for his sake! or that I had any friend
> would be a man for my sake! But manhood is melted into
> cur'sies, valor into compliment, and men are only turn'd
> into tongue, and trim ones too. He is now as valiant as
> Hercules that only tells a lie, and swears it. I cannot be
> a man with wishing, therefore I will die a woman with
> grieving. (IV.i.317-23)

This passage is rich with references to other parts of the
play. Beatrice turns back on Benedick his epithet for her of
"lady Tongue" and generalizes an opposition between
elaborate and effeminate words and simple and manly
blows. In one passionate outburst, she sums up the refusal
to accept a conventional feminine role which has been part

of her character from the beginning. And, in its contemptuous opposition of a more heroic former time to this decadent modern age, the passage is parallel to Benedick's speech about the "time of good neighbors" (V.ii.76-88) which I have discussed earlier. When we read Benedick's speech, we might be amused to notice that he too makes the woman's part to grieve (but not for long!) and the man's to "be the trumpet of his own virtues." But Benedick's later speech is a witty paradox, expressing his hard-won self-confidence as well as recognizing his own absurdity. This of Beatrice seems to be almost pure passion, with only a trace of a rather unpleasant manipulation of her man, and with little or no recognition of the humor in the situation, nor, as I have said, for its possible unpleasant consequences for Benedick.

In any case, there is no moment, here or elsewhere, of self-humiliation for Beatrice quite parallel to Benedick's commitment to her cause at the end of this scene. Beatrice recovers her wit and holds up her end in the spirited wooing dialogues of V.ii and V.iv, but without having "earned" her new sense of proportion in quite the way that Benedick has. Perhaps she earns it, in an indirect and paradoxical way, through her tears shed for Hero, and through the release she gives to her passionate anger in this scene. But Shakespeare seems to allow her to escape unchastized for the sin against love's laws into which these excessive emotions lead her, just as he allows Leonato to escape unchastized for the passionately expressed sin against the faith he should have maintained in his daughter. Beatrice can say later, with appropriate irony, that she loves Benedick "no more than reason" (V.iv.77), but in this scene unreason does not lead her into excess of loving. Far from giving and hazarding all she hath, she here insists upon a complete dominance of her lover.

In order to explore the role of Beatrice further, we must turn to a minor character who is in some respects her double —Margaret.

RAY L. HEFFNER, JR.

Seventh Suspect: Margaret

In the stage directions of the Quarto at the beginning of I.i, and again in II.i, there is introduced a wife for Leonato, "Innogen" by name; she has no lines, and is not mentioned in the dialogue except in Leonato's feeble joke about Hero's parentage. In I.ii, Leonato inquires about a "cousin," his brother Antonio's son; at the end of the scene, he addresses two lines to this "cousin," though there is no reply. As good literary detectives, we might be tempted to hunt for clues associated with these ghostly characters. But they merely indicate that behind the Quarto lay some not-quite-finished authorial draft; these relatives are not only superfluous, but their development as speaking characters would be a positive embarrassment. We have seen that Shakespeare's almost invariable pattern was to provide for the daughter of an angry father no living mother; only *Romeo and Juliet* is an exception, and those plays which lead toward a complete family reunion as a conclusion, like *Pericles* and *A Winter's Tale*—and even here the mother must be miraculously returned from death. If "Innogen" existed, what would there be for her to do? She might add to the sentimental pathos of sweet Hero's preparations for her ill-fated wedding, but in the church scene itself, she could only get in the way. She would either blunt the force of Leonato's passionate—and very masculine—denunciation of his daughter, or that of Beatrice's tearful and total faith in Hero. If, like Lady Capulet, she took her husband's part when the chips were down, she would break the pattern of sexual balance and solidarity which is so important for the play— if only so that Benedick may break it so conspicuously. Bandello's Fenicia may have a mother to comfort her and help to restore her will to live, because her father also believes in his daughter, but Shakespeare's Hero must be denied this consolation. It is only surprising that Shakespeare apparently even considered including "Innogen" in the cast of characters.

206

The same thing can be said of Antonio's son, who cannot remain in the play because the second "Hero," supposedly Antonio's daughter, must be heiress to both Antonio and Leonato. Moreover, if Hero had a young male relative to undertake her quarrel, there would be no reason for Beatrice's fierce demand of Benedick.

If some other characters have little or no function, remaining in the text only in vestigial stage directions or remarks, Margaret is embarrassing because of a superfluity of dramatic functions. Along with Ursula, the other "waiting gentlewoman," she is needed to swell the number of females, both in the masked dance of Act II and in the second masking of Act V. She plays a small but necessary part in the deception of Beatrice in the contrived overhearing scene that begins Act III. In contrast with Ariosto, who emphasizes the role of Dalinda, Margaret's counterpart, and tells most of the story through her lips, Shakespeare seems to minimize or to obscure Margaret's part in the conspiracy. Margaret is never shown discussing the wicked charade with Borachio—indeed, she is never engaged in conversation with Borachio at all, her partner in the masked dance being Balthasar—and Borachio goes out of his way to exculpate her as soon as possible. Nor do we hear how she justifies her conduct to Leonato, after the deception has been revealed. When Margaret is on stage, she behaves as if nothing in which she is personally involved were happening or had happened; she is one of Hero's intimates in the scene just before the denunciation in the church (III.iv), and she can even serve as an intermediary between Beatrice and Benedick *after* her part in the plot against Hero has been announced publicly, though Beatrice and Benedick have not yet heard the news. Of course, Shakespeare must keep Margaret carefully if improbably off stage for the church scene, for there her necessary silence would be impossible to explain.

Though the scene in which Borachio woos Margaret in Hero's clothes is crucial to the plot, there are some indications that Shakespeare himself had not visualized clearly just what is supposed to have occurred. In outlining his plan to Don John, Borachio describes how the Prince and Claudio will "see me at her chamber-window, hear me call Margaret Hero, hear Margaret term me Claudio" (II.ii.42-44). If Margaret did anything of the sort, one would think it would destroy completely the illusion of Hero's disloyalty. But some such innocent charade, in which both partners enacted the roles of their betters, might have been used by Borachio in the difficult task of persuading Margaret to impersonate her mistress. I doubt that even Shakespeare could have given us a convincing scene in which Borachio does so persuade her, and the witty Margaret, who professes so much apprehension, agrees, without smelling a fault. We are asked to believe, almost to take on faith, that such a dialogue does occur, and that nevertheless Margaret "always hath been just and virtuous" (V.i.302).

One reason for this awkward coalescence of several dramatic functions in the role of Margaret, at some expense both to the probability of the plot and to the coherence of the role, is the scarcity of competent boy actors in the Lord Chamberlain's company. But we are quite accustomed, in other plays and in other ways, to seeing Shakespeare make dramatic virtue of theatrical necessity. Does he in any sense make a virtue of the awkward role of Margaret? I think he does, by recognizing that Margaret is a walking paradox, and by assigning to her still another important dramatic function.

In the scene in which Hero prepares for her wedding, Margaret is the one who shocks the bride with her plain speaking about sex. Hero's innocence and shyness are emphasized, but Shakespeare gives Margaret a spirited defense of her freedom of language.

> *Hero.* God give me joy to wear it, for my heart is exceeding heavy.
> *Marg.* 'Twill be heavier soon by the weight of a man.

Hero. Fie upon thee, art not asham'd?

Marg. Of what, lady? of speaking honorably? Is not marriage honorable in a beggar? Is not your lord honorable without marriage? I think you would have me say, "saving your reverence, a husband." And bad thinking do not wrest true speaking, I'll offend nobody. Is there any harm in "the heavier for a husband"? None, I think, and it be the right husband and the right wife; otherwise 'tis light, and not heavy.

(III.iv.24-37)

We might notice that this, like so many things in the play, is a formal paradox, a rhetorical defense of a proposition usually considered indefensible. In it Margaret demonstrates her wit, associates herself with honest sexuality, and assumes the role of one who speaks truth without subterfuge or circumlocution—a role which often creates strong empathy in Shakespeare's plays. And it brings Margaret closer to Beatrice, the loquacious wit, for although Beatrice at the beginning of the play "cannot endure to hear talk of a husband," she has been more an enemy to the hypocrisies of courtship and to the conventional subservience of the female than to honest sexuality. It has been the function of Beatrice to speak truth to Hero, both by urging her cousin to consult her own desire before agreeing to any suitor (II.i.53-56), and by urging both Claudio and Hero to break out of their reticence and speak openly of their love once the match has been made (II.i.305-11).

Margaret is thus the appropriate one of the women to twit Beatrice about her love for Benedick in III.iv; when she does so, both she and Beatrice recognize that Margaret has in part assumed Beatrice's former role:

Beat. I am stuff'd, cousin, I cannot smell.

Marg. A maid, and stuff'd! There's goodly catching of cold.

Beat. O, God help me, God help me, how long have you profess'd apprehension?

Marg. Ever since you left it. Doth not my wit become me rarely?

Beat. It is not seen enough, you should wear it in your cap. By my troth, I am sick.

(III.iv.64-72)

As Beatrice assumes the role of the "sick" lover, who hides her feelings behind a minor prevarication (her stuffy cold is no more to be taken literally than Benedick's toothache), Margaret steps into her shoes as witty commentator, just as Claudio sporadically tries on Benedick's role as "the Prince's jester." Hero cannot do this if the note of reticence in her role is to be maintained, but Margaret is available. And in V.ii, Margaret is an explicit surrogate for Beatrice, as Benedick tries a witty bout with her before taking on Beatrice in the main event.

In some odd way, Margaret is the right woman to test her wits against Beatrice, and to be wooed in her place by Benedick, with sonnets and with suggestive *double-entendres* about loving and fencing, because she has already served as a substitute for Hero, in that scene we never see but whose blatant sexuality so offends Claudio. In both plots, Margaret brings to the surface submerged elements of female sexuality. But she is no scapegoat; far from being banished, she is accepted back into the family, and plays her part in the *kommos* at the end. As a symbol, then, she is quite credible, though as a realistic character her motivations are left unexplored.

At the end of III.iv, Margaret has a long speech in which the themes of appearance and reality in love, and of plain thinking as well as plain speaking, are moralized in quite a paradoxical way.

Beat. By my troth, I am sick.

Marg. Get you some of this distill'd *carduus benedictus*, and lay it to your heart; it is the only thing for a qualm.

Hero. There thou prick'st her with a thistle.

Beat. Benedictus! why *benedictus?* You have some moral in this *benedictus.*

Marg. Moral? no, by my troth I have no moral meaning, I meant plain holy-thistle. You may think perchance that I think you are in love. Nay, by'r lady, I am not such a fool to think what I list, nor I list not to think what I can, nor indeed I cannot think, if I would think my heart out of thinking, that you are in love, or that you will be in love, or that you can be in love. Yet Benedick was such another, and now is he become a man. He swore he would never marry, and yet now in despite of his heart he eats his meat without grudging; and how you may be converted I know not, but methinks you look with your eyes as other women do.

(III.iv.72-92)

Explicating passages of Elizabethan wit is often tedious if not superfluous, but let me say that Margaret covers much ground here. Going well beyond her original pun, and the surprisingly explicit phallic twist which Hero gives to it, she first disclaims any pretense to a "moral" meaning (the implication being that all her meanings are "immoral" or bawdy), and then does a witty turn on the cliché that "thought is free," that even a waiting gentlewoman may think what she pleases. Then she scores a hit by pretending to return to the image which Beatrice had projected of herself and to believe that of course Beatrice is incapable of love. Finally, she places the entire exchange in the most general context by suggesting that for Benedick to fall in love is for him to do no less than to "become a man"; and she gracefully suggests not only that Beatrice may be "converted" but that she has been a true woman all along but has been unwilling to admit it.

No passage is more central for the interpretation of the Beatrice-Benedick plot adopted by most critics, and none is truer to the tone of witty recognition of the simplicities which underlie love's ironies and complexities. It seems to me significant that this speech is given to Margaret, by theatrical necessity a somewhat equivocal character, but one whose equivocal nature is here built into the thematic structure of the play.

If *Much Ado About Nothing* is in part, as both John Russell Brown and Rosalie Colie have suggested, a comic rehearsal for the tragedy of *Othello*, it is not surprising that we can find traces of Margaret's ambiguous role in Emilia. Again we are asked to believe that, though she was persuaded by Iago to steal Desdemona's handkerchief, she did not know what she was doing and was innocent of any real treachery to her mistress. And, in the scene in which Desdemona sings the "Willow Song" as she prepares to wait for Othello in her wedding sheets, it is Emilia who admits that she might "do such a deed for all the world," and then is given a twenty-line defense of the rights, and affections, of women:

> *Emil.* . . . Let husbands know
> Their wives have sense like them; they see, and smell,
> And have their palates both for sweet and sour,
> As husbands have. What is it that they do
> When they change us for others? Is it sport?
> I think it is. And doth affection breed it?
> I think it doth. Is't frailty that thus errs?
> It is so too. And have not we affections,
> Desires for sport, and frailty, as men have?
> Then let them use us well; else let them know,
> The ills we do, their ills instruct us so.
>
> (IV.iii.93-103)

The main purpose of this is to show by contrast how truly remarkable is Desdemona's innocence, as in the parallel scene between Margaret and Hero. But it is also a defiance of all suspicious and philandering husbands on behalf of all wives, which seems fully warranted by the behavior of the men in this play. We seem to hear echoes of other characters in other plays who are allowed for one moment to make a sympathetic case for the outcast: "Hath not a Jew eyes? Hath not a Jew hands, organs, dimensions, senses, affections, passions?" At the same time, within her own play, Emilia's rhetorical questions seem to echo her husband's contemptuous assertions: "Bless'd fig's-end! The wine she drinks is made of grapes" (II.i.251-52).

Both Margaret and Emilia are exonerated of complicity in the villainy of the men to whom they have given their bodies, and perhaps their love, but both are important links in the chain which connects the unconventional wit of a Beatrice, the earthiness of Juliet's nurse, and even the cynical "realism" of an Iago. Shakespeare has no "woman killed with kindness," let alone any Vittoria Corombona or Beatrice Joanna. But he does allow a Margaret or an Emilia or a Nurse, in the privacy of the bedchamber, to set off the purity and fidelity of his heroines by suggesting that a woman *might* be unfaithful to her husband, and might even be justified in doing so. Margaret, like Emilia, is a spokeswoman not only for sexuality but for a fully justified female exposure of that male "bad conscience" which underlies all the cuckold jokes, and all the pernicious distrust.

EIGHTH SUSPECT: THE FRIAR

The most comprehensive reply to those who see Claudio as an unmitigated cad has been provided by John Russell Brown, who argues that the theme of "love's truth" unites the two plots, and that both Claudio and Benedick must come by different routes to the same trust in the inward and imaginative vision provided by love rather than in outward appearances:

> Benedick and Beatrice, trusting their eyes, judgements, and power of speech too much, are taught, through the good offices of their friends, to recognize and give sway to their imaginations; so Benedick is

"converted" (II.iii.23) and finds beauty where he had previously seen a "fury" and Beatrice learns to look as "other women do" (III.iv.92). But even when they are brought, through mutual trust of their own "souls," to admit their love to each other, it again needs the offices of friends before they will admit the folly of their love to the world. Claudio, fearing, with good enough reason, to trust his eyes alone, is an easy prey to his prince's enemies, and accepts outward proof of inward guilt. In so doing he brings suffering on his lady and on himself, but in the end their love is justified by his imaginative recognition of the "sweet idea" of Hero's true beauty. Both pairs of lovers take a long road to the same conclusion.[25]

In developing this interpretation, Mr. Brown puts great stress on the Friar's stratagem of the pretended death of Hero, and on the Friar's explanation of the purpose to be served by the deception:

> She dying, as it must be so maintain'd,
> Upon the instant that she was accus'd,
> Shall be lamented, pitied, and excus'd
> Of every hearer; for it so falls out
> That what we have we prize not to the worth
> Whiles we enjoy it, but being lack'd and lost,
> Why then we rack the value; then we find
> The virtue that possession would not show us
> Whiles it was ours. So will it fare with Claudio:
> When he shall hear she died upon his words,
> Th' idea of her life shall sweetly creep
> Into his study of imagination,
> And every lovely organ of her life
> Shall come apparell'd in more precious habit,
> More moving, delicate, and full of life,
> Into the eye and prospect of his soul,

[25] John Russell Brown, *Shakespeare and His Comedies* (London: Methuen, 1962), pp. 122-23.

Than when she liv'd indeed. Then shall he mourn,
If ever love had interest in his liver,
And wish he had not so accused her;
No, though he thought his accusation true.

(IV.i.214-33)

This is an elaborate and pretty piece of quasi-Platonic psychological theory about how the sentiment of pity can rekindle that of love, and establish in the "imagination" of the lover an "idea" of the beloved that is more beautiful, more powerful, more "full of life," than the living form of the beloved herself. But it is also a scenario, a confident prediction of what *will* happen as a consequence of the Friar's benevolent ruse. And this Friar is just as wrong about what does happen as that other Friar who planned the false death of Juliet. Claudio does not mourn and wish he had not accused Hero, "though he thought his accusation true"; only after the accusation has been shown to be false does he say,

Sweet Hero, now thy image doth appear
In the rare semblance that I lov'd it first.

(V.i.251-52)

Even at this point, her image is restored, but it does not seem to have achieved that transcendent beauty and power which the Friar predicted. Claudio, instead of being overwhelmed by repentance and regret, is still exculpating himself: "yet sinn'd I not, / But in mistaking" (V.i.274-75). In the early part of this scene, when, according to the Friar's prediction, the idea of her life should be sweetly creeping into "the eye and prospect of his soul," Claudio has no thoughts of Hero and, with the Prince, is only concerned with making a hasty withdrawal from Leonato's house.

What actually happens in V.i needs to be more carefully examined. At the beginning of the scene, Antonio tries to ameliorate his brother's passionate grief with Stoic counsels of patience. Leonato with vehemence rejects such

215

counsels, not only for his own case but for all cases of real
"ache":

> for, brother, men
> Can counsel and speak comfort to that grief
> Which they themselves not feel, but tasting it,
> Their counsel turns to passion, which before
> Would give preceptial med'cine to rage,
> Fetter strong madness in a silken thread,
> Charm ache with air, and agony with words.
> (V.i.20-26)

Finding it impossible to control Leonato's passion with
reason, and having been challenged, as a member of the
family, to show a sympathetic passion himself, Antonio
now tries to direct Leonato's "rage" and "madness" outward, and in this he succeeds immediately. When Claudio
and the Prince arrive, the two brothers are ready to vie
with each other in belligerency.

The point I wish to make is that, although both Leonato
and Antonio have ostensibly accepted the Friar's analysis
and agreed to follow his advice, they do not really do so.
Instead of allowing remorse and love to "creep" into Claudio's soul, they drive these soft emotions off with their
challenges. Claudio reacts for a moment with reciprocal
passion, as his hand strays to his sword, but the feeling
which gains the ascendancy is an amused contempt for the
brothers: "We had lik'd to have had our two noses snapp'd
off with two old men without teeth" (V.i.115-16). None
of this can produce the result the Friar anticipated; Don
Pedro speaks for Claudio as well as for himself as he reiterates their conviction that what they did was entirely
justifiable:

> My heart is sorry for your daughter's death;
> But on my honor she was charg'd with nothing
> But what was true, and very full of proof.
> (V.i.103-5)

Not only Leonato and Antonio but also Beatrice and Benedick very conspicuously fail to follow the Friar's plan, though Benedick has urged Leonato to let the Friar advise him, and has sworn his own allegiance. The essence of the Friar's advice is "have patience and endure" (IV.i.254). But as soon as the Friar has left the stage, Beatrice drops her bombshell, "Kill Claudio," and Benedick is forced to commit himself to this bloody course of action in order to prove his love. The announced objective of the Friar's stratagem is the marriage of a repentant Claudio and a rehabilitated Hero; Beatrice's counterplan is obviously subversive of this objective, and thus of her cousin's potential happiness, if the Friar's analysis is accepted.

John Russell Brown's comment on the church scene, attempting as it does to harmonize the two plots around the theme of "love's truth," seems, in its unquestioning endorsement of the feeling from which Beatrice's command derives, not to recognize sufficiently that Beatrice here is a force directing the movement of the play away from a comic conclusion:

> At length Benedick can put a solemn question, asking "Think you *in your soul* the Count Claudio hath wrong'd Hero?" and he receives as solemn an answer: "Yea, as sure as I have a thought of a soul" [IV.i.329-30]. If Benedick truly loves he must—as Claudio must—believe his lady's "soul" against all outward testimony; he had called her inward spirit a "fury," but, if he has truly looked upon her with a lover's imagination, he will have seen the beauty of that spirit and will now trust and obey—and will challenge Claudio. The twin stories of *Much Ado About Nothing* turn on the same point; the very wise and the very uncertain must both learn to trust inward qualities, mere nothings to some other eyes; through a lover's imagination each must recognize inward truth and beauty, and must speak and act from a convinced heart.[26]

26 Brown, p. 118.

Yea, but what if Love's own best interest, soberly considered, prick you off when Love's passionately conceived "inward truth" pricks you on? The carefully contrived Shakespearean situation is too complex in its ironies to be moralized so simply, even with the aid of Mr. Brown's romantic rhetoric.

Leonato repels his brother's reasonable counsel in much the same way that Benedick repels the jests of Claudio and Don Pedro as they comment on the obvious "signs of love" in him. Benedick disguises his lovesickness as "the toothache," and Leonato says:

> I pray thee peace. I will be flesh and blood,
> For there was never yet philosopher
> That could endure the toothache patiently.
>
> (V.i.34-36)

Benedick says, "Well, every one can master a grief but he that has it" (III.ii.28-29). In V.i, Leonato is just as convinced as Beatrice that his "soul" doth now tell him that Hero is belied, and just as convinced that this "inward truth" should lead to violence. I cannot agree with Mr. Brown, then, that Shakespeare organizes *Much Ado* consistently as a sermon to convince us all to trust the "inward spirit"; there is too much evidence that that spirit we have heard "may be a dev'l, and the dev'l hath power / T' assume a pleasing shape" (*Hamlet* II.ii.599-600).

We have seen that the Friar's confident prescription of a way to work gently on Claudio's passion does not work out in practice, partially because the Friar's allies are too distracted by contrary passions to follow his advice. The opposition between reason and passion, and the competing psychologies put forward as ways of understanding and controlling the passions, need to be considered more comprehensively. Toward this end, I should like to introduce the last in my list of "suspects"—Claudio's uncle.

NINTH SUSPECT: CLAUDIO'S UNCLE

There are other characters around whom luscious clues seem to hang like fruit, ripe for the plucking. I have said little about Dogberry, whose verbosity and Poloniuslike pride in his linguistic cunning associates him with Beatrice and Benedick, but who, with his confederates, is also a very particularized version of the Shakespearean wise fool, as the paradox of Borachio emphasizes: "What your wisdoms could not discover, these shallow fools have brought to light" (V.i.232-34). Or, on the other side of that grouping of the talkative versus the silent which seems almost as important for this play as the distinction of the sexes, I have said little about the melancholy Don John, the addition of whom to the plot Professor Prouty considers so important, and who introduces himself by saying, "I am not of many words, but I thank you" (I.i.157-58). But I wish instead to concentrate on Claudio's uncle, who is one of the first persons mentioned in the first scene, but who has no speaking part and is not referred to again. After the Messenger has described how Claudio in the recent action has done "in the figure of a lamb the feats of a lion," this dialogue ensues:

> *Leon.* He hath an uncle here in Messina will be very much glad of it.
>
> *Mess.* I have already deliver'd him letters, and there appears much joy in him, even so much that joy could not show itself modest enough without a badge of bitterness.
>
> *Leon.* Did he break out into tears?
>
> *Mess.* In great measure.
>
> *Leon.* A kind overflow of kindness. There are no faces truer than those that are so wash'd. How much better is it to weep at joy than to joy at weeping!
>
> (I.i.18-29)

Among the standard paradoxes listed in the table of contents of a book by Ortensio Lando which Rosalie Colie calls
"the *Ur*-manual of paradoxy"; and which Anthony Munday
translated in 1593 under the title *The Defence of Contra-
ries: Paradoxes against common opinion* is this: "It is better
to weep than to laugh."[27] Leonato's conclusion is a more
complicated but at the same time a less paradoxical version
of this old chestnut. Applied to literature, the collocation
of joy and weeping can move in the direction of the suggestive remark at the end of Plato's *Symposium*—that "the
same man could have the knowledge required for writing
comedy and tragedy"[28]—and could become the rationale for
the mongrel genre of tragicomedy. Turned around somewhat, it can become the motto for the popular "black"
comedy of the twentieth century. As developed by Leonato,
the emphasis is on overflowing the measure, on the cleansing
effect of tears, and on the perception of truth.

Like the long speech of the Friar on the effect of pity in
reestablishing the idea of the beloved in the soul of the
lover (IV.i.210-43), Leonato's paradox may be considered
as a generalization to be tested by subsequent events. In the
church scene, belief in this generalization seems to be one
of the causes of Leonato's error:

> Would the two princes lie, and Claudio lie,
> Who lov'd her so, that speaking of her foulness,
> Wash'd it with tears? Hence from her, let her die.
>
> (IV.i.152-54)

The Friar has been reading Hero's face rather than Claudio's, where, despite the absence of tears, he finds confirma-
tion of her innocence:

> I have mark'd
> A thousand blushing apparitions
> To start into her face, a thousand innocent shames
> In angel whiteness beat away those blushes,

[27] Ortensio Lando, *Paradossi Cioè, Sententie fuori del comun parere*
(Venice, 1544), cited by Colie, p. 461.
[28] Plato, *Symposium*, Loeb Classical Library; cited by Colie, p. xiii.

And in her eye there hath appear'd a fire
To burn the errors that these princes hold
Against her maiden truth.

(IV.i.158-64)

This seems at least to imply that the science of deducing truth from the external signs of emotion is more complex than Leonato's paradox had indicated. Nevertheless, both the Friar's reading and his observations of human behavior have taught him that there is truth to be found in blushes, in pale innocent shames, and in the fire of an angry eye.

Claudio is not the only one who weeps in this scene. That Beatrice has "wept all this while" (255) is part of the reason why Benedick trusts what she thinks in her soul; and many critics have observed that it takes the solvent of emotional sympathy for Hero's plight to melt the reserves Beatrice and Benedick have built up, and to enable them to declare their true love for each other. But Beatrice moves quickly from wordless tears to a very voluble anger, and the play insists that she is as wrong in her conclusion that Claudio has been "approv'd in the height a villain" (301) as Claudio is in concluding that Hero's "blush is guiltiness, not modesty" (42).

Must we conclude, with Duncan, that "There's no art / To find the mind's construction in the face" (*Macbeth* I.iv.11-12)? No such conclusion is warranted in this play. Despite the skepticism we have learned for all easy generalizations about human behavior, we can observe that both Leonato and Beatrice attempt to go beyond reading the truth of the individual soul in that individual's facial expression, whereas Claudio in his error is the one who insists that Hero's innocence cannot be deduced from "these exterior shows." The paradox of the situation is that Hero is true *and* Claudio is true, though these may seem contradictory propositions.

All three misapprehenders—Claudio, Leonato, and Beatrice—allow the passion of anger as well as the passion of grief to cloud their judgments. And Don Pedro, Antonio, and Benedick, despite their opportunity for a somewhat more dispassionate judgment, are drawn into error by their sympathy for these passionate principals. Only the Friar stands apart, and puts his reading and his observations to good use. If the Friar's plan, based upon the writings of authorities but with his own "experimental seal" (IV.i.166), goes awry, it is mainly because both Beatrice and Leonato are too passionate to accept his counsel to "have patience and endure" (254). As for Claudio, we may still believe that Love once "had interest in his liver," and may again, though this is not established in the way that the Friar had hoped.

The Friar's hoax is not entirely inefficacious. If Claudio is not brought to remorse by the news of Hero's death, Borachio is. His complete confession and his desire for "nothing but the reward of a villain" (V.i.243-44) seem to be motivated as much by repentance as by the evidence which the shallow fools have brought to light.

I characterized the scheme of Beatrice to get Benedick to kill Claudio, in recompense for the death of Hero's reputation, as a "counterplan," working at cross purposes to the Friar's and raising the real possibility of a tragic ending for the play. The continuing deception of Claudio and the Prince after Hero's innocence has been established, the imposed penance of singing an epitaph "to her bones," and the insistence that Claudio agree to marry, sight unseen, a hitherto unknown "cousin" of Hero, all seem to be the brainchildren of Leonato, though he needs the cooperation of all the conspirators to carry them out. The agreement to accept without question a bride of the bereaved father's choosing is in Bandello, and there the wedding is much elaborated, with the revelation that the bride is really Fenicia much postponed. But in Bandello it is "Lionato" who writes the pathetic epitaph for Fenicia's tomb; he uses it to accuse the "harsh bridegroom" of cruelty and lack of faith long before the true facts have come to light. But it is because of the "tearful obsequies" that Claudio's counterpart, Sir Timbreo, "began to feel great sorrow and a heart-stirring such as he never would have thought possible."[29]

Shakespeare rearranges these elements and puts them to different use. Shakespeare's Leonato imposes the tombside vigil on Don Pedro and Claudio because he perceives that they must share with Borachio and Don John the guilt for the slander of Hero, and because they have not suffered enough and are not fully repentant. Bandello's "Lionato" persists in his deception long after Sir Timbreo has fully exhibited his grief and remorse. That part of the penance Leonato imposes is that Claudio must compose the epitaph and apparently also the accompanying dirge seems to me significant, as does the fact that the wedding to the "new Hero" follows immediately upon these obsequies, whereas in Bandello a year intervenes. We have here a brief emblem of the way not only to stimulate grief but to use it productively and to transcend it. Like the Friar, Leonato plans to use one passion to reawaken and to condition another, but he adds the important ingredients of music and poetry, as well as setting the stage carefully, by the monument, at night.

For Claudio to compose both the epitaph and the dirge is for his love to labor "in sad invention" (V.i.283), and Claudio has used the same term—"invention"—for Leonato's effort in devising an appropriate penance. I would connect this with all the efforts throughout the play to find an appropriate, "poetic" formula for expressing deeply felt emotion, and with the conventionalized and often superficial association of love and poetry. I would remember Balthasar's song, "Sigh no more, ladies" (II.iii.62-74), performed with such assumed reluctance, which was really anti-romantic and cynical and thus inappropriate to Claudio's sentimental state, but the inappropriateness of which was unperceived, by Benedick as well as by Claudio and the Prince. I would remember Benedick's contemptuous words

---

[29] Bullough, II, 122.

about Claudio the lover, when Benedick thought he himself
was still heart-whole:

> he was wont to speak plain and to the purpose (like an
> honest man and a soldier), and now is he turn'd ortogra-
> phy—his words are a very fantastical banquet, just so
> many strange dishes.

> (II.iii.18-21)

In the real Claudio of the early acts, of course, we never see
this fantastical love-poet whom Benedick imagines. I would
remember also Benedick the love-poet, whose efforts in this
kind are strategically placed in V.ii, between Leonato's
instructions to Claudio and the actual performance of
Claudio's penance. Benedick gaily promises to write a sonnet
praising Margaret in a high style, but when he tries to
compose a song for Beatrice, he quickly abandons the
attempt:

> Marry, I cannot show it in rhyme; I have tried. I can
> find out no rhyme to "lady" but "baby," an innocent
> rhyme; for "scorn," "horn," a hard rhyme; for "school,"
> "fool," a babbling rhyme: very ominous endings. No, I
> was not born under a rhyming planet, nor I cannot woo
> in festival terms.

> (V.ii.36-41)

There is under all this an assumption (even though Benedick denies that he himself can woo in festival terms) that
the emotions of love are not fully realized unless they are
presented in the disciplined form of poetry. So also, in a
somewhat different way, for the emotions of grief and righteous anger. These must be recognized, controlled, and used;
they cannot be simply exorcised by reasoned philosophy, any
more than the toothache. Thus Leonato uses his "invention"
in devising the two-part tragicomedy for Claudio to act—
and kills his own desire for revenge. Thus Claudio sings his
grief and his repentance, and then is able to face a new day
of matrimony with a restored soul.

The poetry by the tomb is really in three movements, for Don Pedro also has his part. First, the epitaph confesses the slander and establishes, by fitting paradox, Hero's "glorious fame." Then the dirge prays to the "goddess of the night" for pardon for those who slew Hero, and asks "midnight" to assist in their ritual moan. Finally, Don Pedro announces the dawn of the "gentle day" in heightened imagery, rhymed formally as a quatrain:

> Good morrow, masters, put your torches out.
> The wolves have preyed, and look, the gentle day,
> Before the wheels of Phoebus, round about
> Dapples the drowsy east with spots of grey.
>
> (V.iii.24-27)

To those who see a light and comic tone as sustained throughout the play, the image of the preying wolves may seem excessive for the perils of the night—the misapprehensions, the slanders, the excesses of passion—which these characters have now successfully endured. But it is possible to read the play, for all its slapstick and its wit, its irony and its paradox, as a tragicomedy of the passions, which these inflated images summarize effectively.

I hope that a few "morals" have emerged from my detective story. One is that *Much Ado About Nothing* abounds in "moral" generalizations about human behavior, and most of them are rendered suspect by their context in the total pattern of the play, from Margaret's impious remarks about female sexuality, through the Friar's prescription for using pity to produce love (remember Benedick's remark that he weds Beatrice only "for pity"—V.iv.93), to Benedick's final joke that "there is no staff more reverent than one tipped with horn," and including Leonato's initial statement that "there are no faces truer" than those washed with tears. The play forces us to adopt a healthy skepticism toward all such *sententiae*.

The play thus promotes the attitude of the Renaissance

tradition of paradox, and it is replete with paradoxes of all sorts. Indeed, the *sententiae* just mentioned are all stated in paradoxical form, and they are surrounded by many others —the Friar's counsel to Hero, "Die to live"; Benedick's cynical paradox that trust is a transgression; Beatrice's paradoxical demonstration that she cannot marry a man with a beard nor a man without one; and the mind-boggling paradoxes about "nothing" suggested by the title, to name just a few. What Rosalie Colie says about paradox in general is true of this play:

> Paradoxes are profoundly self-critical: whether rhetorical, logical, or epistemological, they comment on their own method and their own technique. . . . The thinking process, examining for the "error" which brought it up sharp against paradox, turns back on itself to see how it got stuck upon the paradox, and if that paradox might have been avoided: a paradox generates the self-referential activity. Operating at the limits of discourse, redirecting thoughtful attention to the faculty or limited structures of thought, paradoxes play back and forth across terminal and categorical boundaries—that is, they play with human understanding, that most serious of all human activities.[30]

Shakespeare's use of paradox in *Much Ado* is related to his use here and elsewhere of the "idea" of the play and the "idea" of the poem, through plays and playlets within plays and through the dramatization of the poetic process. The disappearance of the "subject" in an infinite regress of mirror images is suggested by both techniques. If one were forced to try to define the subject of this play in a phrase, one might do worse than to say it is about the art of paradox, and the paradoxical meaning of that art.

Finally, let me suggest a "moral" which is more positive, as well as more pedagogical. Our several and tentative criti-

[30] Colie, p. 7.

cal analyses seem rather like attempts to put the round earth on a flat map, using Mercator's projection; the latitude and longitude on which we center our attention may be presented accurately enough, but there is great distortion elsewhere. Nevertheless, many of these approaches are really quite useful to teachers and students in their attempts to see the play whole. Certainly the introductions and notes by David Stevenson and Josephine Waters Bennett, the compilations and analyses of sources by Charles T. Prouty and Geoffrey Bullough, the essays by Paul Jorgenson and John Russell Brown, the general approaches of Leslie Fiedler and Rosalie Colie, the very popular modern production by Joseph Papp and A. J. Antoon—all can lead us to see things in the play which we might otherwise have overlooked. Even my own pseudo-Fiedlerian attempts to center the play on the father-daughter relationship, or on Margaret's defense of women's rights, and my suggestion that the play may be analyzed as a tragicomedy of the passions, may add an insight or two. So long as we really reject the analogy of the detective story and do not hope to find a single key figure or nugget of philosophy or ultimate solution of any sort, there is no harm in our continuing to hunt for clues in this or in any Shakespearean play.

ELEVEN

TEACHING *CORIOLANUS*:
THE IMPORTANCE OF PERSPECTIVE

BRIAN VICKERS

THE problems of teaching Shakespeare are, in essence, the same as those of reading and interpreting Shakespeare, whether in private or as a working scholar-critic. The classroom imposes certain limitations on a teacher's method—for instance, he cannot just deliver an interpretation and walk away, as the critic does who publishes an essay or book on Shakespeare: the teacher's audience is ever present, and (hopefully, at least) articulate. If a teacher is any good, and if his pupils are any good, then he is going to have to argue his interpretation out stage by stage, justify it by detailed reference to the text, illuminate it by comparative analysis with other Shakespeare plays, or with any relevant works of literature.

Nor, again, can the teacher assume a wide historical knowledge, or a familiarity with sophisticated modern critical techniques, unless he is so fortunate as to have an advanced class with whom to work. (Rare event in these times of accelerated courses, overcrowded syllabuses, demanding yet unintelligent examination requirements, curricula which permit everything yet fail to offer constructive approaches to literature, since they have been planned by teachers who are afraid of taking responsibility for a structured education.) It is, perhaps, unreasonable to compress a whole feeling of dissatisfaction with the modern university system into one parenthesis, yet it may not be inappropriate to record that in this writer's experience of teaching Shakespeare in Cambridge, England (ten years), America (one summer), and Switzerland (four years) the situation con-

228

ducive to a full mutual experience of a play rarely occurs. Seldom have the teacher and student worked together often enough or long enough to have a proper appreciation of each other's strengths and weaknesses; seldom is there the openness on both sides to challenge opinion without giving or taking offense; seldom are both parties in possession of a wide enough knowledge of the primary and secondary literatures to bring out what is special about the work being studied, what the main problems of interpretation have proved to be, and to what extent the debate, past or present, has been at all relevant. The modern teaching situation, by contrast, is often rushed, inadequately prepared; both teachers and students are being expected to do too much work in too many fields; these fields are not properly related by intelligent and responsible planning of curricula and examination requirements; and the result is often one of monotony and repetition on the one side, haste and confusion on the other. Few university teachers are satisfied with their system, yet few are willing to do anything to change it. We teachers are in danger of becoming a class adept at criticism, yet either unable or unwilling to carry out the consequences of our criticism into action and reform.

That grievance aired, one must of course record that stimulating and mutually rewarding teaching often takes place, and that the classroom—by which I mean an extended seminar or lecture-course devoted to a small number of plays—in fact provides a number of advantages to the understanding of Shakespeare. One for the teacher is that the audience answers back, and while one's thoughts are in the process of development—publish a book, by contrast, and criticism comes too late, when it is impossible to change or improve one's work. For the student the benefit consists in being able to think aloud, to develop his ideas spontaneously yet under stimulus, and to learn not only from the teacher but—more important, since this is a discussion that can and ought to continue outside the classroom—from his fellow students as well. Another advantage for the teacher is that he can experiment with an approach to a play, develop its strengths, cut short its weaknesses, in a way which is clearly impossible in the cut-and-dried form of printed criticism. Above all, the teacher is very favorably placed to innovate in what I shall call multifocal criticism.

I

The deficiency of most Shakespeare criticism, past and present, is that it takes a single view of a play: it fastens on to one aspect, or to one character's interpretation of the proceedings (it takes sides for or against that character), and pushes that view through to the end as if a play were a linear, one-strand narrative, told from a sharply restricted viewpoint. Yet all drama is polyphonic, multifocal. The controlling perspective is that of the dramatist, but a Shakespeare or an Aeschylus or a Chekhov does not present only one view of his characters, or one opinion of them. He shows many aspects of each character, passes many judgments on them in the course of a play—indeed, if he showed only one aspect, passed only one judgment, he would be writing a moral fable only, or a very simple allegory. In creating a highly varied, sharply contrasted group of characters, individual in personality and often clearly differentiated in language and style, he gan give us, in addition, each of the main characters' view both of the whole action and of each of the other protagonists. Not only does he show and judge them, but they all judge each other, by loving, hating, admiring, envying, accepting, believing, criticizing each other. If we were to limit the actors to four, say, and designate them A, B, C, and D, then the possible judgments and perspectives would include

A on B; A on C; A on D
B on A; B on C; B on D,

and so on, assuming that each is an individual unrelated to the others. Given groupings, B and C as husband and wife, say, then we will have, in addition to B on C and C on B (think of Albee, *Who's Afraid of Virginia Woolf?*),

$$A \text{ on } B+C; \ D \text{ on } B+C$$
$$B+C \text{ on } A; \ B+C \text{ on } D,$$

and so on. And of course all such judgments reveal the nature of the personality making the judgment: A's judgment of B will tell us a great deal about A. Further, in the drama as in the novel a writer is able to give us, by exterior or interior monologue, A's own view of himself, his self-presentation, as in the soliloquy, often placed early on as a kind of introduction, or later as a reaction to a development or a crisis.

To give a practical example of multifocal dramatic structure, and to use a simpler model than Elizabethan drama, I take one Greek tragedy, the *Agamemnon* of Aeschylus. If we consider the Chorus, Agamemnon, his wife Clytemnestra, her lover Aegisthus, and Agamemnon's concubine Cassandra, then we can soon verify that a large part of Aeschylus' drama is in fact given up to the presentation of each character's perspective on the others. It is possible to write it out in tabular form:

I. (*a*) Chorus on Agamemnon
   (*b*) Chorus on Clytemnestra
   (*c*) Chorus on Clytemnestra plus Aegisthus
   (*d*) Chorus on Aegisthus
   (*e*) Chorus on Cassandra

II. (*a*) Clytemnestra on herself
   (*b*) Clytemnestra on the Chorus (representing the people of Argos)
   (*c*) Clytemnestra on Agamemnon
   (*d*) Clytemnestra on Aegisthus
   (*e*) Clytemnestra on Cassandra

III. (*a*) Agamemnon on himself
   (*b*) Agamemnon on Clytemnestra
   (*c*) Agamemnon on the Chorus (representing Argos)
   (*d*) Agamemnon on Cassandra

IV. (*a*) Cassandra on Apollo
    (*b*) Cassandra on Agamemnon
    (*c*) Cassandra on Clytemnestra
    (*d*) Cassandra on the Chorus
    (*e*) Cassandra on herself
    (*f*) Cassandra on Aegisthus
V. (*a*) Aegisthus on Agamemnon
    (*b*) Aegisthus on himself
    (*c*) Aegisthus on the Chorus
    (*d*) Aegisthus on Clytemnestra.

While detailed analysis of this sequence could reveal much of Aeschylus' dramatic technique, and of his evaluation of the situation, this would lead us too far away from Shakespeare; but I would note the significance of the fact that section III and section V consist of only four perspectives, instead of the possible five. In the latter case, V, this is because Aegisthus does not mention Cassandra—their paths do not cross, for the prophetess is an actor in Clytemnestra's plot against Agamemnon. Her plot is based ostensibly on the offended feelings of the wife whose husband has taken a concubine, whereas Aegisthus' grievance against Agamemnon is based ostensibly on the family vendetta deriving from the banquet of Atreus. The other case of a missing perspective, III, is Agamemnon's, and there is a terrible irony for the King in that he is entirely unaware of the existence of Aegisthus, the lover whom his wife has taken as solace during the ten long years he has been away at the siege of Troy. Aegisthus moves outside Agamemnon's consciousness, and the King never knows the reason why he is murdered. If we have two examples of a section having less than the expected total of perspectives, we have one instance of an unexpectedly greater total, six instead of five (IV). Cassandra, in her prophetic madness, speaks much of her vindictive pursuit by Apollo, who is venting his frustrated lust on her: these are events from another play, as it were, in a different place and time ("But that was in another country, / And besides, the wench is dead").

Consideration of the past life of Cassandra may throw light on another important aspect of drama, to which Shakespeare was as sensitive as Aeschylus, namely the relation between past and present, between the lives of the characters before this play, as it were: experience which is outside the immediate scope of this dramatic action, yet most relevant to it. One could could represent this visually by a group of overlapping circles:

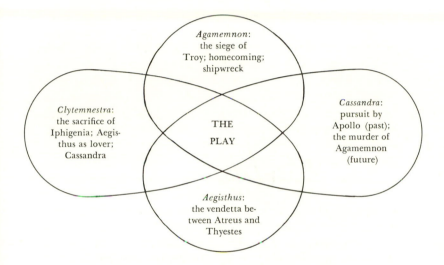

Characters who stand before us have all had a previous existence, which has in some way helped to shape their present selves: in *Coriolanus* Shakespeare shows the formative influence of the past especially clearly.

Two further theoretical considerations emerge from our model, *Agamemnon*. One is the fact that my two diagrams serve to highlight particular structures or connections within the play, but do not of course represent its shape as it is enacted before us, on the stage or on the page. The experience of literature is an experience in time, on an axis from start to finish: it is linear in direction, yet it is polyphonic in experience. If one were to cut a slice through the text at any one point, then we might be experiencing, simultaneously, several different networks of relationship. In the scene where Clytemnestra welcomes Agamemnon, for instance, we could itemize perspectives II (a), (b), (c), (d), and (e); by implication, Clytemnestra approves of III (b), Agamemnon's mistakenly unsuspecting view of her and rejects I (b), and I (c), the Chorus' critical view of her and Aegisthus, also IV (c) and (f), Cassandra's savagely denunciatory view of them both. Yet—a simple point which totally transforms our naive model—the play will show that the Chorus and Cassandra are right to distrust Clytemnestra, Agamemnon wrong to trust her, since in a few minutes she will slaughter both Agamemnon and Cassandra.

In other words, in drama as in life, all judgments are relative; all judgments are to be evaluated according to the person(s) judging and being judged; all judgments are right or wrong, *according to us*. That is, we make up our own minds on the basis of the presentation by the dramatist. In this example, Aeschylus gives us precious little liberty to decide that Clytemnestra and Aegisthus are right, since by a truly overwhelming exploitation of all the resources of drama he presents their act as a perversion of nature.[1] There are plays by Shakespeare in which an equally firm view is presented—no one can admire the usurpers of Prospero's dukedom, for instance, or the murderers of Clarence. But they tend to be early or late plays, both simplified stages: in the mature drama we are given both positive and negative aspects of almost every important action and character. If we are not necessarily asked to sympathize with them, we do at least understand why they have acted in this way —they have been allowed to present their wishes and deeds in their own terms, from their own perspective.

The last point that I wish to make via Aeschylus is that a sequence of judgment that appears very tidy in my itemiza-

[1] I have argued this interpretation of the play in my *Towards Greek Tragedy: Drama, Myth, Society* (London and New York: Longman, 1973), pp. 347-437.

tion of it can be in fact subject to constant change and fluctuation. It is not so all the time, naturally enough. Cassandra's view of Apollo, and Clytemnestra's of Agamemnon are both constant throughout (though of course Clytemnestra's *ostensible* view of her husband is at total variance with her *real* one, a point expressed by Aeschylus in many ways, direct and indirect). Yet Cassandra's view of Clytemnestra and Aegisthus, by contrast, is built up with many hesitations and obscurities—she is, after all, seeing into the future. All the same, it is constant in its moral loathing of the two. Thus our analysis would need to distinguish *information*, complete or otherwise, and *evaluation*, which will be changing as the information comes in. The Chorus, while constant in its fear and disapproval of Clytemnestra, fluctuates in its evaluation of Agamemnon, according to the stage of his career, or the moral complexion of his activities. As king and lord he is admirable; as leader of a life-destructive campaign to avenge a rape he is despicable; as sacrificer of his daughter he is loathsome; as murdered hero he is admirable again.[2] The fluctuations in the Chorus' attitude of course affect us, as do those in Cassandra's: we see the trio of Agamemnon, Clytemnestra, and Aegisthus through their eyes, and we are made by them constantly to revise our judgments, to qualify admiration, to intensify loathing.

The human mind, as it experiences drama, is—or should be—constantly on the alert, feeding in new information about the people or the issues involved, being ready to see things in a new light, and then perhaps to see that light in turn as a false and delusory one. A full moment-by-moment analysis of our experience of a play, keeping all the strands in view, and noting our relationship to each of them and to the interconnections between them, would be a truly formidable task, and is very seldom attempted, at least in my reading experience. True, there are scene-by-scene com-

[2] For substantiation of this point see Vickers, *Towards Greek Tragedy*, pp. 349-88.

mentaries on plays, but these are usually dogged enterprises, elucidating each individual word but rarely (if ever?) seeing the dramatic interconnection. What follows will be a sketch of such a method as it can be applied to a particularly complex play. Already, perhaps, some readers may be having doubts as to the practicability of the analytical method I have been outlining. They may feel the need rather to make things simpler than to expose them in their full complexity; actuated, perhaps, by a spirit of benevolence, they may want to assent to Dr. Johnson's practice:

> I am no friend to making religion appear too hard. Many good people have done harm, by giving severe notions of it. In the same way, as to learning; I never frighten young people with difficulties; on the contrary, I tell them that they may very easily get as much as will do well.[3]

That is a humane attitude, and clearly every teacher would wish to encourage rather than discourage his pupils. But to "simplify" drama is usually to crudify it. In our desire to make a communicable pattern we reduce a play to a single issue, or a few simple points; we make it monofocal rather than multifocal, select one perspective, one aspect presented by Shakespeare, and ignore the rest.

In defense of a mode of criticism which tries to be sensitive to the total system of perspectives I would argue that, as well as approaching nearer to the truth of a play as a whole, this method may complicate the issue but does not confuse it—rather the opposite. By using it we can clarify the components of the scene, and it is a method which is far easier to communicate to students than any other critical approach currently in vogue, because it is more natural. It is difficult —and highly unnatural—to teach students to conceive of the meaning of a dramatic work in terms of the dominant image-patterns; or its "themes"; or its ambiguities; or its

[3] James Boswell, *Journal of a Tour to the Hebrides with Samuel Johnson, LL.D.*, ed. R. W. Chapman (London: Oxford Univ. Press, 1924), pp. 373-74.

irony; or its juxtaposition of metaphor and metonymy; or its use of codes and armatures; or its systematic articulation of binary patterns, at the level of exchange-systems or phonological symmetries. What the truly critical student of drama has to say about the dominant movements in literary criticism in the last fifty years (and my short list refers to work associated with such distinguished critics as Caroline Spurgeon, Cleanth Brooks, L. C. Knights, R. B. Heilman, William Empson, Roman Jakobson, Claude Lévi-Strauss and others), is that they may all have clarified ways in which language works in literature, but that they have seldom contributed to an understanding of how drama works. For instead of responding to the dramatic totality—a representation of human behavior and interplay, using a wide range of notation (visual and linguistic symbolism, scenery, setting, lighting, gesture, movement, grouping)—they have isolated one element only, that of language. Further, and worse still, they have at once severed language from its role in drama by treating it as an element detached from the people who use it, who apply it for purposes of self-presentation, manipulation, denigration, justification, or whatever. In these schools of criticism any animal image is as significant as any other, no matter who uses it, or why, or at what stage in the development of the play; any metaphoric/metonymic usage, any instance of appearance and reality—all are taken as if a drama were a long lyric poem, with a narrator "persona," instead of representing the interplay between fully individualized characters.

Literary criticism often seeks the patronage of another discipline, whether for protection against its feelings of insecurity, or whether as a higher authority which can provide a theoretical justification that literary criticism on its own could not accomplish. The critical method for which I am pleading may also be related to other disciplines, and in pointing to these I also indicate why this method, although undoubtedly demanding patience and thought, is—in my practical teaching experience—immediately comprehensible

to students, even to beginners. The two disciplines I have
in mind are phenomenology and the study of vision, and
what they have in common—at any rate in the rather elementary form in which I would introduce them—is that
they re-create in immediately graspable terms our everyday
experience of life. The most approachable examples that I
would cite, distinguished by clarity of exposition yet without
any falsification of the underlying scholarship, would be on
the one hand Alfred Schutz, in *The Phenomenology of the
Social World*, and on the other Richard Gregory, in *Eye and
Brain: The Psychology of Seeing*.[4] To simplify drastically,
the phenomenologist validates subjective experience, as
against the former philosophical ideals of objectivity or
empathy by showing that all experience is individual, that
we cannot in fact experience life in the same way that another person does since we cannot possibly get inside his or
her brain, or memory, or attitudes. Relations between individuals are interpersonal, intersubjective: our knowledge of
the other person is a compound of deductions and inferences, an interpretation of signs rather than a fixed collec-
tion of facts.[5] Each individual interprets the signs differently. The scientist of vision, similarly, shows that the eye
is not a passive agent of observation but an agency that
interprets, shapes what it "sees" according to its expectations, partly learned in the early stages of development
(babies are in effect *taught* to see, or taught to *interpret*
sight), partly by its memory of past visual experiences. The
eye and brain together make inferences and deductions,
interpret experience, and do so, of course, in the inevitably

4 Alfred Schutz, *The Phenomenology of the Social World*, trans. G.
Walsh and F. Lehnert (Evanston: Northwestern Univ. Press, 1967);
Richard Gregory, *Eye and Brain: The Psychology of Seeing* (London:
Weidenfeld and Nicholson, 1966; rev. 1972). My interest in these two
areas has been much stimulated by my friend and former colleague
Stephen Heath of Jesus College, Cambridge.

5 See the works by Husserl, Scheler, and Max Weber referred to by
Schutz; also Roger Poole, *Towards Deep Subjectivity* (London: Allen
Lane, 1972).

"subjective" context of each individual. It is possible that we all see the world differently, as we certainly experience it individually, and in my teaching experience students readily grasp both the theoretical and practical implications of both disciplines.

This line of thought, especially the project of phenomenology, seems to me extremely fruitful for a new theory of drama as an inter-subjective experience, a system of perspectives in which each interaction defines both subject and object simultaneously and in which the work of a dramatist such as Shakespeare depends on the ability to see with a thousand eyes, and to be seen by another thousand. To see is necessarily to interpret, and, in the area of human behavior, to interpret is to judge. Once we reach an interpretation of the meaning of a sequence of behavior we commonly react at the same time, we go on to make an evaluation of it. When we see the hypocrisy of Clytemnestra, or of Goneril and Regan at the beginning of the play, our suspicions are alerted, without sufficient information to enable us to judge definitely: when we can do so finally, judgment turns into loathing, condemnation. What modern criticism needs is an approach to drama which will be faithful to the realities of vision, interpretation, and evaluation, moment-by-moment, from the perspective of each individual, relationship, or group within the play, and summing all up in an interpretation which, we hope, will be true to that made by the dramatist in the course of shaping his material.

II

Commonly in Shakespeare's tragedies we are made to see the main characters from more than one moral perspective. From one aspect Lear is a petty, vain dotard; from another he is a heroic and abused figure. Macbeth is a murderer, yet has a sensitivity toward experience, including his own perversions, which lift him above everyone else in that play. Even the notionally admirable heroes have their detractors, and thus show that a critical perspective is possible (whether or not Shakespeare included one)—Hamlet still has his critics, so does Cordelia, and even Desdemona. Perhaps only Ophelia of the major characters is never said to have been shown by Shakespeare in a critical light.

This ability or need to present conflicting viewpoints— and not always, *pace* such critics as Coleridge and Cleanth Brooks—to reconcile them, seems indeed to become more and more intense in Shakespeare as his tragic art developed. In the later tragedies—*King Lear, Timon of Athens, Antony and Cleopatra, Coriolanus*—his main characters are presented at one time or another in the most unflattering, disapproving of lights. In all of them they attract comment almost as much off the stage as when they are on it.[6] In *Coriolanus* this method becomes a way of life, for in no other play that I know is the major figure subjected to such a barrage of comment. The cause is partly that divided nature of the hero which made him such a popular historical exemplum, as we can see from Plutarch's grouping of him with Alcibiades—both patriots who turned against their country. But as Shakespeare builds up his story out of Plutarch, with, as Geoffrey Bullough has shown,[7] sideglances at Livy and Lucius Julius Florus, he seems to become alert to the essentially political nature of the conflict in this play, more than in any of the other tragic subjects he treated. His discovery is comparable to that of Dryden's, in the preface to *Absalom and Achitophel*:

> he who draws his Pen for one Party must expect to make Enemies of the other. For *Wit* and *Fool* are Consequents of *Whig* and *Tory*: And every man is a Knave or an Ass to the contrary side.

[6] Some useful comments on this method are made by Maurice Charney in *Shakespeare's Roman Plays* (Cambridge: Harvard Univ. Press, 1961).

[7] *Narrative and Dramatic Sources of Shakespeare*, V (London: Routledge, 1964).

The contrary sides in *Coriolanus* divide up in various ways. There is, first, the external conflict, Romans against Volscians. This campaign—and this alone—unites the state against its enemies. Otherwise Rome is deeply divided, as the traditional authority of the patrician class is for the first time being challenged by the people, who have just had political representatives allotted to them, five tribunes, of whom we see two, Sicinius and Brutus. In this deep-rooted and irreconcilable division, "every man" is indeed "a Knave or an Ass to the contrary side," and none more so than Coriolanus. He, as the leading warrior bringing peace to Rome in the opening battle scenes, becomes the focal point of all the struggles throughout the rest of the play. In Acts I, II, and III he is the patricians' main hope of preserving their power, for if they succeed in having him elected consul then they will put the plebs and their tribunes in the subordinate place for a long time to come. That this would be the result of his election is made clear by the tribunes themselves, speaking together on stage alone, after Coriolanus has been given that name, and an extraordinary public welcome, in recognition of his great feats against the Volscians in Corioli:

> *Sic.*   On the sudden,
> I warrant him consul.
> *Bru.*   Then our office may,
> During his power, go sleep.
>
> (II.i.221-23)

Accordingly they fight against his election with every fair and unfair tactic in the greasy pages of politics, and succeed in having him expelled from Rome. In Acts IV and V, resentful of his country's ingratitude, Coriolanus joins forces with the Volscian general, Aufidius, and returns to Rome for revenge; at the last moment an intercession led by his mother, Volumnia, his wife Virgilia, and his son, young Martius, is successful. Having relented, he returns to the

241

Volscians to explain his deed, but is murdered by Aufidius as ostensible punishment for some secret plot against the state, but in reality to satisfy a purely personal jealousy.

In that brief summary of the action I would stress the roles that Coriolanus is forced to play in so many movements. For Rome he is a war-weapon, a tool to destroy enemies; for the patricians he becomes, in peacetime, a political tool for the same purpose; for the tribunes he is public enemy number one; and, once they have had him expelled, he becomes the public enemy of the whole of Rome. To Aufidius Coriolanus is first enemy; then ally; then enemy again. The action is symmetrical, beginning and ending with Coriolanus alone inside the enemy gates. On the first occasion, simple warfare (I.iv), he triumphs; on the second occasion, the manipulations of politics (V.vi), he is defeated by a plot. As Parolles says, when he is finally exposed, "Who cannot be crush'd with a plot?" (*All's Well* IV.iii.325). Yet Coriolanus seems particularly susceptible to such deception. He is young, innocent, forced into one role on behalf of his class, forced out of it by the opponents of that class. Throughout the whole play Coriolanus is being used for one group, against another: for Rome against the Volscians, for the Volscians against Rome; for and by the patricians at the beginning, against them at the end. As such he is the constant focus of comment and judgment: but, given his status at the center of all the military and political turmoil of the play, everyone is either for him or against him, and so he is hero to one side, knave and ass to the other. The question facing the reader of this play, whose account can we trust? As in politics, one asks: which is true ("more true" or "less true," if we are not naive), the left wing's view of the right, or the right's of the left?

I would state as the key principle of interpreting this play: unless one attends to all the perspectives, one is bound to get it wrong.

To begin with the patricians: their view of the people is unanimous, and unfavorable in the extreme. The patricians' leading negotiator is Menenius, who professes to love the people, yet calls them a "multiplying spawn" (II.ii.78), sees the combat as between "Rome and her rats" (II.ii.162) and describes the tribunes as "the herdsmen of the beastly plebeians" (II.i.95). Cominius calls the people a "tag," or rabble (III.i.247) and we learn from Coriolanus that Volumnia—in the privacy of patrician circles, as it were—

> was wont
> To call them woollen vassals, things created
> To buy and sell with groats, to show bare heads
> In congregations, to yawn, be still, and wonder,
> When one but of my ordinance stood up
> To speak of peace or war.
>
> (III.ii.8-13)

Viewed against this background we can see that in expressing loathing for the people Coriolanus declares the values of his class, but since he is younger than the others, and less tactful, he does so with more violence. They are "fragments," "Our musty superfluity," "rats" (I.i.222, 226, 249); they are "The beast / With many heads" (IV.i.1-2), "measles," or infectious scabs (III.i.78-80), and above all they smell (III.i.66; III.iii.120-23).

Critics who single Coriolanus out as an arrogant patrician should note first that he expresses the social prejudices of the class into which he was born—"us a' th' right-hand file" (II.i.22-23), as Menenius describes them. Yet here is an interesting example of what would seem to be a failure on Shakespeare's part to present the balancing viewpoint. Deliberately disagreeing with his sources, Shakespeare changes the mob from the willing soldiers of Plutarch to a cowardly lot who go reluctantly to battle, and run away from the enemy (I.iv.34-37). They refuse to follow Coriolanus into battle, leave him alone inside Corioli, and when he reappears are found looting (I.v.1-8). Shakespeare writes a comic prose passage to show the mindless and discordant nature of the mob (II.iii.1-39), and their behavior throughout the election scene is foolish in the extreme. Even their own leaders, the tribunes, have nothing but contempt for them (II.i.205-21), and when it comes to rehearsing the mob for their part in the rigged election the tribunes show their low opinion of the people by the lengths they go to in repeating perfectly obvious points (II.iii.155-263; III.iii.1-30). Coriolanus' account of the mob's fickle loyalty (I.i.167-84) is proved true, ironically enough, when he is approaching Rome for his revenge: in the panic within the city the people betray their leaders, putting the blame for Coriolanus' expulsion on the tribunes (IV.vi.139-60)—where, indeed, it rightly belongs. Just before the news of Coriolanus' capitulation they are about to tear the tribunes apart (V.iv.35-39).

To re-create the perspectives given of the Roman people, then, is to note that the right wing's pejorative opinion of them is not matched by any balancing praise. If we turn to the people's view of the patricians we see a curiously parallel one-sidedness. We find resentment expressed by the people and the tribunes, naturally enough, and so clearly that there is no need to quote it. Yet when we look for evidence of fellow-feeling by the patricians toward the people we look in vain. Menenius claims that "most charitable care / Have the patricians of you. . . . [they] care for you like fathers" (I.i.65-77), but this is what oppressing and exploiting ruling classes generally claim—here especially absurdly. The internal unrest in Rome is caused by the famine, and from Plutarch Shakespeare would see that the people's grievances were real and justified—indeed, he retained them. Nowhere do the patricians show any concern for the people's hunger, or go without food themselves. Faced with their insistent claims for food in the opening scene (I.i.15-25, 79-86) Menenius answers them with what purports to be an explanation of the dearth but is in effect a threat—it is in vain to attack Rome, since the state is stronger (65-72), and then he fobs them off with the belly-fable which "serves my purpose" (91), but hardly theirs. Coriolanus also rejects their appeals for food (205ff), only directly, without a manipulative fable. In the later confrontation Coriolanus violently denounces the move to give the people "corn gratis" (III.i.113ff).

The only area in which we can admire the patrician class is in their military dedication to the protection and preservation of Rome—even though that will turn out to mean the sacrifice of Coriolanus himself—and in such related values as valor, loyalty, and service. For everything that concerns their relations with the people their policies would seem to be disastrous, in their combination of deep-rooted class hatred with a confused experiment in democracy (no one seems to know what the new rules are, now that the tribunes have been created). The one person in the play to see the direction these policies will take is, significantly enough, Coriolanus, who in Shakespeare as in Plutarch is given the key statement of the general political situation. (His tragedy is that he cannot "read" political situations when they involve him personally.) He sees, and feels:

> my soul aches
> To know, when two authorities are up,
> Neither supreme, how soon confusion
> May enter 'twixt the gap of both, and take
> The one by th' other.

> (III.i.108-12)

Chaos will come again if the patrician class does not have "the power to do the good it would, / For th' ill which doth control't" (160-61).

When it comes to politics Shakespeare again deliberately balances negative perspectives. We found nothing good to say about the people, and very little to praise about the patricians. In the political arena both sides rehearse their campaigns,[8] and on both sides we find the same false grooming of the protagonists, and the same debased standards.

[8] For a fuller account of this process see Brian Vickers, *"Coriolanus,"* *Studies in English Literature* (London: Edward Arnold, 1976), pp. 26-37.

The tribunes rehearse the mob so that they will shout whatever their leaders tell them to:

> *Sic.* Assemble presently the people hither;
> And when they hear me say, "It shall be so
> I' th' right and strength a' th' commons," be it either
> For death, for fine, or banishment, then let them,
> If I say fine, cry "Fine!"; if death, cry "Death!";
> Insisting on the old prerogative
> And power i' th' truth a' th' cause.
>
> (III.iii.12-18)

This is not democracy but demagoguery—the last two lines are a transparent lie, since the "old prerogative" has only just been established. The hypocrisy is disgusting, the instruction to the actors adjusted to a low level of intelligence ("If I say fine, cry 'Fine!' "). But on the patrician side the hypocrisy is just as bad, the rehearsal just as obvious. Here Volumnia tells her son that he *must* play his role:

> now it lies you on to speak
> To th' people; not by your own instruction,
> Nor by th' matter which your heart prompts you,
> But with such words that are but roted in
> Your tongue, though but bastards, and syllables
> Of no allowance, to your bosom's truth.
> Now, this no more dishonors you at all. . . .
> I prithee now, my son,
> Go to them, with this bonnet in thy hand,
> And thus far having stretch'd it (here be with them),
> Thy knee bussing the stones (for in such business
> Action is eloquence, and the eyes of th' ignorant
> More learned than the ears), waving thy head,
> . . . say to them . . . .
>
> (III.ii.52-58,72-80)

Coleridge praised Shakespeare for the impartiality of his politics in this play. That is a half-truth, though, suggesting that Shakespeare sides with neither party: in fact he does take sides, but against both, condemning them to the consequences of their selfish manipulation of power. Such a society gets what it deserves, total chaos. The tragedy of the play is that while Coriolanus is destroyed the social discords live on, to the next generation. At the end of the play nothing has changed.

III

Approaching *Coriolanus* by reconstituting the perspectives of the interested parties will alert us to the multifocal structure and will prevent us from siding too easily with any one view. All the conflicting groups in the play are trying to dominate each other by using Coriolanus as a tool, for attack or defense. It follows that we cannot take anything that any of them say about him as constituting the truth, for each group has its own image, used for a specific purpose. I will now list the four main images of Coriolanus and briefly analyze their function. (This is an exercise which can be fruitfully done by dividing a class up into groups and having them place themselves in each perspective. I have sometimes found it necessary to have a central group not involved in this project who can detect when the others begin to identify with their perspective, thus losing the self-awareness needed to criticize it.)

(i) *The patricians' image*

For them Coriolanus is a war-tool designed to strike fear into the hearts of the enemy. Menenius and Volumnia mentally tot up the number of his wounds:

> *Men.* Where is he wounded?
> *Vol.* I' th' shoulder and i' th' left arm. There will be large cicatrices to show the people, when he shall stand for his place. . . . He had, before this last expedition, twenty-five wounds upon him.
> *Men.* Now it's twenty-seven; every gash was an enemy's grave. (II.i.146-56)

As I have written elsewhere,[9] they remind us of the killer making a notch on the handle of his gun for each life claimed. All the patricians gloat over Coriolanus' killing powers, and they all exaggerate grossly. Detailed reference to the text will produce a crop of bizarre and fantastic images with which they magnify his exploits beyond the realms of possibility. Lartius does so when he thinks Coriolanus has been killed in Corioli, addressing an epitaph to the hero missing, presumed dead:

> with thy grim looks and
> The thunder-like percussion of thy sounds,
> Thou mad'st thine enemies shake, as if the world
> Were feverous and did tremble.
>
> (I.iv.58-61)

Cominius does so to his face, much to Coriolanus' embarrassment (I.ix.1-85), and with enormous pomp and circumstance to the assembled congregation in Rome (II.ii.37-122), a speech which is so effusive and extravagant that Coriolanus leaves the Senate rather than listen to it. (Critics who accuse Coriolanus of being proud ought one day to notice the complete absence of self-regard which makes him minimize his own exploits and loathe flattery.) What Cominius is doing is what all the patricians do, presenting Coriolanus as the unanswerable Ultimate Deterrent, conceived in nonhuman mechanical terms:

> His sword, death's stamp,
> Where it did mark, it took; from face to foot
> He was a thing of blood, whose every motion
> Was tim'd with dying cries.
>
> (II.ii.107-10)

This is no more than political propaganda, familiar to us today from the exploits of the general-turned-politician, "savior of the people" in peace as in war.

---

[9] Vickers, *The Artistry of Shakespeare's Prose* (London: Methuen, 1968), pp. 395ff.

The basis of the patricians' image of Coriolanus as naked political propaganda is already clear, but two later passages make it overwhelmingly obvious. The first occurs when Coriolanus is returning for vengeance on Rome. Cominius has been to him to plead for mercy, but was rejected: his account of the incident to the tribunes is clearly intended to strike terror into their hearts:

> I tell you, he does sit in gold, his eye
> Red as 'twould burn Rome; and his injury
> The jailer to his pity.
>
> (V.i.63-65)

Menenius then also attempts to intercede, claiming to the guards who bar his way that

> The general is my lover. I have been
> The book of his good acts, whence men have read
> His fame unparallel'd, haply amplified.
>
> (V.ii.14-16)

He has been his panegyrist, as it were, and indeed Shakespeare makes Menenius admit that he has laid on as much praise as would stick, has perhaps even exceeded the mark, and given falsehood the stamp of truth (to paraphrase some rather difficult lines, V.ii.17-22). This propensity to lying exaggeration is given full rein when Menenius, too, returns to Rome with his plea rejected, when he positively wallows in the images of Coriolanus as Ultimate Deterrent in order to terrorize the tribunes still further:

> This Martius is grown from man to dragon: he has wings, he's more than a creeping thing. . . . The tartness of his face sours ripe grapes. When he walks, he moves like an engine, and the ground shrinks before his treading.
>
> (V.iv.12-20)

He has an eye like a laser beam, a voice like a funeral-bell, a "hum" like a troop of artillery (20-21). This is so exaggerated as to be comic. What gives the game away is the claim that Coriolanus "no more remembers his mother now than an eight-year-old horse" (16-17). Events have traveled faster than Menenius' malicious exaggerations, and in the time it has taken him to return from Coriolanus' camp we have seen this supposedly inhuman, thing-like, monster-like juggernaut yield up his conquest and his life to his mother, touched by her appeal to his belief in love and nature. Here as in many places Shakespeare shows us the full complexity of Coriolanus' character, making him a dedicated and violent soldier who is also compassionate, gentle, aware of the sufferings of others, moved by a willingness to repay generosity and love. These are values which he shares, appropriately enough, with his wife, Virgilia, that image of gentleness and constancy, inarticulate in her love but unshakably loyal ("my gracious silence," as he calls her, II.i.175), whose fear and hatred of war stand at the opposite extreme from Volumnia's maniacal reveling in blood and destruction. (Their attitudes are beautifully contrasted in I.iii.) Virgilia highlights an aspect of Coriolanus' character which Shakespeare stresses deliberately and which provides us with a truer perspective, from which the right-wing militarist propaganda can only seem debased fantasies.

(ii) *The people's image*

In the opening lines of the play Shakespeare gives us a mob, rioting over the stage. (This is surely the most *tumultuous* play he ever wrote, people, events, indeed, a whole social structure being in a constant state of turmoil.) Their hatred of Coriolanus is all too evident:

> *1 Cit.* First, you know Caius Martius is chief enemy to the people.
> *All.* We know't, we know't.
> *1 Cit.* Let us kill him, and we'll have corn at our own price.
>
> (I.i.7-11)

As their discussion continues, 1st Citizen is beginning to elaborate—"he's a very dog to the commonalty" (28-29)—when suddenly one of his fellows objects:

> *2 Cit.* Consider you what services he has done for his country?
>
> *1 Cit.* Very well, and could be content to give him good report for 't, but that he pays himself with being proud.
>
> *2 Cit.* Nay, but speak not maliciously.
>
> *1 Cit.* I say unto you, what he hath done famously, he did it to that end. Though soft-conscienc'd men can be content to say it was for his country, he did it to please his mother, and to be partly proud, which he is, even to the altitude of his virtue.   (30-40)

That this account is biased is only what we would expect—yet Shakespeare alerts us to the fact by making the Second Citizen reprove his fellow: "speak not maliciously." To show the extent of the malice one would need to analyze the scenes where Coriolanus goes into battle for the state, and agrees to stand as consul on behalf of his class—in both cases motivated only by a sense of duty, in the first case to Rome and to his general (cf. I.v.9-14; I.vi.66-75), actions of war which have his full support, but in the second very much against his own wishes (cf. II.i.202-4). True, he loathes the people, but that is not "pride" so much as general class-hatred. Where the citizen says that his motives are pride and desire to please his mother, not love of his country, I would agree with the second (his mother's approval), but interchange the other two: patriotism moves him, but not pride. For Coriolanus does not show himself eager to dominate: he willingly accepts second place in the army behind Cominius (I.i.236-39); he does not drink up adulation, but loathes it as false and overdone (I.ix.13-73; II.i.162-69; II.ii.37-77). Having seen both of these reactions with unmistakable clarity we will be amazed to hear the tribunes' account of him:

> *Bru.* The present wars devour him! he is grown
> Too proud to be so valiant.
> *Sic.*   Such a nature,
> Tickled with good success, disdains the shadow
> Which he treads on at noon. But I do wonder
> His insolence can brook to be commanded
> Under Cominius.
> *Bru.* Fame, at the which he aims, ...
>
> > (I.i.264-270)

—who, Coriolanus? we ask in amazement—where? "Think you there was or might be such a man?"

> > (*Antony and Cleopatra* V.ii.93)

> Think you there was or might be such a man?
> > (*Antony and Cleopatra* V.ii.93)

As the tribunes continue, agreeing that Coriolanus accepted second place because he could profit from the mistakes of his general and win greater "Opinion" (I.i.263-72), our surprise turns into recognition: here is political propaganda at the moment of propagation. Here is the image that the tribunes need, the unfavorable image of the opposing election candidate to be built up, hammered home to the voters of their party. So they take it a stage further, adding more smears:

> *Bru.* He's poor in no one fault, but stor'd with all.
> *Sic.* Especially in pride.
> *Bru.* And topping all others in boasting.
>
> > (II.i.18-20)

This exchange is placed after the scene on the battlefield, where Coriolanus rejected the adulation of the army, and just before the homecoming to Rome, where he rejects the adulation of the state. The tribunes' image, which will be broadcast wider yet, is thus shown to be a malicious construct for electioneering purposes. It is the kind of image of the ruling class that has become a cliché in our time.

Whatever the rights or wrongs of contemporary politics we can see how each side in class-warfare *needs* a loathsome image of the other to continue, and intensify, the opposition between them. The enemy must be shown as terrifying and nauseating in order to produce solidarity, a collective and corporate effort to win the class-struggle—by any means, from defamation to manipulation to naked violence, which is roughly the progress of the tribunes' campaign from Act I to Act III.

Summing up my argument so far, I would say that we can accept neither the patricians' view of Coriolanus as an inhuman war-machine, nor the tribunes' view of him as an ambitious, proud boaster. Both right and left have constructed a false image for their own political purposes. A pox on both their houses!

(iii) *Volumnia's image*

Volumnia, in her relationship with Coriolanus, plays two roles, expresses two loyalties—one as mother toward her son, one as patrician woman toward Rome. Shakespeare knew enough about the courage and patriotism of Roman women to see what these virtues could mean in terms of motherhood, and he builds up the image of a life which has always existed *pro patria*, in which the feelings of the mother—if she ever experienced any—have always been sacrificed to the state and its military service. Volumnia tells us so herself, as she sits with Virgilia waiting for Coriolanus to return from the war, and reminisces how she set him on his path years ago, when he was most malleable:

> When yet he was but tender-bodied and the only son of my womb; when youth with comeliness pluck'd all gaze his way; when for a day of kings' entreaties a mother should not sell him an hour from her beholding;

—there Shakespeare sums up all the right, natural human reactions that Volumnia has flaunted, proudly and self-admiringly—

> I, considering how honor would become such a person . . .
> was pleas'd to let him seek danger where he was like to
> find fame. To a cruel war I sent him, from whence he
> return'd, his brows bound with oak. I tell thee, daughter,
> I sprang not more in joy at first hearing he was a man-
> child than now in first seeing he had prov'd himself a
> man.   (I.iii.5-17)

If she had a dozen sons, she "had rather had eleven die
nobly for their country than one voluptuously surfeit out of
action" (24-25). We believe her, since this is a remarkably
convincing picture of the role of the mother in a militarist
state. (Volumnia would have been a natural for a Nazi
propaganda film, from the cradle to the front in a few
heroic images.) Indeed, this aspect of the play seems relatively uncontroversial, since no critic that I know of claims
that Volumnia acted out of mother-love, even though few of
those who cast Coriolanus as the villain militarist have considered the responsibility of his mother for his upbringing.

Yet it seems to me that Shakespeare takes the issue further
than this. He goes on to show Volumnia working herself
up into a trance-like vision of her son beating down his enemies like a harvest-man, his face covered in blood, a sight,
she says (in reproof to Virgilia's horrified "O Jupiter, no
blood!") more beautiful in a man than the gilt on his trophy
(29-43). Shakespeare is giving us a Volumnia moved not in
fact, or not only, by patriotism but by blood-lust, a delight
in death and destruction for their own sake, as we see again
in her exaltation over her son as a death-bringing machine:

> *Men.* Hark, the trumpets.
> *Vol.* These are the ushers of Martius: before him he
> carries noise, and behind him he leaves tears:
> Death, that dark spirit, in's nervy arm doth lie,
> Which, being advanc'd, declines, and then men die.
>
> (II.i.156-61)

Another instance of patrician propaganda for the Ultimate
Deterrent? Yes, but in addition an intense personal gloating

in the account of death itself. Volumnia's image of Coriolanus, then, like the others we have been looking at, exists
to fill a personal need. She projects her longing for power
and fame on to him. This emerges clearly a few moments
later, when she sees this latest victory as earning him the
consulship, the crowning glory of *her* career:

> I have lived
> To see inherited my very wishes
> And the buildings of my fancy; only
> There's one thing wanting, which I doubt not but
> Our Rome will cast upon thee.
>
> (198-202)

It is her dreams that are going to be fulfilled (she hopes),
not his.

Coriolanus respects his mother, of course, kneels to her
like the dutiful son in this scene (171), yet here and elsewhere expresses a certain resentment toward her. She claims
to have a special license "to extol her blood," he says, and
"When she does praise me grieves me" (I.ix.14-15). Face-to-
face with her here, he says that she has no doubt "petition'd
all the gods / For my prosperity" (II.i.170-71)—has peti-
tioned them from the status of an equal, it would seem from
his later taunting of the grief she expresses at his banishment:

> Nay, mother,
> Resume that spirit when you were wont to say,
> If you had been the wife of Hercules,
> Six of his labors you'ld have done, and sav'd
> Your husband so much sweat.
>
> (IV.i.15-19)

That picture intensifies our recognition of Volumnia's
megalomania, and just as telling is his next jibe:

> My mother, you wot well
> My hazards still have been your solace.
>
> (27-28)

She has derived enjoyment and consolation from his dangerous exploits, has satisfied her longing for power vicariously.

Such a relationship is successful—or at any rate rewarding for the dominant person—only so long as the subordinate plays his role obediently. If Coriolanus were to rebel Volumnia would be faced with a crisis (or what would be seen by a normal mother as a crisis): she would have to choose between what was good for her son and what was good for herself—or "for Rome," as she would say. In the play he rebels twice, in fact, and on each occasion she exerts all her pressure to make him conform to her wishes. In both cases he refuses to do what she wants until she pretends to withdraw her love from him: then he suddenly collapses. Ironically, both occasions place him—and her—outside the familiar role of fighter for Rome.

The first sequence concerns his loathing for the traditional custom in which a patrician was elected consul, where he had to bare his wounds before the people and beg their votes. To a man who hates adulation and display, who also hates the people and their "stinking breaths," nothing could be more abhorrent. As we saw earlier, Volumnia presents the ceremony to him as if it had no ethical meaning, as if one could lie without forfeiting one's integrity, as if the same unscrupulous tactics could be applied in peace as in war (III.ii.28-110). Coriolanus agrees, against all his instincts, yet as he does so his loathing breaks forth uncontrollably:

> The smiles of knaves
> Tent in my cheeks. . . . A beggar's tongue
> Make motion through my lips . . . !
> I will not do't,
> Lest I surcease to honor mine own truth,
> And by my body's action teach my mind
> A most inherent baseness.
>
> (115-23)

This is an anguished statement of his deepest feelings, and a normal mother might respect her son's wishes at this crisis in his identity. Yet Volumnia sweeps on, affirming her pride by refusing to "beg" from him, and turning that pride round by transferring it to him:

> At thy choice then.
> To beg of thee, it is my more dishonor
> Than thou of them. Come all to ruin, let
> Thy mother rather feel thy pride than fear
> Thy dangerous stoutness; for I mock at death
> With as big heart as thou. Do as thou list;
> Thy valiantness was mine, thou suck'st it from me,
> But owe thy pride thyself.
>
> (III.ii.123-30)

This is an astonishing claim, to have created, to be alone responsible for, Coriolanus' valor—in taking the credit in this way we see that Volumnia suffers from egomania as well as megalomania. And it is typical of her bullying, personality-crushing methods, that she should describe any attempt to express an independent opinion as "pride," twice over. We know who is suffering from pride here. Crude and fallacious as both charges are, they have the desired effect, as Coriolanus capitulates: "Pray be content. / Mother . . . Chide me no more" (130-32).

When Coriolanus is expelled from the city Volumnia's sympathy goes with him, and her anger is against all those who have frustrated her plans and denied her son reward for all that he has done "for Rome" (thrice repeated: IV.ii.19, 22, 28). As she leaves she calls on the others to "lament as I do, / In anger, Juno-like" (52-55), and the comparison no longer surprises us—we have come to accept her godlike image of herself. Volumnia has formidable striking power, an ego of almost entirely unlimited aggression. She frightens me, and I am not sure that I, too, would not be crushed by her, for she has that perception into another person's weaknesses which only comes through living together in the intimacy of the family, and she exploits her perception with absolute ruthlessness. Here her anger is against the others, but when Coriolanus returns for revenge on Rome, a movement entirely of his own—for the first time in his life carrying out an action not planned, prepared for, and rehearsed by her, an action, furthermore, which gravely compromises her status as patrician woman whose exertions have always been for the benefit of Rome—then Coriolanus can only become the focus of all her fury. Yet, while we note her public reasons we should not lose sight of the more commonplace motive, that of the mother who has always dominated her son.

The confrontation is a scene which is too long to be analyzed in detail here, and in a sense does not need full analysis, since it is one of the most explicit scenes Shakespeare ever wrote—it is as if the whole play had been designed outward from this point. Coriolanus tries to play the role of the heartless revenger, fights against "affection" and "nature," but his innate tenderness and love undermine the role as he is confronted by mother, wife, and son as potential victims of his revenge:

> What is that curtsy worth? or those doves' eyes,
> Which can make gods forsworn? I melt, and am not
> Of stronger earth than others. . . .
>   Like a dull actor now
> I have forgot my part. . . .
>
>   (V.iii.27-41)

The kiss that he exchanges with Virgilia—"O, a kiss / Long as my exile, sweet as my revenge!" (44-45), marks his acknowledgment of those human, family ties that he is incapable of denying. Seeing that, Volumnia is able to start her assault on him, a sequence of over a hundred lines of emotional blackmail, putting the screws on him like an enormous nutcracker, one that finally breaks his will. He fights her off for a long time, until, at the climax of her argument, she again denies him his personality and identity:

> There's no man in the world
> More bound to 's mother, yet here he lets me prate
> Like one i' th' stocks.—Thou has never in thy life
> Show'd thy dear mother any courtesy,
> When she, poor hen, fond of no second brood,
> Has cluck'd thee to the wars, and safely home
> Loaden with honor.
>
> (158-64)

Then follows the final blow, denying him relationship, even:

> Come, let us go.
> This fellow had a Volscian to his mother;
> His wife is in Corioles, and his child
> Like him by chance.
>
> (177-80)

That is the stroke that breaks him up: "O mother, mother! / What have you done?" (182-83). He takes her by the hand to affirm the relationship she has just denied, but it is the gesture of a subordinate, acknowledging the dominant one, who has just crushed him. He goes back to the Volscians, and to his death.

Volumnia can truly be described as having an image of Coriolanus, for it is an image that she claims to have manufactured, as God is said in Genesis to have made man "in his own image and likeness." For Volumnia Coriolanus is a surrogate for her own unfulfilled ambition to dominate and destroy. When the puppet does not obey, it is reproved for its pride; or else its maker disowns it, allows it to be destroyed. (Did she, I sometimes wonder, feel any remorse or regrets before, or after, her triumph?) Clearly whatever Volumnia has to say about Coriolanus can only be understood in terms of her own distorted mentality.

(iv) *Aufidius' image*

Aufidius, general of the Volscians, appears before us first as the enemy leader (I.ii) and, very soon afterward, as the beaten soldier, smarting at his defeat by Coriolanus, and resolving that in future he will put aside "honor" and "equal combat," and destroy him by any means:

> I'll potch at him some way,
> Or wrath or craft may get him.
> (I.x.15-16)

This terrible violation of military codes—"My valor's poison'd" (17), as he rightly says—expresses an underlying hatred and resentment that needs to be kept in mind throughout what follows. Superficially, it would seem that when Coriolanus goes over to the Volscians, Aufidius welcomes him as a long-lost friend (IV.v.101-47). Yet, glad though he is to have such a formidable ally, that mood soon vanishes, and two scenes later we find that Aufidius' envy has returned: he reflects bitterly over Coriolanus' greater popularity with his soldiers, and resolves to destroy him once he has defeated Rome (IV.vii.6-12,17-26,56-57). When Coriolanus is turned back by his mother, in an aside to the audience Aufidius views his ally's betrayal of his contract with the Volscians not as a blow to his country's safety or peace, say, but solely as fuel for his own personal career:

> *Auf.* I am glad thou hast set thy mercy and thy honor
> At difference in thee. Out of that I'll work
> Myself a former fortune.
>
> (V.iii.200-202)

In his wish to destroy Coriolanus to further his own standing Aufidius exists at the same level as the tribunes, cannibals and bloodsuckers all.

All the important discussions of Coriolanus take place outside his consciousness (as with Aegisthus and Agamemnon), as do the plans to destroy him. So we find Aufidius and "three or four Conspirators of Aufidius' faction," as Shakespeare's stage direction has it (V.vi.8), producing their new image of Coriolanus. If you are about to assassinate someone, it is advisable to have a story prepared for your press conference afterward. Aufidius makes up his story, and Shakespeare makes the hypocritical process clear: "my pretext to strike at him admits / A good construction" (19-20) —a most candid admission, off-the-record, of course, that he can put out not a true but at least a plausible story (*"pretext"* might be taken literally here). The story is to be that Coriolanus has stooped to conquer:

> I rais'd him, and I pawn'd
> Mine honor for his truth; who being so heighten'd,
> He watered his new plants with dews of flattery,
> Seducing so my friends; and, to this end,
> He bow'd his nature, never known before
> But to be rough, unswayable, and free.
>
> (20-25)

If we have been at all alert to our experience of the play, here is another place where we must goggle in amazement, as with the tribunes' account of Coriolanus the proud and ambitious boaster. Who is this seducing flatterer? No one we know, surely? And as if to articulate our thoughts for us, Shakespeare makes "Third Conspirator" break in—quite against the "probability" of a hired assassin quibbling over the hirer's assignment—

> Sir, his stoutness
> When he did stand for consul, which he lost
> By lack of stooping—

"That I would have spoke of" (26-28), says Aufidius, cutting him off short before he can make any more uncomfortable remarks. This situation is an exact parallel to that in the opening scene of the play, with "Second Citizen's" equally unlikely interjection—"Nay, but speak not maliciously." In both cases Shakespeare is violating strict motivation in order to point up the malice and distortion that surround Coriolanus on all sides. When Aufidius has carried out his plan, provoked Coriolanus to anger with a series of taunts, and then had him killed, the last prepared press-

261

handout lie is about "the great danger / Which this man's life did owe you" (V.vi.136-37), a cheap, but, as we see to this day, an effective excuse for a political assassination.

Aufidius' image, then, like the others', is a lie designed to further his own ends. Coriolanus is used and exploited by him, as he has been by the patricians, by the tribunes, and by Volumnia. All wish to benefit at his expense. With Aufidius the idea of bloodsucking or cannibalism actually emerges to the surface:

> therefore shall he die,
> And I'll renew me in his fall.
> (V.vi.47-48)

IV

I hope that this rapid survey of the main perspectives on Coriolanus will have done something to validate the critical method I am advocating, and that it will at any rate have begun to clarify this long and complex play. Clearly we cannot accept any of these four views of the central character, since each is constructed to fulfill its own unpleasant purpose. What image do we take, or make, then? Shakespeare is fully aware of the complexities which he has so carefully assembled and integrated, offering several other discussions of the hero's character and motives, such as one by two officers laying cushions in the Senate (II.ii.1-36), another by the servants of Aufidius (IV.v.148-234), and a third by Aufidius himself, a passage of detached, impersonal analysis so lacking in private animus that I suppose we will have to elevate it to the status of "choric commentary" (IV.vii.28-55). It is the privilege of the individual reader to make up his own mind on the basis of all the evidence, but it is the duty of the critic to reveal how he has decided. I have done so in more detail elsewhere,[10] but in order to

---

[10] See Vickers, "*Coriolanus*," pp. 55-60.

THE IMPORTANCE OF PERSPECTIVE

give this essay proper balance I ought perhaps to summarize
that argument here.

My image of Coriolanus, then, starts from a full recognition of his faults. He is violent, intolerant, unreasonable,
and unfeeling in his attitude toward the people. True, that
is an attitude which has been learned from his class, indoc-
trinated by his mother, and which he cannot be blamed for
having originated. True again, we see no side of the people
which would suggest that Coriolanus has overlooked positive and admirable qualities—they are cowardly, greedy,
self-regarding, mindless, easily manipulated by their leaders,
and ready to betray Coriolanus, or Rome, or the tribunes,
just as the occasion demands. Yet their faults, and their
prejudices of the patrician class, are not enough to excuse
altogether Coriolanus' animus against the people.

Coriolanus has all the energy of youth, and all its innocence. He is unaware of the corruption and deception inherent in politics. He is unaware for much of the time that
he is being manipulated—he comes to a recognition of the
fact when it involves his "friends" (the patrician class and
Volumnia), yet he never sees it when it derives from his
enemies (the tribunes and Aufidius). He is so sensitive to
his honor, like all good Renaissance heroes, that one has
only to call him "boy" or "traitor" to make him explode,
and be exploited. He never learns the lesson of not allowing
oneself to be provoked. The only lesson he learns in the play
he learns too late. When he returns to the Volscians after
his capitulation before Rome he tries to gloss over his failure
with the stock strategies of the defeated general, claiming
glory, drawing attention to the great "spoils" he has con-
quered (showing a 33 1/3 percent return on expenditure!),
and speaking for the first time the debased language of the
political soldier (V.vi.70-83). Happily, though, this is another insincere role which he cannot sustain, and when
Aufidius starts insulting him his real self emerges again.
I am glad that he preserved his integrity, even if it meant

263

his death. I can sympathize with him as a political innocent, but not as a political liar.

As a soldier Coriolanus is supreme. Here though, ironically enough, in this area of his unquestioned excellence, the modern reader finds greatest difficulty in relating to him. We are so sick of war, so aware of heroism being used in a manipulative way, that we cannot easily respond to his exploits. The only remedy, as I see it, is to make a great effort of the historical imagination, to pretend that we are dealing with a text as remote as medieval chivalry, or the *Iliad*, say, and to think ourselves back into a world of heroic action. Then I believe that we would appreciate his values of service, valor, loyalty to country and comrades, readiness to sacrifice himself to the group.

Yet I would not base my case for him on military prowess. Where Coriolanus stands out for me is in the fact that he and Virgilia alone in the play display any love or compassion. We see that, besides the violence and fighting, Coriolanus has an innate tenderness, as in the mirror-scene when he wants to repay the kindness once shown him by a poor man in Corioli (I.ix.79-90)—an incident Shakespeare has taken over from Plutarch but has made more affecting by some subtle changes.[11] We note the tenderness with which he greets his wife after his victory (II.i.175-79), and, more moving still, at the intercession before Rome (V.iii.22-48). In the first of these meetings Coriolanus reproves her for showing grief:

Wouldst thou have laugh'd had I come coffin'd home,
That weep'st to see me triumph? Ah, my dear,
Such eyes the widows in Corioles wear,
And mothers that lack sons.

He is the only person in the play to have any feelings to

[11] G. R. Hibbard, in his New Penguin edition of the play, notes that while in Plutarch the host is rich, "By making the man poor Shakespeare increases an audience's sense of Martius's magnanimity and fundamental decency" (p. 205).

spare about the defeated in battle—not for him the inhuman blood-mania of Volumnia. Shakespeare stresses this point when Coriolanus stands before Aufidius' house, about to go over to serve Rome's enemy:

> A goodly city is this Antium. City,
> 'Tis I that made thy widows; many an heir
> Of these fair edifices 'fore my wars
> Have I heard groan and drop.
>
> (IV.iv.1-4)

Coriolanus is the only character in this world to think about others. Whereas the rest place themselves first, exploit him for some debased material gains, he alone lives according to ideals of humanity and love.

This last point emerges most fully in the confrontation. There is an awful discrepancy between Volumnia's ruthless extortion of respect and obedience, and his yielding to the reciprocal ties of human affection. She offers mere bullying, he real love. The core of the play is his struggle against his natural instincts:

> But out, affection,
> All bond and privilege of nature, break!
> Let it be virtuous to be obstinate. . . .
> my young boy
> Hath an aspect of intercession, which
> Great Nature cries, "Deny not." Let the Volsces
> Plough Rome and harrow Italy, I'll never
> Be such a gosling to obey instinct, but stand
> As if a man were author of himself,
> And knew no other kin.
>
> (V.iii.24-26, 31-37)

"As if": he knows that the idea is impossible, that his mother is "the honored mould / Wherein this trunk was fram'd" (22-23), and that he must acknowledge her. His struggle against "Great Nature" is doomed to failure, since he is deeply identified with nature, affection, and love. The prin-

ciple by which he lives is " 'Deny not.' " As ever in Shakespearean tragedy, it is the greatest sources of love that are
destroyed.

V

My evaluation of this play has been developed over many
years of reading and teaching it. Obviously I have not expected everyone to agree with my account, although I hope
that more people will come round to my way of thinking.
(A critic knows that not everyone will accept his argument,
yet he would be dishonest if he did not believe that it was
right.) In my teaching experience some people have stopped
short at the last stage, and we have generally agreed to
differ, in that I hold a more favorable view of the hero than
they do, or are yet prepared for. (One must not expect to
change everything overnight.) Yet it has been for me a very
striking fact that once the play has been analyzed in this
way, and the malicious and self-seeking nature of the main
images of Coriolanus exposed, then no members of the class
have continued to think that the accounts given by Volumnia, Cominius, Menenius, Aufidius, the tribunes, or the
plebs can in future be taken as objective and unbiased comments. We have come to see that Coriolanus seems to be
the focal point of comment but that in fact rays of light
directed toward him miss the target, illuminate rather those
who cast them. Coriolanus becomes a mirror which reflects
their own images, gives us a standard by which we can
measure their distortion of his image, and their reasons for
wanting this distortion.

It may seem to some of my readers that I have labored the
point of perspective; to others my account may seem so
instantly persuasive that they cannot imagine why I needed
to go into at this length. My reply would be, in general
terms, that the approach is, so far as I know, a new one, and
needed some justification; and that this is a long and complex play. But specifically I would answer that this play has

been, and continues to be, the most misjudged of the major tragedies precisely because critics have been, so far, impervious to the existence of this structure of perspectives. A very brief reference to some of the leading accounts of the play will show that critics have accepted one unsympathetic image of Coriolanus without inquiring into who has created it and for what motive. A large group of writers, for instance, have accepted the right-wing Ultimate Deterrent image at face value, as if this were Shakespeare's considered conclusion about his hero. Thus one critic describes him as a "human war-machine," a "mechanical warrior, a man turned into an instrument of war,"[12] another sees him as a "mechanical juggernaut,"[13] yet another as "an automaton in fight, a slaying-machine of mechanic excellence."[14] As recently as 1970, in an article in that quasi-official journal of American English teachers, *PMLA*, a writer argued that "Coriolanus' claim to godlike independence of the complicated inner conflicts of man—reason, loyalty, compassion"— I should add that this supposed "independence" is nowhere justified by reference to the text—"makes him a kind of Bergsonian automaton, fearsome—as Menenius says: 'When he walks, he moves like an engine, and the ground shrinks before his treading.' "[15] This is to betray a disabling unawareness of dramatic context.

If one thing has emerged from this account it is that we cannot trust the patricians' image of Coriolanus, and that not only they but every other power-group have been utterly discredited by Shakespeare. All are seen to be untrust-

[12] D. A. Traversi, *An Approach to Shakespeare* (London: Sands, 1957), pp. 226ff.

[13] D. J. Enright, "Coriolanus," *The Apothecary's Shop* (London: Secker and Warburg, 1957), pp. 32-53. This essay originally appeared in *Essays in Criticism* 4 (1954), and was well criticized in that journal (5 [1955], 18-31) by I. R. Browning, in an essay called "Coriolanus: Boy of Tears."

[14] G. Wilson Knight, quoted in Enright, p. 39.

[15] Katherine Stockholder, "The Other Coriolanus," *PMLA* 85 (1970), 228-36.

worthy, loathsome in their self-regarding, manipulative, and exploiting attitudes. Yet the same writer, bent on registering the most unsympathetic image possible of Coriolanus, simply takes over their criticisms and endorses, indeed approves of their viewpoint and their actions. She believes that "The plebs have underlying justification for withdrawing their voices" (p. 232), and writes neutrally of the tribunes' "strategy for defeating Coriolanus," in which the hero, rather, is to blame, since "he unconsciously gives the tribunes the tool with which to destroy him" (p. 233). Volumnia is said to embody "the values of her country's tradition," but with no consideration of the nature of these values the critic at once uses her as another stick with which to beat Coriolanus:

> She is not lovable, but always admirable [sic!], strong, and, unlike Coriolanus, free to use the strength of her personality in whatever way will serve her ends.
>
> (p. 235)

There the critic seems to me to have totally evaded the issue of what "values," what "ends," Volumnia works for. This is to close a blind eye to human evil.

The question of means, as well as ends, must be considered, and I hope I have made it clear that in reconstructing a perspective we are inescapably involved in a process of evaluation: one cannot describe the tribunes' perversion of ethics and politics neutrally, or at least not without condoning that kind of behavior. Too many modern critics flunk the task of evaluating perspectives. William Rosen says that the tribune Brutus "is not treacherous and irresponsible, as most critics have suggested; his analysis, from his own vantage point, is quite valid."[16] Maurice Charney finds that "In their perspicacity and shrewdness the Tribunes resemble Aufidius, whom they also follow in being able

---

[16] *Shakespeare and the Craft of Tragedy* (Cambridge: Harvard Univ. Press, 1960), p. 194. Rosen also describes Coriolanus as "a mechanical being" (p. 187).

to turn their insight to practical effect"[17]—well, yes, but what are the moral qualities of their shrewdness and practicality? A scholar whom I much admire has written an essay "In Defence of the Tribunes."[18] All these approaches derive from what I would call false or transferred perspective: having taken sides against Coriolanus they have no option but to endorse the viewpoint of his enemies. When the *Dies Irae* tolls for literary critics, I for one would not want to be on the side of the tribunes—nor, for that matter, on that of the patricians.

To be neither on the right hand nor on the left: is there a middle point? Or must we move outside the system altogether? My judgment would be that the structure of perspectives created by Shakespeare eliminates practically everyone in the play as a focus for our approval or identification. In the face of a continuing critical disapproval of Coriolanus (still based on his manipulators' allegation of his pride),[19] I would side with one of the very few approaches to the play which has grasped the full significance of Shakespeare's design, an essay by the late Una Ellis-Fermor which, although brief, remains a most penetrating evaluation.[20] She showed that the values of the patricians are base, "crude and coarse-

---

[17] *Shakespeare's Roman Plays*, p. 188.

[18] Kenneth Muir, in *Essays in Criticism* 4 (1954), 331-33.

[19] Thus Muir: Shakespeare "shows the hero as inordinately proud" ("Shakespeare and the Tragic Pattern," British Academy Shakespeare Lecture, 1958, *Proceedings of the British Academy* 44 [1959]); Rosen agrees with previous critics "that he is an unsympathetic character, and that chief of his glaring faults is inordinate pride" (p. 161). Richmond Lattimore, having rightly demolished the concept of "tragic flaw" in Greek tragedy, concludes: "Yet I do know one tragedy in which the pattern of tragic flaw is classically seen, a master-pattern practically all-sufficient . . . *Coriolanus*; here pride, contempt for his fellow man, is the sole and sufficient cause of the great man's downfall" (*Story Patterns in Greek Tragedy* [Ann Arbor: Michigan Univ. Press, 1964], p. 22). Such references could be duplicated many times over.

[20] "Coriolanus," in *Shakespeare the Dramatist*, ed. Kenneth Muir (London: Methuen, 1961), pp. 60-77.

grained," a compound of "restless ambition" and political corruption. Coriolanus "is right" to want to reject the hypocritical role that the patricians have cast him in, "though he cannot communicate his reasons to them," and the "disquiet and disgust" that he feels for their values shows that his "ideals" could never be satisfied by their ignoble behavior. In his paradoxical greeting to his wife, "My gracious silence, hail!", Miss Ellis-Fermor argued that we can find the partly formed expression "of two things deeply hidden in the mind of Coriolanus, of a longing for the balancing silences, graces, and wisdom banished from the outer world but vital to wholeness of life, and an acknowledgment, albeit inarticulate, that in Virgilia these values were preserved" (p. 74). Using the method I have been outlining here we could say that the image that these two have of each other is the only true perspective in the play, the only one not falsified for purposes of manipulation, domination, power, or gain. As such it is the only source of human values which is able to offer a living alternative to the brutality, violence, and corruption all round them. Their values are not strong enough to overcome, but then in tragedy the good never is. All that we can do is to care for the good, and to recognize evil when we see it.

V. SEEING AND HEARING
THE PLAY

TWELVE

"THIS WIDE AND UNIVERSAL STAGE":
SHAKESPEARE'S PLAYS AS PLAYS

JAY L. HALIO

INEVITABLY, the teacher of Shakespeare is pitched into a quandary. On the one hand, he recognizes that seeing Shakespeare's plays staged or on film provides the utmost delight to audiences from all walks of life. (Often, at places like Ashland, Oregon's Shakespeare Festival, I have observed this phenomenon—people arriving from all over the West Coast and beyond, from small villages and big cities, from universities and shops, factories and farms, sitting enrapt at a dramatic performance of a tragedy or history, or breaking out into genuine laughter and delight at a fast-paced comedy.) On the other hand, in the classroom the teacher finds his students grappling arduously with the texts of the very same plays, stumped by the language, the long dramatis personae (especially in the histories), or the sheer complexity of "interpretation." If honestly answering, few students —or teachers, either—would admit that they *read* Shakespeare for pleasure. It is work, hard work; and though it has its rewards, most would rather see a play than study it.

Thanks to the increasing availability of films, recent television productions, and touring companies, seeing Shakespeare's plays is becoming more and more feasible for students and their teachers. To some extent, this new availability of films and performances threatens to supplant the old reliance upon a close reading of the text followed by lectures and discussions—the usual format for undergraduate courses in Shakespeare. "Threatens" is, admittedly, a loaded word and reveals my own predilections, I suppose, although the main thrust of what I want to say here is to defend the use of Shakespeare in performance as a teaching technique. But there is no point in evading at the outset the concern that without proper care the study of Shakespeare could degenerate into entertainment without insight, a joyful but vacuous apprehension of the plays leading to, at best, a sophisticated appreciation of staging techniques or, at worst, a debased taste for gimmickry and horseplay. Alas, our modern theater is not free of such degeneracy, its many superb accomplishments not withstanding.

What to do? I have two suggestions, neither of them especially original but each tested over a period of years with my own students with sufficient success to encourage me to recommend them to others. The first concerns the *critical* use of Shakespeare in performance. The other involves the students' own performance of scenes from Shakespeare.

I

The critical analysis of Shakespeare's plays in performance requires, first of all, a coming to grips with the question of the text. One need not subject undergraduates to the mysteries of Bowers and Hinman to arouse in them an intelligent awareness of the flexibility rather than the sanctity of Shakespeare's scripts. Seeing a play in performance usually brings up the question anyway: Why is the acting version different from the modern edition used in class? Probably it is better to anticipate the question rather than find oneself in the position of explaining or justifying after the fact. *Hamlet* offers an excellent reference point, and students are duly impressed when they are told that the version in their modern editions is one that Shakespeare himself never saw or hoped to see performed. It then becomes necessary to explain briefly the fact of modern conflations, or the variations between the quartos and the folio; but the matter rapidly becomes something much more than merely antiquarian or academic. It can relate to any show currently being prepared for Broadway or London's West End. Shakespeare revised—as Tennessee Williams, Arthur Miller, and almost everyone else in the contemporary theater revises his plays, usually before opening night, but not invariably. Revivals, then as now, may also be the occasion for revision, as J. M. Nosworthy has shown in the case of *Macbeth*.[1] (Again, the *Macbeth* that we have is not the same play that Kings James and Christian saw during the initial performance at court. Unfortunately, no quarto exists to show us what that version was like, and the apparent failure of Middleton's *The Witch* at the Blackfriars Theatre in 1609—if we accept Nosworthy's argument—is responsible for the revival and revision of Shakespeare's play, complete with flying machines, Hecate, elaborate costumes, and a couple of borrowed songs.) Given this background, students find modern renderings of Shakespeare's work less guilty of some suspected violation or sacrilege. An uncut *Hamlet* is as unthinkable, practically speaking, in our day as it was in Shakespeare's, even though his plays and Jonson's seem to have exceeded the usual two hours' traffic of their contemporaries.[2] But for a modern audience it is just as unthinkable to expect a cutting of the text to follow the exigencies of 1603 or 1623 rather than the demands and constraints of our own time, or the interpretation that a producer or director has seen fit to develop out of the wealth of Shakespeare's materials. Our criticism must follow, then, not the divergence from the originals, for that is only to be expected, but the end-product of those divergences—the play that has emerged. The various films of *Hamlet* by Olivier, Richardson, Kozintsev, and others, or the latest production at Stratford-upon-Avon (choose any or all three locations) must be

---

[1] In *Shakespeare's Occasional Plays* (London: Edward Arnold, 1965).
[2] See Alfred Hart, "The Length of Elizabethan and Jacobean Plays," *Shakespeare and the Homilies* (Melbourne: Melbourne Univ. Press, 1934), pp. 77-95.

judged on their intrinsic merits, their use or adaptation of Shakespeare, not their fidelity to an original script which, in fact, no longer exists (and what if it did?).

All this may sound like heresy to purists, but to students it awakens a keen sense of existential realities and plain common sense. "Museum Shakespeare" is not for young minds. But where does all this leave us in relation to the carefully edited modern texts used in our classrooms? It leaves us precisely where we want to be, with a sharper focus on what is actually happening in the plays. We can ask, without fear of raising merely abstract considerations, what happens to the play if Hamlet's last soliloquy is omitted. What is lost? What is gained? How is the structure seriously altered if a production (like Tony Richardson's) follows the First Quarto's sequence of events for Acts II and III rather than the sequence as it appears in Q2 and F? Such questions need not be directed to forming evaluative judgments, at first anyway, but rather to perceiving that the plays do have an essential structure which, when altered, alters much of their significance.[3] By comparison and contrast, the student is led back to the texts and forward to modern interpretations. In this process, the plays come alive as never before.

In the process, too, the student will become aware of the important differences between filming Shakespeare's plays and staging them. This is something that should be stressed, as the two media, though related, are extremely unlike in many respects. The camera eye is far more selective than a staged production, and often, as Grigori Kozintsev has said, it must translate Shakespeare's language into visual equivalents.[4] Hence, while many films of *Hamlet* sacrifice about half the text, they are not necessarily shorter than a staged

[3] For a fuller discussion of this point, see my essay, "Essential *Hamlet*," *College Literature* 1 (1974), 83-99.

[4] "'Hamlet' and 'King Lear,'" in *Shakespeare 1971: Proceedings of the World Shakespeare Congress*, ed. Clifford Leech and J.M.R. Margeson (Toronto: Univ. of Toronto Press, 1972), p. 191.

version cut very conservatively. But perhaps all this is more a matter for film critics to take up,[5] and lest I digress, I ought now to focus on another aspect of the text, the distinction to be made between versions of Shakespeare's plays and adaptations of them.

The distinction is easy to draw in a crude way—no one would confuse *Your Own Thing* with Jonathan Miller's production of *Twelfth Night* for the Oxford-Cambridge Players in 1970/71. The distinction becomes more difficult when one tries to refine it—more difficult and less useful. In a narrow sense, any divergence from the basic text, or' change of setting and costume, results in an adaptation. Practically every modern production is, in that sense, an adaptation. It is important to recognize, however, that such departures are not a new thing in Shakespearean production; they are perfectly traditional. Just as Shakespeare's company acted Roman tragedies in contemporary costume rather than classical dress (though there may have been some suggestion of a toga over doublet and hose), so the Restoration and the eighteenth century acted the same plays in the elaborate wigs and dress of those times. All of these efforts emphasized the contemporary relevance of the action, but it is probably nearer the truth that the issue as an issue never arose, and I doubt that this has much to do with whether or not these periods had developed an adequate historical sense. Thus when students see one of Shakespeare's plays performed in "modern" dress, as in the *Antony and Cleopatra* done on the Bankside in London in August 1973, or in a costume and setting which only generally suggests a distant time, as in Peter Hall's film of *A Midsummer Night's Dream*, they may be assured that these productions, following old precedents, neither revolutionize nor desecrate Shakespeare in our time.

Of course, adaptation can go much further, as the refer-

[5] See, e.g., the various essays in the Shakespeare number of *Literature/Film Quarterly* 1 (Fall 1973) or *Focus on Shakespearean Films*, ed. C. W. Eckert (Englewood Cliffs: Prentice-Hall, 1972).

ence to *Your Own Thing* suggests and as many Restoration
and later productions attest. Joseph Papp's adaptation of
Two Gentlemen of Verona was not the first to interpolate
much new material and thus radically alter what Shakespeare left. In effect, a new work emerged, in this instance a
rock musical. Papp's production of *Much Ado About Nothing*, on the other hand, more closely followed the basic text
—the settings, costumes, and music being the chief altera-
tions (the scene was set in a small town in America of the
Gay Nineties). The result of this version was to present the
play in a fresh—and refreshing—perspective, not to develop
it into something else.[6] The most useful arbiter in making
these distinctions seems to be the quantity and quality of
the departures from Shakespeare's texts and the amount of
new materials added. Thus Booth's *Hamlet* of 1860 is, like
the Folio's of 1623, a version of Shakespeare's original;
whereas Cibber's *Richard III* (1700) or, more obviously,
Davenant's *The Law Against Lovers* (1662), based on
Measure for Measure, are adaptations.

II

These points being made, the analysis of particular productions should proceed. Ultimately, it probably does not matter very much whether students see the plays before or after
they read them, although it is true that the initial effect of
the production or the text will be different according to
which precedes the other. (I have not experimented adequately with the results of the different sequences to offer
any meaningful data, but the matter might be worth exploring.) At any rate, eventually the student will have to

[6] A more extreme example is Peter Brook's *Midsummer Night's
Dream*, staged by Britain's Royal Shakespeare Company (1970). Does
his interpretation amount to a refreshing version or a radical adaptation? For contrasting views, see Peter Thomson, "A Necessary Theatre:
The Royal Shakespeare Season 1970 Reviewed," and John Russell
Brown, "Free Shakespeare," *Shakespeare Survey* 24 (1971), 125-26,
131-35.

compare the production he has seen with the modern edition he has read, possibly going on to compare several productions to each other as well as to the text. He is now in an excellent position to analyze both the play and his own responses to it, responses which have become all the more vivid and personal because he has actively engaged in witnessing the play in action, in performance.

Doubtless there will be parts of the play he will fail to grasp completely, but far fewer parts than if he had not seen the play at all. The more interesting questions arise when he confronts problems of interpretation or adaptation. Consider, for example, the recently televised production of the National Theatre's *The Merchant of Venice*, directed by Jonathan Miller with Laurence Olivier as Shylock. Instead of a sixteenth-century setting, the scene is mid-Victorian Venice, or a Venice much more like London than Italy. Why? What is the value of moving the setting up two and a half centuries? Before these questions can be answered, the basic interpretation of the production must be weighed, for setting, costume, musical accompaniment (itself an interesting aspect here), and especially the acting must be taken into account as an integrated whole, not as separate parts. Unavoidably, the interpretation of Shylock is of central importance, for it influences everything else, for better or for worse. Aware of the diversity of possible interpretations, from the comic villain of the original productions to the tragic hero more sinned against than sinning in nineteenth-century performances, Olivier attempted to present Shylock in a still different way, although his interpretation was surely meant to be more sympathetic than not. Yet it stops far short of Irving's tragic figure. To Olivier,[7] Shylock is someone who has tried to place himself on a level with British aristocracy, emulating their manner of social

[7] According to many newspaper accounts and articles in *TV Guide*, etc., at the time of the showing. See also Fred Hechinger, "Why Shylock Should Not Be Censored," *The New York Times*, 31 March 1974, Section 2, pp. 23, 47.

conduct (including elocution) and using his accumulation of wealth to offset a racial handicap which, paradoxically, he never consciously regrets or laments. A "professional" as well as a professed Jew, Shylock in this interpretation is also a social climber. And the greatest wound to him midway in the play, upon which the action is made to turn (again, in this interpretation) is the logical elopement of his daughter with a Christian: logical, because it is predicated upon everything that Shylock has apparently sought (i.e., acceptance in the Christian world); cruel, because it suddenly and savagely forces to the surface his essentially ambivalent attitude toward himself and his race. Appropriately, then, the historical setting is that of an England still unwilling to allow a Rothschild to take his (elected) seat in Parliament, the England of the mid-nineteenth century. But much more significantly, the whole conception of the play, and particularly the characterization of Shylock, gives ample opportunity for a complex rendering that is more faithful to the fundamental contradictions and complexities of Shakespeare's text than many other interpretations permit.[8] By comparing the performance with the text, the student is moved to ponder these complexities—and others —through the kinds of questions that naturally arise in his mind during his own study or during classroom discussions.

Not that Jonathan Miller's production eschews simplifications at one or two key places, even as it adds complications or mystifications at others. The whole Jessica-Lorenzo plot is altered in tone, especially in the last act, from what we might ordinarily expect from reading the text. The role of Launcelot Gobbo is reduced to almost nothing, eliminating the low comedy that might otherwise interfere with rather than enhance the more solemn tone of this production. Shylock's desire for vengeance against Antonio (and by extension all his Christian set) is made more plausible and sympathetic, although not finally acceptable, by the omis-

[8] See Norman Rabkin, "Meaning and Shakespeare," in *Shakespeare 1971*, pp. 89-106.

sion of his key speech at I.iii.41-52 ("How like a fawning publican he looks," etc.). Not until Jessica's elopement profoundly upsets him does he think of Antonio's forfeiture as his revenge.[9] The point is easily made to students, but it is better to let them grasp it for themselves. As L. C. Knights has indicated, we do not always want to be standing, pointer in hand, directing our students' attention to what is significant.[10] We must allow them to enjoy the thrill of discovery for themselves if ever they are to value learning at all. Tentative, gently probing questions may help guide the less apt, but even for these students the plays in performance tend to provide more than adequate prompting when comparisons to the text are invited.

The part in Jonathan Miller's *Merchant* that has aroused most controversy and mystification, at least among my undergraduates, is the ending. Jessica's preoccupation, her refusal to blend in with the general reconciliation and joy of the other couples, as she walks apart from them with the document Nerissa has handed her from Shylock, is underscored most emphatically by the loud intoning of the Mourner's Kaddish in the background. Clearly, this is Miller's addition to Shakespeare's script, just as Shylock's anguished offstage scream at IV.i.400 is his interpolation, both apparently designed to complicate the otherwise festive situation and attitude of the Christians who, under Portia, have triumphed in love and wealth and wit. But whom is the Kaddish sung *for*? For Jessica, because she has married out of her faith? But mourning her would be the role of her parent, and Shylock has himself ostensibly accepted conversion, too (IV.i.394). For Shylock then? If not for his apostasy, for his death? He is admittedly ill when we last see him

[9] The cue for this interpretation is actually in the text, in the Salerio-Salanio dialogue of II.viii, all of which, like II.vi, is omitted. See especially II.viii.25-26.

[10] Knights, "The Teaching of Shakespeare," in *Manner and Meaning in Shakespeare*, ed. B.A.W. Jackson (Hamilton, Ont.: McMaster Univ. Library Press, 1969), p. 14. The whole essay, which emphasizes ways of *reading* the texts, is well worth study.

helped offstage, but we have no other indication of his death, and in any event he has no son to mourn him, only his daughter Jessica, a convert. It is just possible that all of these questions miss the point, or rather they make a somewhat different point, very much worth making to students whose bent unfortunately tends to be literalistic. Does it really matter whom the Kaddish is for, specifically? Is not its function rather to remind us that the problems raised in this play have not really been solved satisfactorily, that the play remains, what in Miller's interpretation it started out to be—a "problem" play? Or like the passing bell in Donne's meditation, is the Kaddish sung, not for Shylock or Jessica, but for us?

The larger question—by what right has Miller introduced the Kaddish at all—is more difficult and problematical, and here much critical agreement is unlikely. To be sure, this is a clear example of adaptation, justified—if at all—by the exigencies of a modern interpretation for a modern audience knowledgeable, as surely Shakespeare's audience was not, in the significance of the Mourner's Kaddish. But the criterion for judgment remains here as for all other aspects of adaptation and interpretation in this and similar productions— the intrinsic dramatic effect. Taking liberties with Shakespeare's texts cannot *in itself* be used as a judgment against a production; the result of the liberties taken—whether they enhance the play in a meaningful and (given the contours of the specific interpretation—itself to be judged by related criteria) legitimate way—should remain the basis for evaluation. We must not be stuffy about this. Otherwise, we shall misprize some of the best efforts of the modern theater and, in the process, lose some of our best students as well.

Other recent television productions raise similar issues and controversies, all of them worth exploring in class. The Richard Chamberlain/Peter Wood *Hamlet* a few years ago as well as the New York Shakespeare Festival's production of *Much Ado*, both of them also set in the nineteenth century, although at either end of it, presented extremely interesting versions of these plays, excellently well acted, staged, and filmed for the small-sized screen. Quite a different kind of television experience, however, was the New York Shakespeare Festival production of *King Lear*, which filmed a live performance of the play at the Delacorte Theater in Central Park (August 1973). How different or how successful this production was technically as compared to other productions made expressly for television may not arouse quite as interesting discussion among students as the way Lear was acted by the fine black actor, James Earl Jones. Lear's daughters were accordingly also played by black actresses. The fact of their blackness is, or should be, an irrelevance in any serious discussion of the merits of the performance, but it does raise the issue which Joseph Papp, the producer, has also confronted in many other productions (most notably in *Two Gentlemen of Verona*): how can Shakespeare's plays be made more accessible to audiences of a far more heterogeneous kind than Shakespeare could have envisioned at the Globe? I do not mean heterogeneous as to class, for of course, Shakespeare's audience was mixed in that sense; I mean heterogeneous in that and every other sense—culturally and racially, above all. Adaptation, making plays into rock musicals, seems to be one route; the use of black and Puerto Rican actors in a mixed cast seems to be another; and, as in *Two Gentlemen*, these approaches may be combined. It should be noted that very little adaptation as such seems to have been made in the performance of *King Lear*, and the acting was sustained at a very high level. Indeed, the quality of the acting and the staging—besides the overall rendition or interpretation of the play—becomes the only acceptable aesthetic basis for evaluation, although in the final analysis some account of the social effectiveness or accessibility of the production should (to be logical) also be measured.[11]

11 To judge from only a few performances that I have attended, I cannot personally attest to seeing many people from other than the white middle-class segments of the population, but it is obviously

III

Another strategy for awakening in students a keener appreciation of Shakespeare as a poet and dramatist involves them in acting out scenes from the plays. There are many ways of instituting this procedure, with different ends in view. After several years of experimentation, I have found that the requirement of a scene or parts of scenes lasting at least fifteen or twenty minutes and staged entirely by students in small groups of five, six, or seven members each, works well. In my experience it has proved more valuable than the traditional term paper, and apart from the benefits in the study of Shakespeare, there are others as well, of which more in a moment. The requirement can be simply stated, and yes, I am convinced it should be a requirement, not an option. Moreover, while it may substitute for a term paper, it should not be used to replace a reasonable amount of shorter papers and/or essay examinations during the term. (I tend to favor the one-page critical essay, which can easily be assigned four or five times during a semester without unduly burdening either student or teacher—as opposed, say, to two or three 500-word or longer essays.) Each group of students must choose a scene that it wishes to present, either from a play studied in class or from one selected and read on their own (advantages and disadvantages either way usually balance out). Lines *must* be memorized. And the audience must consist of at least one—the instructor. Everything else is optional: costumes, scenery, sound effect, invitations (for a larger audience), and so forth. One group even chose to have a cast party after the presentation!

After the initial groans and gripes, the feelings of bewilderment and even fear among students who have never attempted a project of this kind, it is amazing how the

---

absurd to generalize from such meager data. Important to consider, too, would be the influence of these stage productions on the touring companies that frequently visit the schools of New York City.

groups begin to pitch in and get into the spirit of cooperation and adventure. Some reassurance at the outset is of
course well-advised: they are not expected to put on a professional performance. It is understood that most of them
are not drama majors. But if they are truly to understand
Shakespeare's plays *as plays*, reading them or seeing them
performed by professional troupes is not quite enough.
They must get into the act themselves. There are some
things that cannot be taught; they can only be learned.
Granted it is a sink or swim situation, many students discover that swimming is not so difficult after all.

I know of no other way to impress students with the
fundamental values of Shakespeare's language and dramatic
art than this technique. Analyzing a passage on paper in an
essay or examination paper is one thing; analyzing it for
performance is another—but it is directly related to the
first. The processes are connected, or should be, as the students become aware of the whole range of human attributes
that acting Shakespeare requires—thinking, feeling, sensing,
projecting. To help in this awareness, that is, to help students more fully recognize and evaluate what they have
been doing, the last part of the assignment is essential. Once
the scene has been performed, the instructor should allow
enough time afterward to sit down with the group and discuss the experience they have had. Why was the particular
scene chosen? What rationale was found for its particular
interpretation? Were any alternative interpretations considered and rejected? Why? These are just a few queries that
can launch a stimulating conversation during which the
instructor as well as his students stand to profit immensely.

Students will naturally profit in other ways, too, ways in
which, after he has made the original assignment, the instructor cannot and should not have a significant part.
Working in small groups,[12] students will be compelled to

[12] Groups may be assigned arbitrarily or, preferably, allowed to form
themselves according to the students' common interests in certain
plays or types of plays. Always there seem to be a few left over who,

deal with the dynamics of group activities—making a selection, casting, and countless other decisions; dealing with less cooperative members of the group, or with problems arising from those who drop the course midway during rehearsals; discovering from each other the ability to make contributions to mutual understanding and enlightenment that they had not realized were latent in themselves or their classmates; discovering, also, that learning can go forward without lectures or a classroom or even an instructor. By the end of the term, if the instructor is fortunate, he will discover that he has become superfluous. Which is another way of saying that both he and his students have done their work and done it well.

In the past, I have usually waited until the last weeks of the term for the student scenes to be presented, but some of my students have recently questioned the advisability of waiting so long and have suggested, instead, that the projects come due by the middle of the semester. In this way, they argue, the benefits of their experience can accrue much earlier and so carry forward to the further understanding and appreciation of plays remaining to be read, seen, and perhaps also acted later on. The arguments strike me as valid, and I regret that my teaching assignments and other duties have not yet permitted me to experiment in this direction. It would be very illuminating to see—as I have not yet had an adequate opportunity to see within the earlier format I have described—what effect the acting project has on the students' grasp of the plays they read afterward, whether they act out parts of them or not. What new kinds of insights do they seem to be acquiring, once they have had the experience of performing a scene or combination of scenes? How much more sensitive do they become to the qualities of language, to dramatic verse, as well as to the deeper psychology in the plays? Do they feel more

---

in the latter instance, must depend on the instructor to form them into groups or integrate them into smaller groups already formed.

comfortable amidst alternative or even conflicting interpretations of the same play? My guess is that the acting projects occasion generally positive responses to all of these questions, but it is not much more than a guess based on several student comments and the insufficient testimony of final examinations. Moving the acting projects up closer to the midway point of the term would afford some time to investigate more closely the actual facts, as well as affording the students the benefits that everyone so far seems agreed would accrue. The logistics need not appear formidable, if one allowed for enough flexibility of scheduling within a two- or three-week period.

Not surprisingly, undergraduates tend to favor scenes from the comedies and tragedies for their presentations. Among the many that stand out in my memory are a rather spectacular and original staging of the Graveyard Scene from *Hamlet*, an energetic Trial Scene from *The Merchant of Venice*, and a hilarious Dueling Scene from *Twelfth Night*. Scenes from *The Winter's Tale* and *The Tempest* have often proved popular and successful: I have seldom seen a more stately Hermione or a more comical and outlandish Caliban than these students have provided. Interestingly (and very gratifying, too), the student groups have not found it necessary—if they thought of it at all—to ape professional performances they may have seen or heard; usually, they have found their own way of doing things. (Since no grades as such are given for these presentations, the incentive for doing the project for its own sake is strengthened.) A lecture hall resembling a small enclosed amphitheater and equipped with apparatus for dimming all but the stage lights provides a suitable theater. A few props may be used, but little other scenery; students prefer to concentrate on costumes and musical effects for whatever embellishments they want. The best work, of course, comes when the groups find themselves developing into true ensembles, but sometimes a presentation that leans heavily on the abilities of a single student can work well, too. Recognizing that they had a voice major in their midst, one group elected to perform the Mad Scenes from *Hamlet*, Act IV, and rarely have Ophelia's songs been sung with such grace and beauty. Another undergraduate group decided to introduce a Marx Brothers routine into scenes from *Twelfth Night* with a startling, uproarious, but by no means inappropriate effect. Where doubling of roles has been necessary, this has been accomplished simply and swiftly. Students find no problem (despite initial trepidation) in effecting these transitions, or in using women for men's parts, and vice versa. Shakespeare's play world is play, after all, though the kind of play that students seldom realize can be as significant, enlightening and enjoyable as they discover it to be in developing their presentations.[13]

IV

I end where I began: the function of attending or participating in Shakespeare's plays in performance should lead to the same goal—a heightened awareness of the plays as living artifacts in which any student, if he is willing to make the effort to free himself of unnecessary prejudice or inhibition, can find himself in the happy situation of enjoying and learning simultaneously. The study of the text remains, as it should, foremost in importance, but the perspective has shifted—for the better, I believe—from an abstract consideration of words on a page to a vital absorption into the dynamics of art. As teachers we have to be concerned with both how and what our students are learning—and whether they are learning at all. But as teachers we recognize, also, that how and what, especially in the humanities, often come to the same thing. Hence the significance of a technique that fosters the play of active intelligence and sensibility, as

[13] For a recent discussion on this basic approach, published well after this essay was written, see Malcolm G. Scully, "Teachers of Shakespeare Using New Techniques," *The Chronicle of Higher Education*, 11 October 1976, p. 5.

against other techniques which promote a more passive acceptance of second-hand insights, however authoritative. Finally, the strategies I have advocated have in addition this virtue—perhaps their most important one—that they restrain in us the inveterate tendency to impose upon our charges critical schemata or other formulations which, no matter how useful, students are inclined to take as ends in themselves.[14] Viewing and performing Shakespeare's plays will make them far more accessible than any critical schema can do, at the same time allowing for free and honest responses to the worlds of complexity they contain. The critical intelligence is and must be still engaged, but more willingly and fully engaged in the abundance of all that Shakespeare has to offer. To help bring our students to this experience is surely the greatest service we can render.

[14] Knights, p. 15.

THIRTEEN

THE TEACHER AS POETIC ACTOR*

G. WILSON KNIGHT

IN OUR time we have heard much, from T. S. Eliot and others, of the "dissociation of sensibility," which is supposed to have dated from the seventeenth century. What is meant is the split between intellect and emotion, which may also take the form of the opposition of reason and occult recognition. Pope was aware of the disruption in his plea for acceptance of instinct as against reason in Epistles II and III of his *Essay on Man*; at the conclusion to *The Dunciad* he foresees the breakdown of our culture coming about through this very split. It is sometimes assumed it has invalidated all our endeavors, including subsequent poetry; but his is a grave error, for wherever poetry has been authentic we have a healing of the wound. This is, indeed, what poetry is *for*: to heal the wound, which has in fact existed long before the seventeenth century, dating back to the origins of the intellect.

When making the persons of his drama speak in poetry, the poet is making them, heroes and lesser persons alike, speak from beyond this "dissociation of sensibility," and therefore, in part, from a height overlooking their immediate concerns. It can happen in a prose play too: as Bernard Shaw said toward the end of his preface to *Saint Joan*, the people are made to speak as if they realized, as the real persons would not have realized, the further implications of their actions: "The things I represent these three exponents of the drama as saying are the things they actually would

---

* Excerpted and amended from a book in preparation, *Shakespeare's Dramatic Challenge.*

have said if they had known what they were really doing."[1]
According to Granville-Barker, people in poetic drama have
to express both what is known to them and also truths
about themselves that they do *"not know"*: "all of which
things, diverse and contradictory, must be expressed at one
and the same time" and "in one and the same fashion."[2]

That Shakespeare's dramatic poetry entwines so regularly
the colloquial with the rhetorical establishes a needed relation with ordinary life so that we are invited to participate
in a progress from normal behavior patterns toward what
may be termed a "higher consciousness" or even a higher
common sense. With Shakespeare's heroes this higher consciousness is not only present in the poetry, but the nature
and use of it is carefully, as it were, exposed before us. The
heroes not only see themselves as the action matures with a
new clarity, but also become more objectively philosophical
and selfless, while through that very selflessness a new thing,
which we may call the "soul," is being born. At the opening
to his *Preface to Hamlet,* Granville-Barker sees Shakespeare's imagination beginning to give his persons, through
their poetry, "something like an immortal soul."[3]

Such a view of poetry makes strong demands on the imagination; and the best way to vitalize the imagination is
through the art of public reading. Without that it will
remain undeveloped. Educationally what we have to do is to
draw out, educe, from the student powers usually dormant.
So the sensitive teacher will do well to alert the student to
the infinite variety of intonation needed for the speaking
of Shakespeare or indeed poetry in general. He may be re-
ceptive to advice and proceed, as he thinks, to implement it.

[1] George Bernard Shaw, preface, to *Saint Joan* (New York: Brenta-
no's, 1924), p. lxxviii.

[2] Harley Granville-Barker, *On Poetry in Drama* (London: Sidgwick
& Jackson, 1937), p. 34.

[3] Harley Granville-Barker, *Prefaces to Shakespeare: Hamlet* (Princeton: Princeton Univ. Press, 1946), p. 29.

Here, however, there may be a catch. He may not be able to hear what he is actually doing. I mean, he may well think that he is expressing the needed variations; they are in his head, and in speaking he hears them, as it were, within his head; but they are not being projected to the hearer outside. The only way to bring this home to him is to get him to listen to his own speaking on a tape; and he may then be shocked to discover how little he is conveying of the variegated powers he thought that he was expressing.

He may raise objections. He may say, "The meaning is in the words; surely all one wants to do is to speak them audibly, and the audience will respond. We do not want to be accused of gilding the lily." One fallacy here is obvious: what audience is he thinking of? People in one room? People in a hall? In a large theater? Correct speaking will vary the emphasis far more powerfully for a large audience than a small one, and without such variation he will not grip them, or even be audible, since audibility depends very largely on the audience getting the phrase-units, not only the words, and feeling the relevant meanings. There is another difficulty. He may be reluctant to delve into his deeper self and draw from it the emotional resources that are needed; he may have inhibitions about getting the required tones and resonance, thinking them too emotional, or, put otherwise, fearing to reveal the soul of the poetry, as something almost indecent. The answer to this is clear. Suggest to the student that he may well be right, and say that he can, if he likes, so speak the lines. But ask him at least to speak them with full depth and variation, to show that he *can* do it; and let him hear the results. If they are negative, the obvious implication is that his excuses are merely a veil to his real reason: the inability to speak his lines correctly. I am assuming that such variations will be given while maintaining full respect to metrics.

I cannot overemphasize the value for the student in imaginative apprehension of a series of such trials; if he draws out from himself the richer music of speech, he will begin to enjoy the use of powers hitherto dormant and will advance in his understanding of literature. If he fails, he will remain, to that extent, in an unimaginative state. I believe the answer to many of our literary problems in education is to be found in making the student listen to his own voice.

An easy way to see what may be demanded is to consider certain of Shakespeare's longer speeches, and see how they build up and flower in the process.[4] As a start, I point to Henry IV's sleep speech in 2 *Henry IV* (III.i.4-31). The King is at first weak, through sleeplessness:

> How many thousand of my poorest subjects
> Are at this hour asleep! O sleep! O gentle sleep!
> Nature's soft nurse, how have I frighted thee,
> That thou no more wilt weigh my eyelids down,
> And steep my senses in forgetfulness?

The voice breaks; he is almost in tears. He next reasons, with a firmer voice:

> Why rather, sleep, liest thou in smoky cribs,
> Upon uneasy pallets stretching thee,
> And hush'd with buzzing night-flies to thy slumber,
> Than in the perfum'd chambers of the great,
> Under the canopies of costly state,
> And lull'd with sound of sweetest melody?
> O thou dull god, why li'st thou with the vile
> In loathsome beds, and leavest the kingly couch
> A watch-case or a common 'larum-bell?

That is comparatively straightforward, and will be spoken normally, though with a momentary access of vocal gran-

---

[4] I have often made these the subject of a lecture, as printed in *The City of London School Chronicle* 1 (July 1970). The readings were broadcast, under the title "Shakespeare's Rhetoric," on the BBC (1963, repeated 1964). There is a tape of them made by Sound Seminars, Cincinnati; it was marketed until recently by McGraw-Hill in New York and England, but they have now been transferred to Jeffry Norton, Publishers, Inc., 145 East 49th Street, New York.

deur for the "perfum'd chambers." But now the speech
starts to burgeon out, to flower:

> Wilt thou upon the high and giddy mast
> Seal up the ship-boy's eyes, and rock his brains
> In cradle of the rude imperious surge,
> And in the visitation of the winds,
> Who take the ruffian billows by the top,
> Curling their monstrous heads and hanging them
> With deafing clamor in the slippery clouds,
> That with the hurly death itself awakes?

Sleep is a great power, by hyperbole imagined here as a yet
greater power than death, as indeed it may be, or as great
anyway, since we do not know what sleep is or where we
go to in sleep, perhaps to the Elysian fields of death itself.
Such thoughts multiply from inspection of the poetry. But
what of the sleepless King and his broken voice? We have
completely forgotten them. The actor will be concentrating
only on the poetry, and giving it all the strength at his
disposal. The fourth line here goes quickly, but we slow
down for the fifth, the voice rising on "top." From "curling"
to "slippery clouds" a maximum of power will be needed,
an especially heavy stress falling on the delaying and ob-
structive syllable of "deafing clamor," followed, in the next
line, by an awed quiet, for death.

Now the speech continues, still quiet, and a little wistful,
for what follows:

> Canst thou, O partial sleep, give then repose
> To the wet sea-boy in an hour so rude,
> And in the calmest and most stillest night,
> With all appliances and means to boot,
> Deny it to a king?

We can enjoy the second vowel of "repòse," which speaks
volumes; and also the phrase "wet sea-bòy," accenting
"bòy," and so to the final couplet:

> Then happy low, lie down!
> Uneasy lies the head that wears a crown.

We return to the quiet accents of the opening, after our tumultuous adventure. But this is the point I would drive home: the psychological situation gives birth to a poetic splendor, which in manner of execution has little in common with the psychological situation we started with.

This buildup is usual in Shakespeare's long speeches. We have it in *Richard II* in John O'Gaunt's "This royal throne of kings" speech (II.i.40-66), where colloquial intonations should allow for an old man's quavering repetitions:

> This royal throne of kings, this sceptred isle,
> This earth of majesty, this seat of Mars,
> This other Eden, demi-paradise,
> This fortress built by Nature for herself
> Against infection and the hand of war,
> This happy breed of men, this little world,
> This precious stone set in the silver sea,
> Which serves it in the office of a wall,
> Or as a moat defensive to a house,
> Against the envy of less happier lands;
> This blessed plot, this earth, this realm, this England,
> This nurse, this teeming womb of royal kings,
> Fear'd by their breed, and famous by their birth,
> Renowned for their deeds as far from home,
> For Christian service and true chivalry,
> As is the sepulchre in stubborn Jewry
> Of the world's ransom, blessed Mary's Son;
> This land of such dear souls, this dear dear land,
> Dear for her reputation through the world,
> Is now leas'd out—I die pronouncing it—
> Like to a tenement or pelting farm.

We may be excused for wondering whether the old man will ever get to the point. He repeats himself rather like Polo-

nius, though the characterization of age must not be overdone, or it spoils the content; a reminder here and there is
probably enough. There is a purpose in it all, over and
above the "characterization." England's glory has been defined, almost overdefined, and then a new voice takes over:

> England, bound in with the triumphant sea,
> Whose rocky shore beats back the envious siege
> Of wat'ry Neptune, is now bound in with shame,
> With inky blots and rotten parchment bonds;
> That England, that was wont to conquer others,
> Hath made a shameful conquest of itself.

We forget about the "characterization." All the compacted
force possible is needed for the scorn of "inky blots and
rotten parchment bonds;" and then the final, sedate and
withering, judgment. All the pauses, withdrawings, and
repetitions of the earlier lines are preparatory to, and built
into, this firm ending.

We have this kind of thing often. Henry V's "Crispin"
speech starts weakly, talking of honor with a seemingly
deliberate lack of conviction, until it takes fire at "This day
is call'd the feast of Crispian" (IV.iii.40). On the stage,
King Henry may be supposed to find the name when looking
over some papers, to which he has turned in embarrassment
at finding his first words inadequate. The reaction of those
around him first in doubt, and gradually enthusiasm,
should be evident. The *name* is so important that the speech
finally doubles it, in:

> And Crispin Crispian shall ne'er go by,
> From this day to the ending of the world,
> But we in it shall be remembered.
>
> (IV.iii.57-59)

We may almost say, that so far as the play is concerned, the
Battle of Agincourt was won by the poetic radiations of the
word "Crispin." Its sound obliquely suggests "Christian."

A particularly fine example of the buildup toward revelation occurs in Macbeth's soliloquy, "If it were done" (I.vii.1), rising by degrees to the vision of Pity striding the blast. *Antony and Cleopatra* (IV.xiv.35-54) has another. Antony has just heard of Cleopatra's supposed death. He speaks in turn to Eros, his armor-bearer, to Mardian who has brought the news, to himself, to his armor, and to Cleopatra. Note that "keep" means "withstand" and that after "battery" we understand "coming":

> Unarm, Eros, the long day's task is done,
> And we must sleep. [*To Mardian.*] That thou depart'st
> hence safe
> Does pay thy labor richly; go.   *Exit Mardian.*
>   Off, pluck off,
> The sevenfold shield of Ajax cannot keep
> The battery from my heart. O, cleave, my sides!
> Heart, once be stronger than thy continent,
> Crack thy frail case! Apace, Eros, apace.
> No more a soldier. Bruised pieces, go,
> You have been nobly borne.—From me awhile.
>   *Exit Eros.*
> I will o'ertake thee, Cleopatra, and
> Weep for my pardon.

Though the disjointed addresses all radiate from his concern at the news, which is central to them, they remain disjointed. Now he indulges in a complex thought:

> So it must be, for now
> All length is torture; since the torch is out,
> Lie down and stray no farther. Now all labor
> Mars what it does; yea, very force entangles
> Itself with strength. Seal then, and all is done.

Temporal existence has become unbearable; life is self-contradictory; force of biological existence is mastered by the "strength" of spiritual compulsion. So to the climax, in utter simplicity:

> Eros!—I come, my queen!—Eros!—Stay for me!
> Where souls do couch on flowers, we'll hand in hand,
> And with our sprightly port make the ghosts gaze.
> Dido and her Aeneas shall want troops,
> And all the haunt be ours. Come, Eros, Eros!

He wants Eros to come and kill him. See how the germ of Elysian expectation flowers out. The speech starts with abrupt addresses, follows up with complex thought, and then comes the resolving and revelatory climax.

The actor should act not the character alone, but the poetry; and especially toward the close, whether of speech or play, the poetry more than the character. Bernard Shaw has a helpful comment here, giving Mrs. Patrick Campbell advice on the acting of Lady Macbeth:

> When you play Shakespeare, don't worry about the character, but go for the music. It was by word music that he expressed what he wanted to express: and if you get the music right, the whole thing will come right. And neither he nor any other musician ever wrote music without *fortissimi* and thundering ones too. It is only your second rate people who write whole movements for muted strings and never let the trombones and the big drums go. . . .
>
> If you want to know the truth about Lady Macbeth's character, she hasn't one. There never was no such person. She says things that will set people's imagination to work if she says them in the right way: that is all.[5]

"There never was no such person": that is true. Lady Macbeth exists only in the realm of fiction, and so do all the people and events in Shakespeare; but the poetry is a present reality to be experienced by us in a way that the rest

[5] Alan Dent, ed., *Bernard Shaw and Mrs. Patrick Campbell: Their Correspondence* (New York: Knopf, 1952), pp. 218-19.

cannot be. Shaw's words may be an overstatement, but it is
an overstatement that states an all-important truth. I myself
found Macbeth a not too arduous part to perform for the
very reason that so much depends on the poetry. A. C.
Bradley's fine study of *Macbeth* is mainly a study in poetic
psychology; it was bound to be that. Performance, given a
just poetic projection, is comparatively easy. The sharp in-
terchanges of *Othello* and *King Lear* are more demanding;
the poetry has more variation, and you have to consider
other performers. Macbeth talks mainly to himself.

It is not quite so simple as Bernard Shaw implies. The
just speaking of the poetry has its difficulties; nor is it only
the speaking of the poetry, but the acting of it that is required. This should happen, all the time, in subtle, or at
choice moments extreme, ways. What we should be doing is
performing the part not of an ordinary man, but of a poetic
man. I have recently twice been pained by performances of
Hamlet by eminent young actors. The verse was split up
quite intolerably. I do not suggest that they were impervious
to the poetry, or unable to speak it: they were just aiming
at the wrong thing. Faced by the complexities of Hamlet
and his various worryings and muddles, they thought, How
should such a man speak? Obviously, they concluded, in a
muddled fashion. The result was a sequence of discon-
tinuities and jolts. Instead, they should have regarded their
task as one presenting a man who says things like:

> The undiscover'd country, from whose bourn
> No traveller returns . . .
>
> (III.i.78-79)

and,

> Absent thee from felicity a while,
> And in this harsh world draw thy breath in pain.
>
> (V.ii.347-48)

Hamlet as a "character" may be confused, but his poetry
is not; he is less a "character" than a poetic voice, speaking

from a height overlooking his problems. That is our primary fact. It may be untrue to life; people do not speak like
that, but there it is, and we have to make what we can of it.
If we succeed, we end up by having a supreme experience.

When Shakespeare wants a realistic utterance, he uses
prose, as in Hamlet's Nunnery dialogue with Ophelia
(III.i.89-149). It is also true that he can endue prose with
poetic properties, as in his lines on the heavenly firmament
(II.ii.295-303).

All the obvious reservations are admitted. It is as important to intershade the colloquial accents as to do justice to
the poetic. In his "Seneca in Elizabethan Translation,"
T. S. Eliot describes how the Elizabethans learned from
Seneca the skills of declamation: "The art of dramatic language, we must remember, is as near to oratory as to ordinary speech or to other poetry." But they did not stop there:
"Their subsequent progress is a process of splitting up the
primitive rhetoric, developing out of it subtler poetry and
subtler tones of conversation, eventually mingling, as no
other school of dramatists has done, the oratorical, the con-
versational, the elaborate and the simple, the direct and the
indirect; so that they were able to write plays which can still
be viewed as plays, with any plays, and which can still be
read as poetry, with any poetry."[6] There is a continual
interaction. I have often drawn attention, in my *Shakespearian Production* and elsewhere, to Hamlet's words to
his mother:

> Look here upon this picture, and on this,
> The counterfeit presentment of two brothers.
> See what a grace was seated on this brow:
> Hyperion's curls, the front of Jove himself,
> An eye like Mars, to threaten and command,
> A station like the herald Mercury
> New lighted on a heaven-kissing hill,
> A combination and a form indeed,

[6] T. S. Eliot, *Selected Essays* (New York: Harcourt, Brace & World,
1960), pp. 75-76.

Where every god did seem to set his seal
To give the world assurance of a man.
This was your husband.

(III.iv.53-63)

It starts colloquially, more or less, but in the third line rises.
After that, the quality of each god is to be reflected not
only in the voice but in the eye and facial expression of the
actor, with swift changes that yet do not impede the poetic
flow. At "A combination" we return to a more colloquial
utterance. It is like an airplane, taking off for flight, and
returning to the ground.

Shaw's advice to attend to the music is good, but the
word "music" contains manifold implications: vowel-color-
ing; vocal height or depth according to the nature of the
thought being expressed; alteration of speed, with continual
variation between the colloquial and the rhetorical and between natural stress and metrical beat; and all in strict
obedience moreover to the things and qualities which the
poetry, moment by moment, handles; and all distinctly audible. I say "distinctly," since it is not enough to ask a
member of the audience, "Could you hear that?" What one
should ask is, "Could you hear that without straining?"
Any effort devoted to listening takes from the psychic resources needed for the audience's enjoyment and experience.

The language, too, must be not only spoken but lived.
T. S. Eliot, in his essay on Seneca writes well of Greek
tragedy, whose physical actuality he contrasts with Seneca's
verbal art:

Behind the drama of words is the drama of action, the
timbre of the voice and voice, the uplifted hand or tense
muscle, and the particular emotion. The spoken play, the
words which we read, are symbols, a shorthand, and often,
as in the best of Shakespeare, a very abbreviated shorthand indeed, for the acted and felt play, which is always
the real thing. The phrase, beautiful as it may be, stands
for a greater beauty still.[7]

[7] Eliot, pp. 53-54.

The physical and emotional elements of the acted play are felt as a "greater beauty" than the words: though the words are there too, to give them point.

When Hamlet in a soliloquy says,

> And can say nothing; no, not for a king,
> Upon whose property and most dear life
> A damn'd defeat was made
>
> (II.ii.569-71),

his eye should momentarily light up and his face glow for the memory of his father, and then cloud quickly for the "damn'd defeat." Such a lightning transition would be impossible in normal behavior. The poetry directing us, we make a leap of imaginative apprehension to what is behind the poetry. As Richard II has it:

> And these external manners of laments
> Are merely shadows to the unseen grief
> That swells with silence in the tortur'd soul.
>
> (IV.i.296-98)

The externals of first facial expression and gesture and next of words—for gesture tends to precede speech—are no better than "shadows" of the soul-reality within. That soul-reality we should intuit from the words, and from that soul-reality we should, as actors, work. This is what I mean by acting the kind of man—he has never actually existed, of course—who speaks in poetry.

At choice moments—not always, necessarily—the actor's broader gestures should be made to correspond closely to the verse. *Othello* provides an example:

> *Iago.* Patience, I say; your mind perhaps may change.
> *Oth.* Never, Iago. Like to the Pontic Sea,
> Whose icy current and compulsive course
> Nev'r feels retiring ebb, but keeps due on
> To the Propontic and the Hellespont,
> Even so my bloody thoughts, with violent pace,

Shall nev'r look back, nev'r ebb to humble love,
Till that a capable and wide revenge
Swallow them up.

(III.iii.452-60)

At this crest of passion Othello has, we may suppose, his
hand out, back of hand uppermost. It is then drawn away
and out, imitating the course of the sea being described;
but it must be timed exactly to correspond to the 3½ lines
of the movement, finishing with it. Though a passionate
speech, it must be disciplined in the action, and the passion
carried into the extended simile. This does not mean that
gestures would be found to illustrate everything. I once
heard an actor illustrate Richard II's

With mine own tears I wash away my balm
(IV.i.207)

by pointing to his eyes, which struck me as unnecessary.
Wide gestures should be used with reserve.[8]

Here is a passage that makes my argument clearer. George
Henry Lewes is writing in the last century of Salvini's
Othello:

> I remember nothing so musically perfect in its *tempo* and
> intonation, so emotionally perfect in expression, as his
> delivery of this passage—the fury visibly growing with
> every word, his whole being vibrating, his face aflame, the
> voice becoming more and more terrible, and yet so com-
> pletely under musical control that it never approached
> a scream.[9]

The concluding words are important: it is a highly disciplined business, though "control" may not be the right
word, unless, as here, it is grouped with "musical." The

8 For further discussions on poetic acting, see my *Shakespearian
Production* (London: Routledge, 1954), especially pp. 52-55, 236-41,
279-80, 316.

9 George Henry Lewes, *On Actors and the Art of Acting* (London:
Smith, Elder, 1875), p. 269.

actor's voice should never shout, unless a shout, as a shout, is particularly demanded. Its volume and intensity should compass the needed power without that: and indeed, it will be a greater power, since a shout has none, or little. Observe that the whole body is being used. Poetic acting is not a matter solely of voice or even of face and hands, but of the "whole being."[10]

The actor will vary ordinary behavior, for much of the time, with a more poetic, or symbolic, action. Shakespeare's use of prose indicates how nearly he approaches, when he wishes to, normal behavior, and much of the verse demands nothing excessively grandiose. But it should be ready for it when it comes, and the total performance should be suffused with imaginative apprehensions.

To return to our earlier argument. I would assert that the primary need for actor or for literary student alike is to listen to his own vocal dramatization—which the *Four Quartets* need every bit as much as Shakespeare if a public reading is attempted—and see how it works. If it fails I suggest that they should break down their inhibitions and labor for success.

[10] A good way to see what this means is to study.the various pictures of Beerbohm Tree; see Hesketh Pearson, *Beerbohm Tree* (New York: Harpers, 1956) and *Herbert Beerbohm Tree*, ed. Max Beerbohm (London: Hutchinson, n.d.). See also my *Shakespearian Production* (enlarged 1964). I have presented a full study of bodily action in "Symbol of Man," as yet unpublished.

FOURTEEN

SOME PROBLEMS IN
TEACHING SHAKESPEARE'S PLAYS AS
WORKS OF DRAMA

BERNARD BECKERMAN

IN *Hamlet*, Shakespeare tells us the story of the elder Hamlet's death three times. First, he has the Ghost, like a messenger from purgatory, reveal the fact and manner of the murder. Next, as a preface to the play-within-the-play, he introduces a dumb show to illustrate the same events in mime. And lastly, by means of dialogue and gesture, to the accompaniment of the young Hamlet's compulsive chorus, he dramatizes the story as the prince has grafted it upon the stock of the old chestnut, *The Murder of Gonzago*. In all three versions Shakespeare uses the same datum. We do not find here the multiple angles of vision with which we are so familiar in the work of Pirandello or in the tour de force of *Rashomon*. Instead, we find reinforcement of a single point of view though cast in different dramatic forms. That is why the three tellings together provide a cogent example of the transformation of story into drama.

For the "raw" audience, that is, for the playgoers at the first performance in Shakespeare's day as well as for many of our own students, the Ghost supplies the details of an event unknown beforehand. The Ghost, of course, has two kinds of listeners. He has "his son," who is to revenge the unnatural death of the father. He also has the theater audience—those who hear him doubly—in the way the son does in hearing of the murder and as "gods" aware of both the Ghost's telling and the son's hearing. The audience's double awareness, however, is not shaped merely by what information it learns but also by the way that the information is transmitted.

In the first telling of the murder, the story is distilled by the Ghost's fierce need to reveal the crime and the obstacles he had to overcome in order to reach his audience. In many respects he serves as a classical messenger reciting unfortunate events and catastrophic results. In the way that Shakespeare has arranged the recital, he has clued us to the emphasis he intends at the same time as he takes us up the ladder of anguish to a simple climax. The Ghost reveals his murder, then the identity of the murderer, next—in the longest section—both his dismay at his wife's infidelity and the way the murder was accomplished, and ends with a demand that Hamlet avenge him by punishing the murderer but sparing the wife-mother. The Ghost's speeches thus follow the sequence of first revealing the two major facts (Shakespeare gives this information quickly), then depicting the response to the facts as details are sketched in, and finally setting a task to be drawn from the revelation. In the course of these speeches we, the audience, learn necessary expository material but in a manner that stresses the fall from the ideal to the grotesque. The charge to Hamlet is for him, as a man, to punish Claudius but for heaven and not man to punish Gertrude. It is a double-edged, essentially contradictory charge that imposes a paradoxic demand upon Hamlet, a condition evident to the playgoers if they recall his opening soliloquy expressing horror of his mother's marriage to his uncle.

The second telling, in the form of the dumb show, is oddly enough the most comprehensive. Like the first telling, it involves the three principal figures: King, wife, and poisoner. Unlike the first, this recital treats the relation of King and wife more fully. Not only the murder but even more so the wife's initial affection and ultimate betrayal are presented. For us as readers only the outlines of the story emerge from the dumb show. We have no precise way of knowing how the actors played it, whether, for instance, their style of performance in the dumb show differed from their style in the rest of the play. We can assume, however, that the inclusion of the dumb show is purposeful and that therefore a connection exists between its inclusion and its rendition. Without attempting to resolve the dispute over what that purpose was, we can still guess at several possible effects. Like the Ghost's recital, the dumb show also has two audiences. Of those among the on-stage audience, we know Ophelia sees the dumb show and is puzzled by it. We have no direct evidence that Claudius sees it. Verisimilitude suggests he does not. Dramatic construction would argue that he does, that indeed he suspects the intent toward which the mime is pointed, and steels himself to withstand the covert accusation. In this interpretation the dumb show has a complex and significant effect upon the "stage audience."

But we must also assume that the dumb show has something to tell us, the actual audience. We already know all the essential facts of the story so that the informational value is secondary. This version does, of course, direct our attention to the importance of the Queen's role in the events, making clear that Hamlet considers her an implicit rather than an explicit accomplice. More than that, though, the dumb show gives us a full account of the play to be presented so that we can learn precisely how Hamlet has mounted his attack upon Claudius. According to the way it is performed, the dumb show also characterizes the quality of that attack. Too often, unfortunately, productions of this scene utilize a quaint or deliberately theatric style, thereby stressing the histrionic rather than psychological quality of the action. In doing so, such renditions tend to trivialize a statement that has a deadly yet ambivalent aim.

The third and last telling is, on the contrary, deliberately archaic. At least the language is. Not only in comparison to the surrounding verse but in contrast to the verse used in the Pyrrhus speeches, the poetry of the play-within-the-play is ostentatiously patterned and ceremonial. No longer is the main intent of the recital the provision of information, either to the on-stage or to the off-stage audience. Instead, the performance is a testing. Its archaic form emblematizes the relationship of the Player King and Player Queen. They are consecrated as an icon of professed devotion. By adopting this style, Shakespeare deliberately shifts our attention from the interplay between the Player King and Queen to the impact these two have upon the real King and Queen. In this telling, the event that was so much in the forefront of the Ghost's story, the murder itself, is hurriedly enacted as Hamlet propels it with his insistent commentary until he forces Claudius to lose control.

From these three versions we can see that the raw material of narrative which Shakespeare uses in each instance is much the same. How he uses it and what form it assumes differ considerably. Moreover, the impact upon us as upon Claudius is a consequence not merely of the facts but of the shaping of the facts. Two interconnected factors operate in determining the dramatic features of these scenes. In a very general way, the differing context of each telling helps to fix the possible effect it may have. The initial appearances of the Ghost, the awesome puzzle of his presence, and the frantic chase over the battlements all build melodramatically to the revelation itself. Thus, we the audience along with Hamlet are brought to hear the Ghost's tale in a heightened state. The preparatory sequence of excitation serves as a ground for the unfolding story, a quite different ground from the anticipatory but still preliminary phase of Hamlet's plot evident in the dumb show. In each case the context provides a frame of possibilities within which the situation can unfold. All three versions share two common contexts: the story of the King's murder and its telling to an audience-within-an-audience. They also differ in their contexts: in respect to the point in *Hamlet* when they are introduced and in respect to the forms through which they are expressed.

The frame thus established by the context sets the scene's

limits. Its dramatic character is the result partly of the activity chosen by the dramatist in each instance and partly of the way that activity is shaped. It is evident from the second telling through dumb show that each activity offers possibilities but also has limitations. The dumb show permits Shakespeare to sketch the broad outlines of the entire history of the murder and subsequent wooing. Messengers' speeches, on the other hand, traditionally afford time for the expression of a messenger's feelings and therefore its use in *Hamlet* provides an outlet for the Ghost's anguish. How Shakespeare modulates each of these activities finally determines the artistic form that emerges.

Before attempting to delineate that artistic form further, I should like to make some general observations about the perception of Shakespeare's dramaturgy. Having three versions of one event, as we have in *Hamlet,* facilitates the recognition of Shakespeare's theatrical strategy. One treatment helps illuminate another. Through comparing the various tellings we can readily see the relation of story to dramatic realization as well as the connection between the form of that realization and audience response. But what is relatively easy to discern when contemplating three versions is not so perceptible when reading or studying an individual scene. Our own habits of thought as well as the inherent nature of the dramatic medium pose problems.

In trying to teach or study the distinctively dramaturgic features of Shakespeare's work, we encounter four impediments. First, we find it difficult to isolate the exclusively dramatic elements of a play. Traditionally, we are accustomed to discussing theme, by which term we sometimes mean topic, sometimes concept. We gravitate easily to the analysis of trope, imagery, and diction. We are ready to interpret a Shakespearean work by the light of psychoanalysis or theology. We can even read character without the restraints of context, abstracting the total being from the stage play so that the personality transcends its medium.

But when we come to deal with what we consider to be the characteristic dramaturgic features of Shakespeare's plays, we do not exhibit so sure a touch.

One way we try to deal with the drama is through imagining or reconstructing its staging. By clothing the words in sound and movement, we feel that we are taking a step from literature to theater. And in part we are doing so, because we are placing ourselves in a position where, supposedly, we have to grapple with the vagaries of drama. But being in a position to deal with a problem does not itself mean that we actually deal with it. Performing, itself, does not guarantee that we shall either recognize or realize the dramatic form inherent in the text. Indeed, strong feeling exists among many theater directors that the text is merely a point of departure for the creation of a new event, that there is no *a priori* form beyond what is currently performed. My argument is quite contrary. The shape of a potential event inheres in the text. A director may choose to alter that shape, but he cannot assume that it does not exist. In my opinion, engagement in theatrical performance, whether as student, actor, or playgoer, is a necessary adjunct to but no sufficient substitute for a critical understanding of dramaturgic behavior.

To gain that critical understanding, we must recognize the dramatic object. It is not the narrative. Narrative is not exclusive to drama, but shared by romance and epic, history and cinema. Episode or incident is also shared by more than one medium. It is when we come to enacted incident that we begin to focus on drama. And it is when we concentrate on the distinctive style and form with which the incident is elaborated or structured that we begin to attend to the aesthetic of drama. Form is embedded in a Shakespearean text and though it permits, even more invites, variation, it also has a primary integrity of its own.

One of our difficulties in recognizing the dramatic element—perhaps our greatest difficulty—is our failure to distinguish the subject of an incident from its dramatic rendition. Even those critics who are especially concerned with Shakespeare's dramatic artistry have this problem. One of the most recent—and effective—of these critics, Emrys Jones, illuminates Shakespeare's craftsmanship by comparing parallel incidents from early and late plays. Yet even as he does so, he tends to rely on similarity of subject matter as the basis for comparison. This method is especially evident in his comparison of two son-mother scenes: Hamlet and Gertrude (*Hamlet* III.iv) and the Bastard and Lady Faulconbridge (*King John* I.i). Whatever differences there are in the two scenes are discussed in relation to poetic expression rather than dramatic development or quality.[1] What is ignored or, more correctly, not perceived, is that the incidents have similarities in subject matter but not in dramatic activity or in shape of that activity. As a result the critic reaches questionable conclusions about Shakespeare's craftsmanship and intent.

The second impediment is a partner to the first. It is the inability to perceive movement behind language. Since the drama is essentially dialectic, it relies on contrasting impulses. To distinguish these impulses, we have to pay attention not only to what a line of Shakespeare means or how it is delivered but even more to the impulses that pass between one line and the next and ultimately to the pattern of impulses coursing through a scene. In the Ghost's tale the initial revelations of fact serve as background for the pain and horror experienced by the Ghost as he remembers Gertrude's postmortem desertion and then his fatal nap in the orchard. The words and images of his report are the surface manifestation for the remembered anguish that he relives and which mounts in intensity until the scene reaches a climax, not in the specter's words but in Hamlet's cry:

> O, horrible, O, horrible, most horrible!
> (I.v.80)

[1] Emrys Jones, *Scenic Form in Shakespeare* (Oxford: Clarendon, 1971), p. 101.

In that cry Hamlet assimilates his father's pain. The words, in themselves, are undistinguished. Yet coming as they do at the crux of the Ghost's reaction, they express the deepest revulsion at the same time as they mark an end of the reaction to what has passed. They are followed by directions for the future. The Ghost has successfully transferred the burden of revenge from himself to his son. A careful examination of the dynamics of the Ghost-Hamlet scene reveals how artfully Shakespeare has shaped the action by alternating active reports or injunctions with revelations of reactive states. The final, specific charge to Hamlet thus comes at the culminating point of the preceding intensification and clearly encapsulates the paradoxic action Hamlet will pursue throughout the rest of the play. On stage this dynamic quality of drama is conveyed to us directly through the performers' presence and enactment. This same quality also inheres in the text, is intimated by it, and remains to be discerned by us.

When we read a play for the first time, especially if we are unused to reading plays, we find it difficult to be fully aware of its dynamic movement. It is even more difficult to cultivate that awareness in reading Shakespeare's plays. The words are unfamiliar for one thing. For another, the plays are so rich in variety of impulses that readers have problems distinguishing the primary dramatic movements from the secondary. I would call the Ghost's compulsion to tell his tale before dawn the ground of the primary movement. That movement itself lies in the alternation between telling the facts and revealing inner distress, with the latter action becoming increasingly dominant until Hamlet shares that distress in his climactic cry of "O, horrible!" The subsequent setting of limits to the act of revenge is accompanied by a reduction of emotional intensification. This broad pattern has secondary impulses such as the Ghost's repeated challenge to Hamlet: "If thou didst ever thy dear father love," ". . . duller shouldst thou be . . . wouldst thou not stir in this," and "If thou hast nature in thee . . ." (I.v.23,

32-34, 81). Such secondary impulses function within the context of the primary movement of a scene—what followers of Stanislavsky sometimes call the spine of a scene—but it is the primary line that determines the dramatic shape. The Ghost-Hamlet scene thus relies on the activity of the messenger's report. It is unusual in that the locus from which the messenger comes and the locus where the reported act occurred are not the same. This unusual feature allows for a more complex reactiveness on the Ghost's part as he elaborates the report itself.

In defining the primary movement of an incident, I do not mean to suggest that there is only one possible interpretation of a scene. Exactly what emphasis the reader or actor is to give the Ghost's emotional state depends on one's temperament or outlook. Is the Ghost spiteful? Does he recall his wife's remarriage with hate or with sadness? These questions are open to interpretation. But however they are answered, each reader and actor must still deal with the sequence Shakespeare chose in revealing the fratricide and the way that sequence moves to the particular limitation set upon the punishment of Gertrude. That is why appreciating the dialectic of a Shakespearean scene requires a niceness of perception so that we can distinguish between the central scheme in a dramatic movement and the variations organically suggested by that scheme.

In trying to cultivate this discernment, we encounter the third impediment. As a literary document the Shakespearean play has a richness and therefore an autonomy of its own. As a theater text, on the other hand, it requires enactment. Unfortunately, performances of plays being studied are not always available. Too often students have no idea how a play appears on stage. As a result, teachers of Shakespeare face a serious problem in providing concrete theatrical illustration of comments they may make about a play. By contrast, teachers of music have at hand recordings of the best musicians. In addition, they themselves can usually illuminate a point by using the piano. Theoretically, teachers of Shakespare have the same resources. They too can play recordings or read a scene aloud. But Shakespeare recordings do not bear the same proximity to the plays that musical recordings bear to the actual performance of a score. And teachers are seldom skilled enough to illustrate their remarks through comparative readings of their own. It is true, the teacher can utilize class members to perform scenes, and there is considerable value to be gained by the student actor's effort to perform the text. In the main, however, it takes highly skilled actors to illustrate Shakespeare's drama effectively.

The availability of oral or visual examples of the text in itself does not assure critical understanding. It is the way the examples are used and the critical apparatus brought to bear that counts. Actually, the development of adequate means for illustrating the text must go hand in hand with the cultivation of awareness of dramatic movement. The awareness stimulates the need for more refined examples. The availability of refined examples sharpens the awareness. Ultimately, however, recordings, films, and playgoing are only as good as the teacher who uses them.

The fourth and last impediment is the absence of a satisfactory vocabulary with which to talk about the drama. Without a vocabulary it is difficult to identify the recurrent elements in Shakespeare's scenes. Happily, some rudimentary work in identifying the elements is occurring. Such studies as Wolfgang Clemen's *Shakespeare's Dramatic Art* and Robert Y. Turner's *Shakespeare's Apprenticeship*, for example, help us identify the parts of plays with similar activities: messenger scenes, confrontations, persuasions, etc. Increasing sensitivity to these scene types is an important first step to understanding their inner dynamics. In order to go beyond this preliminary typology, however, we need to utilize terms that enable us to distinguish the constituent energies in a scene. I will cite one term as an example.

A key concept in the dialectic of drama is resistance. For an impulse to be communicated its counterforce must be suggested. Shakespeare often commences a scene by having a character begin a mid-speech entry arguing against an implied resistance. Roderigo's "Tush, never tell me!" that opens *Othello* is a clear example of a line that is itself a resistance to Iago's unheard but implied urging. As Shaw commented in his preface to *Mrs. Warren's Profession*, it is the "very resistance of fact and law to human feeling which creates drama."[2] In each of the various tellings of the elder Hamlet's murder, the resistance has a different quality. The Ghost faces an external resistance, the need to finish his message to Hamlet before dawn. An analogous, but more central resistance is the cosmic prohibition against revealing the details of his torment. Both are concrete resistances that accentuate the Ghost's need to gain Hamlet's aid. In the dumb show the strongest and most significant resistance is produced by the miming Queen, first in her protestation of her love and then in her seeming to be "harsh and unwilling awhile" (stage direction, III.ii.135) when the Poisoner woos her. During the play-within-the-play sequence, the resistance shifts from the performance of *The Murder of Gonzago* partly to Gertrude's disapproval of the Queen's protestation but mainly to Claudius' attempt to retain his self-control. These contrasting resistances of King and Queen give us a clue to the split concern of Hamlet and the difficulty he has in obeying the double-edged charge of the Ghost.

As I have already observed, the four impediments are interdependent. They all have to be overcome simultaneously if we are to develop the sharper perception we need to articulate the dramatic movement in Shakespeare. It is, of course, this sharper perception that is our goal. The result of a more exact description of the dramatic movement is the ability to connect the artistic form of a play to its larger implications. In order to achieve this kind of critical understanding, we need the same kind of compara-

[2] George Bernard Shaw, preface, to *Mrs. Warren's Profession*, in *The Bodley Head Bernard Shaw* (London: Bodley Head, 1970), I, 251.

tive material that is available to us in *Hamlet*. We have to
see how Shakespeare plays one scene against another within
a single play, how he treats analogous scenes in different
plays, and indeed how he compares to other playwrights
of his day in the handling of similar material. Through such
comparative reading we can sharpen our sense of Shakespeare's drama and overcome the lack of critical tools that
now limits us.

ANNOTATED BIBLIOGRAPHY

ANDREW M. McLEAN

THE essays in this volume, and those mentioned below, make it clear that there is no single or best way to teach Shakespeare. The problems teachers have presenting Shakespeare in the schools are similar to the problems encountered by the college professor teaching a sophomore Shakespeare class. Recent workshops have indicated that when teacher and professor come together to discuss the teaching of Shakespeare, they realize how many pedagogical problems they have in common. The following selected bibliography, which supplements my checklist in the *Shakespeare Newsletter* 25 (April 1975), brings together various approaches and methods which have been tried in the school and university.

Albert, Richard N. "An Annotated Guide to Audio-Visual Material for Teaching Shakespare," *EJ* 54 (November 1965), 704-715. Reprinted by NCTE with index of producers and distributors.

Alvarez, A. "How to Read a Poem (III). Shakespeare's *The Phoenix and the Turtle*," *Mandrake* 2 (Autumn & Winter 1955-56), 395-408.

Anderegg, Michael A. "Shakespeare on Film in the Classroom," *L/FQ* 4 (Spring 1976), 165-175.

Andrews, Tom, and Jan Austell. "Who Are These People?" *Media and Methods* 5 (1968), 27-29, 35. Contends that students viewing Zeffirelli's film become more involved in the text of *RJ*.

Atthill, Robin. "Set Books: XII: *2 Henry 4*," *Use of English* 9 (Summer 1958), 253-258. Presents teaching *2H4* in correct perspective (which requires some knowledge of *1H4*, *H5*).

Barber, C. L. "On the Use of Talking Passages," *SNL* 25 (April 1975), 11. Considers "how quotation, reading from the text, can best counter tendencies toward empty abstraction."

Barnes, T. R. "Set Books: XI. *JC*," *Use of English* 8 (Summer 1957), 233-236. Questions whether "What is this play about?" is as valid a beginning as asking "How much of this play can this particular class be expected to understand, and what aspect of it will, for a start, appeal to them?"

Barry, Jackson G. "Shakespeare with Words: The Script and the Medium of Drama," *SQ* 25 (Spring 1974), 161-171. Places emphasis on how "the scenes and its speeches are created out of the possibilities provided by a stage and actors."

Bender, Robert M. "Shakespeare Illustrated: A Report on Some Recent Experiments in Teaching," *SNL* 25 (April 1975), 20. Advocates use of media, especially of slides (including over 800 of an entire production of *TN*), synchronized with a professional recording of the play.

Berkeley, David S. *A Guide to Shakespeare's Comedies and Histories*. Stillwater: Oklahoma State University Bookstore Press, 1964. Lists questions on plays for students to answer. There is a separately published *KEY* providing answers.

—————. *A Guide to Shakespearean Tragedy*. Stillwater: Oklahoma State University Bookstore Press, 1960. Contains study questions on *RJ, JC, Ham, Mac, Lear, Oth*, and *AC* in addition to general information on tragedy. There is also a *KEY* (1961) to the answers available.

Berkelman, Robert. "The Drama in Shakespeare's Sonnets," *CE* 10 (December 1948), 138-141. Suggests we should think of the sonnets as "marvelously condensed dramas," especially sonnets 129, 144, 30, 73, and 146.

—————. "Teaching *H5*," *CE* 13 (November 1951), 94-99. Points out difference between jingoism of portions of *H5* and the muted power of Gaunt's tribute to England in *R2*.

Berman, Ronald. *A Reader's Guide to Shakespeare's Plays*. Glenview, Ill.: Scott, Foresman & Co., 1973, rev. ed. Provides a "descriptive bibliography" of prime importance.

Blinderman, Abraham. "I Actually Know Not Too Much on Shakespeare," *CE* 37 (December 1975), 353-357. Comments on student response to three questions about what they know about or have read by Shakespeare.

Bonjour, Adrien. *The Structure of JC*. Liverpool, 1958. Offers a valuable detailed reading of *JC*.

Bose, Amalendu. "Teaching of Shakespeare," *Indian Literature* 9, no. 2 (1966), 77-84. Argues that teachers must generate in a student's mind a sense of the drama of the work—to counter lack of available theater.

Bowden, William R. "Teaching Structure in Shakespeare: *1H4, TN, Ham*," *CE* 23 (April 1962), 525-531. Conveys sense of structure with analysis by means of parallel columns which give students whole perspective of the play and a sense of the skill with which dramatist manipulates multiple plot. Outlines three plays.

Bridge, G. F. "Shakespeare in Schools," *Journal of Education* 68 (London: August 1936), 525-528. Advocates teaching pupils from cut versions.

Brown, J. R., ed. *Shakespeare in Performance: An Introduction Through Six Major Plays*. New York: Harcourt, Brace Jovanovich, 1976. Presents texts in center column, with gloss on right and a running theatrical commentary on left.

Calitri, Charles. "*Mac* and the Reluctant Reader," *EJ* 48 (1959), 254-261. Argues that Shakespeare must be presented to the reluctant reader in familiar terms.

Camp, Gerald M. "Shakespeare on Film," *Journal of Aesthetic Education* 3 (1969), 107-120.

Chapman, Frank. "*1 Henry 4*," *Use of English* 5 (1953), 12-15. Summarizes for teaching purposes the approach of L. C. Knights to the play.

Clark, William R. "Poems for Study: Sonnet 116," *Clearing House* 34 (January 1960), 316. Gives short explication.

Clayton, Thomas. "How Many Beds Did Shakespeare Share?: Lexis, Praxis, Opsis and The Teaching of Shakespearean Drama," *SNL* 23 (April 1973), 12. Suggests differences in teaching-emphasis of how plays are presented "through words (lexis) as through the action (praxis) and its incorporation in vary[ing] spectacle (opsis) implied by the words and the very design of plays."

Clemen, Wolfgang. *A Commentary on Shakespeare's Richard III*. London: Methuen, 1968. Gives excellent scene-by-scene commentary.

Cleve, Charles Fowler Van. *The Teaching of Shakespeare in American Secondary Schools: A Survey of Methods Employed by 363 Superior Teachers* (1962). Indiana Council of Teachers of English, Research Study no. 1, 1970. Reports on ten of the most used techniques: six are teacher-initiated, the remainder are pupil activities.

Cohen, Lauren W. "*RJ*: Living Is Being Relevant," *EJ* 59 (December 1970), 1263-1265; 1269. Teaches play to tenth grade in all-black inner-city public school.

Colijn, I. *An Introduction to Shakespeare: For Secondary Schools*, Zutphen: Thieme, 1958.

Crompton, Donald W. "Shakespeare in the Sixth Form: The Problem of Modern Criticism," *Use of English* 10 (Spring 1959), 171-180. Contends modern critics have made Shakespeare more difficult:

   1) by demanding much closer study of the poetry as poetry;

2) by talking in terms of abstract associations rather than in terms of concrete characteristics;

3) by virtually demanding that *all* the plays be read if one is to appreciate fully the Shakespearean experience.

Crompton, Louis. "Literature and Our Gay Minority," *Iowa English Bulletin* Yearbook (Fall 1973), 11-13. Uses Shakespeare's *Sonn.* as illustration of classroom attitudes toward literature.

Dachslager, E. L. "On Teaching *Ham*," *CEA Critic* 33 (1971), 8-11. Gives students awareness of the quality of the play which makes it difficult—if not impossible—to teach.

Danker, Frederick E. "Composition Themes from *Hamlet*," *EJ* 51 (November 1962), 571-573.

Davies, Derek J. "Getting Shakespeare Taped," *Use of English* 7 (Spring 1956), 184-188. Suggests teacher tape recording of play, tailored to class needs.

Davis, Jack M. and J. E. Grant. "A Critical Dialogue on Shakespeare's Sonnet 71," *Texas Studies in Literature & Language* 1 (1959), 214-232. Uses Shakespeare's sonnet to illustrate a variety of critical approaches.

Devine, Mary E. and Constance M. Clark. "The Stanislavski System as a Tool for Teaching Dramatic Literature," *CE* 38 (September 1976), 15-24. Asks students to write a Stanislavskian analysis of character; uses *Ado* to illustrate.

Dietrich, Daniel J. "An ERIC/RC5 Review: On Teaching Shakespeare," *The Leaflet* 72 (May 1973), 31-34. Provides a brief review of 14 books or essays.

Donne: 1967-71; Steinbeck: 1962-71; Shakespeare: Films and Recordings. Two Author Bibliographies and an Audio-Visual Checklist. San Angelo, Tex.: Angelo State University, 1972. Furnishes a checklist of Shakespeare films and recordings with rental and purchase sources.

Duke, Charles R. "Shakespearean Drama," in *Creative Approaches To The Teaching Of English*, ed. R. Barid Shuman. Ithaca, Ill.: Peacock, 1974, pp. 63-71. Discusses problems students have with Shakespeare's language and background. Bibliography and audio-visual resources listed.

Duncan, Charles F. Jr. "A Blackboard Model of Shakespearean Irony," *CE* 34 (March 1973), 791-795. Diagrams ironies useful to teachers of Shakespeare.

Dunning, Stephen. *Teaching Literature to Adolescents: Poetry.* Glenview, Ill.: Scott, Foresman & Co., 1966, 66-69. Examines Sonnet 73 for "Skeleton statements" of meaning in the sonnets.

Eagleson, R. D. "Propertied as all the tuned speres": Aspects of Shakespeare's Language," *Teaching of English* 20 (1971), 4-15.

Eaves, Morris. "The Real Thing: A Plan for Producing Shakespeare in the Classroom," *CE* 31 (February 1970), 463-472. Restages college freshman production from *1H4* and *TN*.

Eckert, Charles, ed. *Focus on Shakespearean Films.* Englewood Cliffs, N.J.: Prentice-Hall, 1972. Contains an excellent filmography and annotated bibliography.

Elliott, G. R. *Dramatic Providence in "Macbeth": A Study of Shakespeare's Tragic Theme of Humanity and Grace.* Princeton: Princeton University Press, 1958. Gives scene-by-scene analysis and focuses on how dramatic tension is achieved in the play.

Emslie, MacDonald. "*Ham* & Hamilton," *English Language Teaching* 23 (1969), 289-298. Enlivens *Ham* for first-year university students.

————. "Set Books: VI. *AYL*," *Use of English* 6 (Winter 1954), 99-104. Contends: "What the play has to say is to be found in the way 'characters' move from one world to another within the play, in the way they behave in these different worlds, and in the remarks which relate one world to another."

Enright, D. J. *Shakespeare and the Students.* New York: Schocken, 1970. Discusses *Lear, AC, Mac* and *WT* as "plays about people" with scene-by-scene analysis growing out of author's teaching experiences.

Evans, Bertrand. *Teaching Shakespeare in the High School.* New York: Macmillan, 1966. Defends choice of Shakespearean plays for study (Chapters 1-8) and discusses best method for presentation and which editions to use. Gives notes on teaching fourteen plays (Chapters 9-11) and discusses teaching the sonnets (Chapter 12). A controversial book; see rev. by G. Veidemans, *EJ* 56 (April 1967), 626-628.

Fagin, N. Bryllion. "Segregated Shakespeare," *Commonweal* 71 (1960), 591-592. Considers problems of teaching Shakespeare to black college students in the segregated South.

Felsher, Roy L. "Two Shakespearean History Plays/Grade 9: *R3, H5*," in *Teaching Literature in Grades Seven through Nine*, ed. Edward B. Jenkinson and Jane Stouder Hawley. Bloomington: Indiana University Press, 1967, 117-143. Provides excellent discussions.

Focus: Teaching English in Southeastern Ohio 2 (Spring 1976): Teaching Shakespeare issue, ed. James E. Davis.

Geduld, Harry M. *Filmguide to Henry V.* Bloomington: Indiana University Press, 1973. Outlines the film and gives useful information concerning production. See review by A. McLean in *L/FQ* I (Fall 1973), 377-380.

ANDREW M. McLEAN

Gillie, Christopher. "The Tempest," *Use of English* 7 (1955), 37-41. Warns against approaching play only as allegory or fairy story with good poetry; recognizes that the "unreality" of the play is found in the place (magical island) and in the magicianship of Prospero and Ariel.

———. "*TN*," *Use of English* 4 (Spring 1953), 136-140. Argues that *TN*, commonly regarded as a safe introduction to Shakespeare, is more complex and interesting than is usually recognized.

Goldstone, Richard H. "Experiments with Audio-Visual Aids: I. In Teaching Shakespeare," 13 (1952), 319-322. Describes use of Verdi's *Otello* in teaching Shakespeare's play to college sophomores.

Griffin, Alice. *Rebels and Lovers: Shakespeare's Young Heroes and Heroines: A New Approach to Acting and Teaching.* New York: New York University Press, 1976. Edits *MND*, *RJ*, *1H4*, *Ham* following original punctuation of Quartos in order to restore proper reading of the text "by defining blocks of thought as well as by indicating tempo and cadence."

Halio, Jay L. "Essential *Hamlet*," *College Literature* 1 (1974), 83-99. Argues that the complex, even contradictory movements of the play must be preserved.

Hanke, Jeanette J. "*Romeo & Juliet* and the Disadvantaged," *EJ* 59 (February 1970), 273-276. Involves small groups of students enacting and discussing scenes.

Harrison, G. B. "The Teaching of Shakespeare," *EJ* 52 (September 1963), 411-419. Approaches the play in terms of Shakespeare's craftsmanship with emphasis on the plot, characterization, and diction.

Hayden, Howard. *The Immortal Memory: A New Approach to the Teaching of Shakespeare.* London: Dent, 1936. Pp. viii, 87. Presents "a living picture of Shakespeare" for teaching of pupils between 14-16 years old the "dramatic form" worded within episodes from Shakespearean plays. Suggests that "first each scene should be treated as a form-room play to be produced as simply or as elaborately as may be convenient." Also contains suggestions for "follow-up" lessons.

Hedberg, Johannes. "Enjoying a Shakespeare Sonnet in Class," *Moderna Språk* 59 (1965), 5-10. Vitalizes the Shakespearean poem by cutting away the "boils and abscesses."

Hellenga, Robert A. "*Hamlet* in the Classroom," *CE* 35 (1973), 32-39. Invites student and teacher to explore play together.

Hill, Alma Blinn. "Hamlet as an Undergraduate," *CE* 36 (1974), 122-125. Comments on R. Hellenga's discussion of *Ham* in the classroom.

322

Hill, Knox C. "Drama and Fiction," in *Interpreting Literature.* Chicago: University of Chicago Press, 1966, pp. 51-98. Suggests procedures reader may profitably follow in studying *Mac.*

Hinman, Myra. "Teaching *1H4* to Beginning College Students," *SQ* 25 (Spring 1974), 153-160. Recommends reading *1H4* first for plot and character, and provides emotional and atmospheric cues to the play.

Hodgins, Frank and Audrey. "Teaching Guide for *R3*," *EJ* 45 (1956) 138-140, 144.

Hoetker, James, and Alan Englseman. *Shakespeare's Julius Caesar: The Initial Classroom Presentation. An Introduction to Theatre.* Vol. 2, rev. ed. St. Ann, Miss.: Central Midwestern Regional Educational Library, 1969.

Holland, Norman N. "*JC*: A Close Reading," in *Steps to Reading Literature 1*, ed. B. Spacks et al. New York: Harcourt, Brace & World, 1964, pp. 101-150. (Accompanies *Adventure to Appreciation.*) Presents four units for programmed instruction for grades 10-12, and gives "summing up" suggestions for discussion and composition.

Holt, B. E. "A Modular Approach for Teaching Classical Literature in Inner-City High Schools," *DA* 36 (1975), 3355A-3356A. Offers strategy to teach *Hamlet*, among other "classics," to students who read several years below grade level but are otherwise normally intelligent.

Homan, Sidney. "A Cinema for Shakespeare," *L/FQ* 4 (Spring 1976), 176-186. Explores unanswered questions about Shakespeare on film.

Hook, Frank S. "So You're Going to Teach Shakespeare?" *EJ* 56 (November 1967), 1120-1126, 1205. Contends: "If a teacher is to get student response to the majesty and passion of Shakespeare's world, then the teacher must remove historical barriers through informed study."

Howes, Alan B. *Teaching Literature to Adolescents: Plays.* Glenview, Ill.: Scott, Foresman & Co., 1968, pp. 35-73. Offers excellent suggestions for teaching *JC* (pp. 35-39), *Ham* (pp. 49-54), *1H4* (pp. 57-61) and *Mac* (pp. 65-73).

Hudson, Arthur K. *Shakespeare and the Classroom.* London: Heinemann (1954) 1966. Pp. xii, 116. Compiled for the Society for Teachers of English. Argues Shakespeare should be stage centered for school children. Audio-visual listing, pp. 108-112.

Jackson, Elizabeth. "The Kittredge Way," *CE* 4 (May 1943), 483-487. Summarizes teaching method of George L. Kittredge.

ANDREW M. McLEAN

Jacobs, Elizabeth R. "Shakespeare without Tears," *CE* 15 (March 1954), 347-348. Suggests that the more "academic" the approach to Shakespeare, the more successful the college course in preparing secondary school teachers.

Jamison, William A. "The Case for a Complete Shakespeare," *SQ* 25 (Spring 1974), 258-259. Reports on teaching all the plays over a two-term period, allowing sophomore students exposure to the context of the Shakespeare canon.

Jones, Patricia. "A Slanguage of Shakespeare," *Clearing House* 39 (December 1964), 247-249. Suggests teenage slang can be used to overcome language difficulties in *AYL*.

Jones, William M. "Teaching Shakespeare's Insubstantial Pageant," *English Record* 21 (1970), 4-10. Recommends emphasis on the Elizabethan imagination, the "setting by sensation" which provides dramatic compression, and costuming.

Jones, Whitney, ed. *New Approaches to Shakespeare in the Classroom: A Workshop for High School English Teachers.* Laurinburg, N.C.: St. Andrews College, 1975. Digests workshop; see *SNL* 25 (April 1975), 12.

Jorgens, Jack L. "A Course in Shakespeare on Film," *SNL* 23 (November 1973), 43.

———. *Shakespeare on Film.* Bloomington: Indiana University Press, 1976. Details sixteen major films; an appendix provides credits and outlines of the major films.

———. "Shakespeare on Film: A Selected Checklist," *L/FQ* 4 (Spring 1976), 191-193.

Joseph, Bertram, "The Problem of Bradley," *Use of English* 5 (1953), 87-91. Commends Bradley's "character" approach as eminently teachable and satisfying.

Kiley, Frederick S. "Fate's Midnight: A Teaching Guide for *Macbeth,*" *EJ* 49 (February 1960), 589-592. Assesses T.V. production of *Mac* featuring Maurice Evans and Judith Anderson and furnishes six questions for discussion.

———. "Teaching Guide for *The Tempest,*" *EJ* 49 (1960), 341-350.

———. "Teaching Guide for *TN,*" *EJ* 46 (1957), 582-585. Reviews William Nichols' T.V. adaptation, starring Maurice Evans, and offers "Topics for Discussion."

Knapp, Peggy Ann. " 'Stay Illusion,' or How to Teach *Hamlet,*" *CE* 36 (September 1974), 75-85. Presents arguments of contrary scholarship to enrich student understanding of the play.

Knights, L. C. "The Teaching of Shakespeare," *Use of English* 19 (Autumn 1967), 3-16; reprinted in *Stratford Papers 1965-1967,* ed. B.A.W. Jackson. Hamilton, Ont.: McMaster University Library Press. Shannon: Irish University Press, 1969, pp. 1-20.

Addresses poetry and the formal structure of Shakespeare's plays.

Kozelka, Paul. "A Guide to the Screen Version of Shakespeare's (and Orson Welles's) *Othello*," *Audio-Visual Guide* 22 (October 1955), 31-40.

———. "A Guide to the Screen Version of Shakespeare's (and Olivier's) *R3*," *Audio-Visual Guide* 22 (April 1956), 51-57.

Leas, Susan E. "Richard III, Shakespeare and History," *EJ* 60 (December 1971), 1214-1216, 1296. Explores the writing of history in regard to *R3* as way of preparing to read play.

Lederer, Richard H. "*JC*: An Approach to the Teaching of Drama," *English Leaflet* 64, no. 1 (1965), 13-18. Demonstrates selective process by comparing *JC* with source in Plutarch.

Leeb, David. *Permanent Key-Indexed Study Guide to Shakespeare's JC*. New York: Research Associates Inc. of America & Bantam Books, 1966.

Levin, Harry. *Shakespeare and the Revolution of the Times: Perspectives and Commentaries*. New York: Oxford University Press, 1976. Discusses Kittredge's teaching methods as well as his own (Introduction).

Lewin, William. "Guide to the Technicolor Screen Version of Castellani's *RJ*," *Audio-Visual Guide* 21 (December 1954), 19-28.

Lewis, Roger, "An Approach to *Hamlet* with College Students," *Use of English* 25 (1973), 21-26. Describes a student production aimed at involving the audience in a discussion of the play after its showing and assesses what they learned in the process.

L/FQ 1 (Fall 1973) and 4 (Spring 1976). Furnishes essays on various film adaptations.

Lytle, Clyde F. "The Effectiveness of Stage Presentation as a Supplement to Classroom Instruction in Shakespearean Drama in the Secondary School." Ph.D. Diss., New York University, 1943.

MacFadden, Fred R. "Report on Opportunities for Teaching and Researching the Literature of Shakespeare Using the Computer," *Computer Studies in the Humanities and Verbal Behavior* 4 (1973), 3-8. Lists sixty-eight research projects in Shakespearean stylistics and pedagogy adaptable to some kind of computer processing.

MacIsaac, Warren J. "Viva Voce: On Speaking and Hearing Shakespeare's Sentences," *SQ* 25 (Spring 1974), 172-187. Suggests exercises with Kökeritz's pronunciation records and selections from Houseman-Mankiewicz *JC* film: "A speaking-hearing experience of the plays we teach is of the first importance."

Mack, Maynard. "Teaching Drama: *JC*," in Edward J. Gordon and Edward S. Noyes, eds., *Essays on the Teaching of English*. New York: Appleton-Century-Crofts, 1960, pp. 320-336. Asks "Why?" in the first scene of the first act: in *JC* the first episode "dramatizes instantaneously the oncoming theme of the play: that a man's will is not enough."

MacLean, Hugh. "Shakespeare in the Classroom: Titles and the Text," *English Record* 23 (Fall 1972), 27-33. Emphasizes importance of first teaching the significance of the full titles of Shakespeare's plays.

MacLeish, Archibald. "The Proper Pose of Poetry," *Saturday Review* (5 March 1955), pp. 11-12, 47-49. Analyzes Sonnet 116 to answer the question "What is the language of poetry?"

Maloney, H. "Suggestions for Teaching the Television *Mac*," *Clearing House* 25 (November 1960), 187-188.

———. "Teaching Shakespeare on Film: A Checklist," *Teaching Shakespeare: Ideas for the Classroom* 1 (Fall 1976), 6-8.

Manvell, Roger. *Shakespeare and the Film*. New York: Praeger, 1971. Surveys Shakespearean films, with a bibliography and filmography.

Marder, Louis. "The Responsibility of the Shakespeare Teacher," *Oklahoma English Bulletin* 1 (Fall 1964), 1-7.

———. "Teaching Shakespeare: Is There a Method?" *CE* 25 (April 1964), 479-487. Reprinted in *Shakespeare in School and College*. Urbana, Ill.: NCTE, 1964, pp. 46-54. Posits structural approach as "an interesting and effective way of entering the heart of the play and working through it."

———. "A Working Method for Teaching Shakespeare," *SNL* 25 (April 1975), 10. Uses themes, images, plot, etc. "to get into the plays via the analysis, and illustrate how all the elements illuminate and enhance the play, making it relevant to our lives, more comprehensible, and therefore more pleasurable and edifying." See bibliography in this issue for listing of other pedagogical essays and notes by Marder.

Marsh, Philip M. *How to Teach English in High School and College*. New York: Bookman Associates, 1956. Shows how to teach literature (pp. 77-102); includes mock dialogue of teacher presenting *1H4* (pp. 93-97), suggestions for class play-acting, and a sample Shakespeare test combining the essay and objective test (pp. 97-102).

Mary Cleophas, R.S.M. "Absent Thee from Felicity," *CEA Critic* 27 (October 1964), 1, 4-5, 8. Provides three possible classroom approaches to *Hamlet*.

Matthews, Charles, and Margaret M. Blum. "To the Student of Poetry: An Essay on Essays," *CEA Critic* 35 (1973), 24-27. Uses Sonnet 116 to generate suggestions for students writing essays on poetry.

McDonald, Daniel. "Anyone Can Teach Shakespeare," *Journal of General Education* 22 (October 1970), 187-192. Avoids textual and historical matters, and sticks to discussion of plot, characters, and themes, in the contention that "A good generalistic teacher can indeed teach Shakespeare."

McLean, Andrew M. "Bibliography on Teaching Shakespeare," *SNL* 25 (April 1975), 13-15. Contains over 135 annotated entries.

———. "Shakespeare-Media Symposium," *SNL* 25 (April 1975), 12. Describes workshops on teaching *Hamlet*, the use of film as teaching device, and media materials available to the teacher.

———. "Teaching Shakespeare on Film: A Checklist," *Teaching Shakespeare Newsletter* 1 (Winter 1976).

McNamee, Lawrence F. "New Horizons in the Teaching of Shakespeare," *CE* 23 (April 1962), 583-585. Advocates auditory approach.

Menezes, A. "Has Shakespeare Fallen on Evil Tongues?" *Literary Criterion* 6, no. 1 (Mysore: 1963), 79-85. Describes teaching Shakespeare to college students in India.

———. "Writing Papers for an S/F Course," *Shakespeare on Film Newsletter* 1 (December 1976), 8.

Mersand, Joseph. *Teaching Drama in the Secondary School, 1880-1937.* Metuchen, N.J.: Scarecrow Press, 1969. Contains a useful survey of important educators' suggestions for teaching Shakespeare in the schools.

Meszaros, Patricia K. "Notes on a Workshop Approach to Shakespeare," *SQ* (Spring 1974), 188-197. Convenes students in a rehearsal room to block scenes while listening to a recording.

———. "Prolegomena for a Student's Dramatic Edition of Shakespeare with an Edition of *MND*," *DA* 32 (1971), 3261-A.

Miller, Helen Rand. "*Othello* in a Community College," *EJ* 39 (April 1950), 218-219. Gives composite of student papers and describes experience in teaching *Othello* to college sophomores.

Milward, Peter. "Teaching Shakespeare in Japan," *SQ* 25 (Spring 1974), 228-233.

Mizner, Arthur, ed. *Teaching Shakespeare: A Guide to the Teaching of Mac, JC, MV, Ham, RJ, MND, Oth, AYL, TN, R2, 1H4, Temp.* New York: New American Library, 1969. Equips each play with an introduction and follows with act and scene descriptions to furnish "a discussion that represents as closely as possible the actual teaching of the play."

Morris, Peter. *Shakespeare on Film*. Ottawa: Canadian Film Institute, 1972. Rev. ed. Furnishes annotated filmography of Shakespearean sound films 1929-1971, plus a short essay discussing Shakespearean films, 1889-1971. Reprinted in *Films in Review* 24 (March 1973), 132-163.

Motter, Charlotte Kay. *Theatre in High School: Planning, Teaching, Directing*. Englewood Cliffs, N.J.: Prentice-Hall, 1970. Gives suggestions for presenting Shakespeare on the stage (Chapter 14).

Mroczkowski, P. J. "Comparative Reception of *King Lear*: An Experiment in International Education," *SQ* 25 (Spring 1974), 234-247. Polls responses by Polish, French, and English University students to *Lr*.

Muller-Schwefe, Gerhard. "Shakespeare in der Universität," *Praxis des neusprachlichen Unterrichts* 12 (Dortmund: 1965), 1-7.

Murphy, Geraldine. "Advanced Play Reading: Shakespeare," in *The Study of Literature in High School*. Waltham, Mass.: Blaisdell, 1968, pp. 285-299. Discusses *JC* as entree to Shakespeare.

Neumeyer, Peter F. "Teaching Shakespeare: An Anti-Method," *Clearing House* 38 (April 1964), 478-480. Sets "A smorgasbord of twenty-one approaches for selection by teacher."

Niles, Carl E. "A Study of Factors Influencing Student Attitude toward the Study of Shakespearean Drama," *DA* 32 (July 1971), 309-A-310-A. Ph.D. diss., University of Tennessee. Attempts to discover causes for student apathy toward Shakespeare.

Nye, R. A. "Shakespeare in the Seventies: ERIC Report," *Speech Teacher* 20 (November 1973), 348-355. Reviews twelve works on Shakespeare and Education.

O'Malley, R. "Set Books: VIII. *Macbeth*," *Use of English* 6 (Summer 1955), 230-234. Contends: "With almost any class an *intelligent* interest in the play can soon be created." Includes a list of fifteen points to discuss in III.ii.

Ornstein, Robert. *Shakespeare in the Classroom*. Urbana, Ill.: Educational Illustrators, NCTE, 1960. Furnishes an important discussion of classroom Shakespeare.

———. "Teaching *Ham*," *CE* 25 (April 1964), 502-508. Reprinted in *Shakespeare in School and College*. Urbana, Ill.: NCTE, 1964, pp. 30-36. Surmises that "like Hamlet, we might conclude that our task is not to analyze or dissect but to comprehend—to gain that sense of the whole, which makes so many of the speculations and hypotheses of the past seem irrelevant."

Partridge, Edward. "Re-presenting Shakespeare," *SQ* 25 (Spring 1974), 201-208. Prefers "the sensuality of the theater before the tranquility of the study: students need to interrelate the auditory, the semantic, the architectonic, the choreographic, and scenic elements of a play."

Pennel, Charles A. "On Introducing Shakespeare: *R3*," *CE* 26 (May 1965), 643-645. Takes advantage of beginning with *R3* and the melodrama genre.

Perrine, Laurence. "When Form and Content Kiss/Intention Made the Bliss: The Sonnet in *RJ*," *EJ* 55 (October 1966), 872-874. Shows that I.v provides lines in sonnet pattern which make a good exercise in questions of accident or design.

Poley, Irvin C. "Drama in the Classroom," *EJ* 44 (1957), 148-151. Gives pedagogical hints on the teaching of Shakespeare.

Powell, Neil. "Liking It," *Use of English* 26 (Autumn 1974), 3-8. Represents *AYL* for teaching at 0 level fifth-form boys.

Rao, V. Scrinivasa. "Shakespeare and the Indian Graduate," *Literary Half-Yearly* 1, no. 1 (Bangalore: 1960), 69-70. Appeals for a comparative study of the experience of Shakespeare students throughout India and wherever English is not the mother tongue.

Ratliff, John. "A Shakespearean Bibliography," *Arizona English Bulletin* 7 (1964), 15-19. Contains an annotated bibliography for high school teachers.

Rehfeldt, W. "Die Shakespeare-Lekture im Englischunterricht der Oberschulen," *Fremdsprachenunterricht* 1 (Berlin: 1957), 83-88.

Richmond, Hugh M. "Shakespeare College at Berkeley," *SNL* 25 (April, 1975), 19. Reports on an innovative undergraduate interdisciplinary experiment.

Rodgers, Bertha. "Introducing *JC*," *English Leaflet* 31 (February 1932), 169-171. Argues that teachers should place active responsibility upon students.

Rodgers, William H. *Shakespeare and English History*. Totowa, N.J.: Littlefield, Adams, 1966. Presents synopsis of each play and succinct discussion of the historical facts and Shakespeare's alteration of them.

Roemer, Michael. "Shakespeare on Film: A Filmmaker's View," *SNL* 26 (May 1976), 26. Questions entire concept of films as a means of presenting and teaching Shakespeare.

Rolo, J. C. "Teaching Shakespeare in India," *Literary Criterion* 6 (Mysore: 1963), 75-78. Advocates reading several plays rapidly rather than one or two with pseudo-scholarship.

Rosenheim, Edward W., Jr. "Reading Dramatic Literature," in *What Happens in Literature: A Guide to Poetry, Drama, and Fiction.* Chicago: University of Chicago Press, 1960, pp. 93-124. Concerns *RJ*.

Rostron, David. "Some Approaches to Teaching Shakespeare," *Use of English* 26 (Spring 1975), 222-228. Commends role playing, constructing a scenario, and presents ten approaches to the text.

Rowe, D. F. "Set Books x: *Henry V*," *Use of English* 7 (Winter 1956), 106-110. Provides list of twenty-seven questions for pupils to answer.

Roy, Phil A. "Shakespeare is not Dead! (A High School Semester Course in Shakespeare Studies)," *Arizona English Bulletin* 14 (February 1972), 16-22.

Sargeant, Seymour H. "Julius Caesar and the Historical Film," *EJ* 61 (February 1972), 230-233, 245. Compares Shakespearean dramatic techniques with those of the historical film.

Sauer, E. H. "New Methods of Teaching Shakespeare," *Ohio Schools* 18 (April 1940), 162-163.

Schevill, James. "Bright enigma, all thy puzzles glitter," *Teachers College Record* 65 (April 1964), 591-602. Records species of balance, rhythm, and lyrical technique as illustrated by use of song (*TN*), "poetry of soliloquy" (*Oth V*), and treatment of Falstaff.

Schoenbaum, Samuel. "The Teaching of Shakespeare," *University of Kansas Bulletin of Education* 17 (1963), 108-114. Suggests that American students may enjoy and profit from "the close, rigorous reading of texts" and that English majors should "come to grips with the complexities and obscurities of diction, syntax and allusion."

Shakespeare Newsletter 23 (November 1973): Shakespeare on Film issue.

Shakespeare Newsletter 25 (April 1975): Teaching Shakespeare issue.

Shakespeare on Film Newsletter, ed. B. W. Kilman and K. S. Rothwell. 1 (December 1976).

Shakespeare Quarterly 25 (Spring 1974): Teaching Shakespeare issue.

Shakespeare in School and College. Urbana, Ill.: NCTE, 1964. Collects nine essays from April issues of *CE* and *EJ*. See Marder, Ornstein, and Viedemanis.

BIBLIOGRAPHY

Shand, G. B. "Classroom as Theatre: A Technique for Shakespeare Teachers," *English Quarterly* 8, no. 1-2 (Canada: Spring-Summer 1975), 13-19. Evaluates student acting exercises.

Silber, Joan E. "Cinematic Techniques and Interpretations in Film and Television Adaptations of Shakespeare's *Hamlet*," *DA* 34 (1974), 5370-A. Analyzes five productions made for TV or the cinema.

Simon, Henry W. *The Reading of Shakespeare in American Schools and Colleges: An Historical Survey*. New York: Simon and Schuster, 1932.

――――. "Why Shakespeare?" *EJ* 23 (May 1934), 363-368. Lists "bad" practices in the study of Shakespeare's plays.

Skoller, Donald B. "Problems of Transformation in the Adaptation of Shakespeare's Tragedies from Play-Script to Cinema." Ph.D. diss., New York University, 1968. Studies in sensitive detail the textual and cinematic values of Shakespeare.

Smith, Hallett D. "Teaching Shakespeare's *1H4*," *English Leaflet* 62 (Spring 1962), 7-17. Argues that *1H4* can be taught "to high school students as readily as to college freshmen" and focuses on poetic and comic language found in the play.

Smith, Winifred. "Teaching Shakespeare in the School," *EJ* 11 (June 1922), 361-364. Includes a college teacher's plea for changes in secondary schools' approach to Shakespeare.

Sonntag, Wolfgang. "*Macbeth* in Englischunterricht, Forschung-Methodik-Praxis," *Die neueren Sprachen* (August 1965), pp. 353-368. Suggests method of teaching *Mac* with appropriate questions to elicit student response.

Styan, J. L. "Direct Method Shakespeare," *SQ* 25 (Spring 1974), 198-200. Concedes that classrooms are hardly theaters, but urges active student participation, however imperfect the performance, as better than a stale intellectual approach.

――――. "Shakespeare Teaches Shakespeare," *SNL* 25 (April 1975), 16. Reiterates that "students can learn much from performing bits of the play in class."

Svendsen, Kester. "Formalist Criticism and the Teaching of Shakespeare," *CE* 27 (October 1965), 23-27. Argues for "the primacy of formalist literary theory in teaching Shakespeare to beginners."

Swander, Homer. "Teaching Shakespeare as Performance," *SNL* 25 (April 1975), 19. Prepares students "for those meetings of actors and audiences for which play scripts are written."

Taaffe, James, and John Lincks. "Reading the Poetry of William Shakespeare," in *Reading English Poetry*. New York: Free Press, 1971, pp. 1-15. Comments upon selected sonnets and songs.

331

Taylor, Richard V. *Shakespeare for Secondary Schools.* London: Macmillan, 1961; New York: St. Martin's Press, 1964. (Earlier issued as *Shakespeare for Senior Schools,* 1937.) Includes adaptations of seven plays.

Teaching Shakespeare: Ideas for the Classroom 1 (Fall 1976). Published by Scott, Foresman & Co.

Teaching Shakespeare: Resource Units in Language Arts for Secondary Schools. New York Board of Education of the City of New York, 1970.

Templeton, Robert G. "The Problems of Teaching Shakespeare," *English Leaflet* 48 (1949), 83-109. Presents detailed analysis of M.I.T. reading sessions of *1H4* which used various teaching approaches and devices.

Thomas, Cleveland A. "A Focus for Teaching *Hamlet,*" *EJ* 47 (1958), 8-14, 40. Approaches play as theater to question what weakness in Hamlet's nature contributes to his downfall.

Tough, A. J. "Introducing Shakespeare," *Use of English* 11 (Autumn 1959), 23-25. Begins with blackboard diagram of Shakespearean stage and explains its use and the behavior of spectators, before proceeding to readings.

Tucker, Nicholas. "Shakespeare and Film Technique," *Use of English* 14 (1962), 98-104. Applies film principles (the cut, lighting, camera angle and distance) to teaching Shakespearean play.

Veidemanis, Gladys. "Shakespeare in the High School Classroom," *EJ* 53 (April 1964), 240-247. Reprinted in *Shakespeare in School and College.* Urbana, Ill.: NCTE, 1964, pp. 55-62. Discusses practical problems of attention, verse, emphasis.

————. "Special Techniques in Teaching a Shakespeare Play," in *Literature Study in the High Schools,* by Dwight L. Burton. New York: Holt, Rinehart and Winston, 1970, 3d ed., pp. 152-154. Suggests three to four weeks to study play and focus on inner conflicts of characters and the consequences of their actions.

Waddington, Raymond B. "Shakespeare's Sonnet 15 and the Art of Memory," in *The Rhetoric of Renaissance Poetry,* ed. T. O. Sloane and R. B. Waddington. Berkeley: University of California Press, 1974, pp. 96-122. Discusses relevant historical contexts and uses Sonnet 15 to illustrate how certain kinds of reflective lyrics should be read.

Walsh, William. "Shakespeare in the Classroom: An Approach," *Journal of Education* 84 (London: January 1952), 16, 18. Anchors discussions in specific places "in the text."

Warner, John M. "Shakespeare's 'Winter' and 'Spring' and the Radical Teaching of Poetry," *CEA Critic* 34 (March 1972),

16-19. Offers two poems as "a simple exercise that reveals the acuteness and complexity of poetic seeing."

Williams, Clyde V. "Buffalo Bill Might Be Defunct, But the Bard Isn't: An Essay on Relevance," *Cimarron Review* 21 (1972), 30-36. Explores the relevance of *Ham* by reference to *Rosencrantz and Guildenstern Are Dead* and *Hair*, "both of which illustrate to us that the modern artist finds in Shakespeare a continuing source of creative inspiration."

Williams, Deborah A. "Shakespeare in the High School Classroom," *SQ* 25 (Spring 1974), 263-264. Describes a three-day unit developed by the Folger Shakespeare Library to introduce Shakespeare to high school urban-minority students, using actors, slides, and discussion.

Wood, Stanley. *The New Teaching of Shakespeare in Schools (with illustrations from the plays JC and MND)*. London: Gill, 1947. Centers "new teaching" in the child and gives lessons on *JC* (pp. 13-20) and *MND* (pp. 20-26) with tips on how not to teach (pp. 33-34).

Woodbridge, Elizabeth (Mrs. E. Morris). *The Drama: Its Law and Its Technique*. Boston and Chicago: Allyn and Bacon, 1898. Adapts and modified Freytag's *Technique of the Drama* (1863) to make it suitable for college students, and generously samples Shakespeare's plays.

Yoshio, Nakano. "English Literature in Japan," *Japan Quarterly* 6 (1959), 165-174. Includes notes on the teaching of Shakespeare's plays and Shakespeare in the Japanese theater.

NOTES ON CONTRIBUTORS

BERNARD BECKERMAN, Professor of English and Chairman of the Theatre Arts at Columbia University, is the author of several books on drama, including *Shakespeare at the Globe* and *Dynamics of Drama*. He has been Director of the Hofstra University Shakespeare Festival, recipient of the American Shakespeare Festival and Academy award, and President of the American Society for Theatre Research.

DAVID M. BERGERON is Professor of English at the University of Kansas. He has been a Folger Shakespeare Library Fellow and a Fellow of the American Council of Learned Societies. He is the author of *English Civic Pageantry 1558-1642*, and, most recently, *Shakespeare: A Study and Research Guide*. He is the editor of *Research Opportunities in Renaissance Drama*.

D. ALLEN CARROLL edited *Skialetheia: or A Shadow of the Truth, in Certain Epigrams and Satyres* for the University of North Carolina Press. He is Associate Professor of English at the University of Tennessee.

PAUL M. CUBETA is Professor of English and Vice President of Middlebury College and Director of the Bread Loaf School of English. He is the editor of *Modern Drama for Analysis, Twentieth Century Interpretations of "Richard II,"* and has published articles on Ben Jonson and Marlowe.

JAY L. HALIO is Professor of English and Associate Provost at the University of Delaware. Twice a Fulbright-Hays Senior Lecturer, he is the author of many articles and reviews and has edited old-spelling critical texts of *King Lear* and *Macbeth* as well as *Twentieth Century Interpretations of "As You Like It"* and *Approaches to "Macbeth."*

A. C. HAMILTON, formerly a Huntington Library Fellow and Visiting Overseas Fellow of St. John's College, Cambridge, is the author of *The Structure of Allegory in "The Faerie Queene," The Early Shakespeare,* and, most recently, *Sir Philip Sidney*. He is Professor of English at Queen's University, Ontario.

RAY L. HEFFNER, JR., former President of Brown University, is now Professor of English at the University of Iowa. A 1960 Guggenheim Fellow, he has also been an administrative officer at Indiana University and at Iowa, and is the author of studies of Ben Jonson and Shakespeare.

334

NOTES ON CONTRIBUTORS

Robert B. Heilman was Chairman of the English Department at the University of Washington for many years. A recipient of numerous awards, honorary degrees, and fellowships, he is the author of several books, including *This Great Stage: Image and Structure in "King Lear"* and, more recently, *The Ghost on the Ramparts*.

G. Wilson Knight is Emeritus Professor of English Literature, Leeds University. He has acted in, produced, directed, and taught Shakespeare's plays throughout the English-speaking world. His numerous books include *The Wheel of Fire* and *Shakespearian Production*.

Andrew M. McLean co-edited the "Teaching Shakespeare" issue of the *Shakespeare Newsletter* and is consulting editor of the *Teaching Shakespeare Newsletter* and review editor for *CLIO*. He was a research fellow at the University of Louvain and is Assistant Professor of English at the University of Wisconsin-Parkside.

Norman Rabkin has edited and written books on Shakespeare and the Renaissance drama, among them *Shakespeare and the Common Understanding*, and, most recently, in collaboration, *Drama of the English Renaissance*. A former Guggenheim Fellow and Senior Fellow of the National Endowment for the Humanities, he is Professor of English at the University of California, Berkeley.

Winfried Schleiner is Associate Professor of English at the University of California, Davis. A former Folger Shakespeare Library Fellow and Huntington Library Fellow, he is the author of *The Imagery of John Donne's Sermons*.

John W. Velz, formerly a Fellow of the National Endowment for the Humanities and of the Folger Shakespeare Library, is the author of *Shakespeare and the Classical Tradition: A Critical Guide to Commentary 1660-1960*. He is Professor of English at the University of Texas, Austin.

Brian Vickers formerly held appointments at the Universities of Cambridge and Zürich and is now Professor of English at the ETH, Zürich. He is the author of several books, among them *The Artistry of Shakespeare's Prose* and *Shakespeare: the Critical Heritage* (in six vols.; i-iv published), and *Shakespeare: "Coriolanus."*

Albert Wertheim is Associate Professor of English at Indiana University. He has served as Director of the Indiana-Purdue Overseas Study Program in Germany and is a former Folger Shakespeare Library Fellow.

335

INDEX

Adams, Henry, 140
Aeschylus, 230-35, 239, 260
Albee, Edward, 231
Alcibiades, 240
Antoon, A. J., 185-89, 196n, 227, 282-83n
Ariosto, Ludovico, 95n; source of *Much Ado*, 181, 191-93, 207
Ashland Shakespeare Festival, 273
Aubrey, John, xi
Auden, W. H., 183-84
audience, xii; *Hamlet*, 305-9; as judge, 234-36; of plays-within-plays, 156, 163-67, 172; Shakespeare's and modern, 283; speaking to, 292
Augustine, St., 98

Bacon, Francis, 144
Baker, Stewart A., 79
Baldensperger, Fernand, 81n
Bandello, Matteo, 181, 191-93, 196n, 206, 222-23
Barber, C. L., 77, 141n
Barry, Jackson G., 154
Barth, John, 81
Beaumont, Francis, 155
Beckerman, Bernard, 77
Beerbohm, Max, 304n
Belleforest, François de, 181
Beller, Manfred, 81n
Bennett, Josephine Waters, 178-81, 197, 202, 227
Bethell, S. L., 43n
Beverley, Peter, 181
Bible, 45, 122, 141, 155, 259
Bisanz, Adam J., 81n
Blackfriars Theatre, 275
Booth, Edmund, 278
Boswell, James, 236n

Bowers, Fredson, 274
Bradbrook, Muriel C., 87-88
Bradley, A. C., 299
Brook, Peter, 278n
Brooks, Charles, 80n, 84, 92
Brooks, Cleanth, 16, 55, 237, 240
Brown, Arthur, 154n
Brown, John Russel, 60, 212-15, 217-18, 227, 278n
Brown, Rollo W., 63n
Browning, I. R., 267n
Bullough, Geoffrey, 86n, 98n, 99n, 180-81, 191n, 192n, 196n, 223n, 227, 240
Burton, Richard, 60
Burton, Robert, 84-85

Campbell, Mrs. Patrick, 298-99
Carroll, Lewis, 195
Chamberlain, Richard, 282-83
Chambers, E. K., 28n, 104
Chambers, R. W., 99-100
Chapman, R. W., 236n
Charlton, H. B., 58
Charney, Maurice, 240n, 268-69
Chaucer, Geoffrey, 68, 81-82, 194
Chekhov, Anton, 49, 230
Chettle, Henry, 81
Chrestien de Troyes, 81-82
Cibber, Colly, 278
Cinthio, Giraldi, 98-99
civic pageants, 155-56
Clemen, Wolfgang, 314
Coleridge, S. T., 46, 58, 240, 246-47
Colie, Rosalie, 78, 180, 212, 220, 226-27
comedy, farce, 197; Italian, 33n; and melodrama, 181-82; New Comedy, 28, 33n, 44, 77; Old

comedy, farce (*cont.*)
  Comedy, 77; and pastoral,
  139-44; resolution, 150; and
  tragedy, 34-35, 50-52, 103-10,
  142-48, 150-52, 167, 212-13, 220;
  tragicomic convention, 31
commedia erudita, 77
costume, 277
Cunningham, J. V., 104

Davenant, Sir William, 278
Dekker, Thomas, 81
De Quincey, Thomas, 58
de Rougemont, Denis, 48
Donne, John, 79
Doran, Madeleine, 153
Dowden, Edward, 111
dramatic illusion, 153-73
Draper, John, 85n
Dryden, John, 137, 240-41
Dumas, Alexander, 58
dumb show, 155; in *Hamlet*,
  305-9
Dusinberre, Juliet, 79n, 84n

Eliot, T. S., 58, 110, 112, 113,
  290, 300-301, 304
Elizabeth I, 156
Ellis-Fermor, Una, 59, 269-70
Empson, William, 237
Enright, D. J., 267
Epstein, Joseph, 25
Evans, Bertrand, 160n, 170

farce, and melodrama, 197
Faucit, Helen, Lady Martin, 80-81
Fiedler, Leslie, 189, 193-94, 227
Flahiff, F. T., 78
Florus, Lucius Julius, 240
folklore, 141-42
fortune, 141-42, 146, 149
Frost, Robert, 138, 152
Frye, Northrop, 31, 33n, 35n, 68,
  103, 104, 112, 127-28

Gardner, Helen, 144
Garrett, John, 55n, 59n
Globe Theatre, xii, 143-44
Goethe, Johann Wolfgang von, 32
Golding, Arthur, 45
Goldman, Michael, 77
Granville-Barker, Harley, 291
Greene, Thomas, 82-83, 184
Greenfield, Thelma, 157
Greer, Germaine, 79-92 *passim*
Gregory, Richard, 238
Guilpin, Edward, 184

Halio, Jay L., 276n
Hall, Peter, 277
Hankins, John Erskine, 45n
Harington, Sir John, 95, 181, 191n
Hart, Alfred, 275n
Hart, H. C., 107
Hauptmann, Gerhart, 87
Hazlitt, William, 97
Heath, Stephen, 238n
Hechinger, Fred, 279n
Heilman, Robert B., 55, 62, 237
Heine, H., 80, 81
Hewes, Henry, 186-87
Heywood, Thomas, 44
Hibbard, G. R., 264n
Hillier, Richard L., xv
Hinman, Charlton, 72, 274
Holinshed, Raphael, 45, 119, 180
Homer, 264
Horace, 70
Hosley, Richard, 157n
Hotson, Leslie, 70
Houghton, W., 81-82
Housman, A. E., 13
Hunsdon, Henry Carey, 1st Lord,
  70
Husserl, Edmund, 238n

inconsistencies in plays, 166-67,
  195
Irving, Henry, 279

Jakobson, Roman, 237
James I, 119, 130, 275
Jameson, Anna B., 80, 81
Johnson, Samuel, 58, 68, 236
Jones, Emrys, 311
Jones, James Earl, 283
Jonson, Ben, 7-8, 69-70, 76, 155, 184-85, 275
Jorgenson, Paul, 179, 180, 227

Kittredge, George Lyman, 7, 63
Knight, G. Wilson, 31, 35n, 107n, 112, 267, 293n
Knights, L. C., 237, 281, 289n
Kohl, Herbert, 73
Kökeritz, Helge, 133n, 135n
Kott, Jan, 13
Kozintsev, Grigori, 275-76
Kyd, Thomas, 70, 157, 159

Lando, Ortensio, 220
Langland, John, 102-3
language in drama, 311
Lattimore, Richmond, 269n
Lawrence, W. W., 107n
Lever, J. W., 107, 112
Lévi-Strauss, Claude, 237
Lewes, George Henry, 303-4
liebestod, 36, 48
Livy, 240
Lodge, Thomas, 88-91, 184
Lowes, John Livingston, 46
Lyons, Bridget Gellert, 86n

MacCarthy, Desmond, 54-55
Mack, Maynard, 36, 139
Mackintosh, Elizabeth, 177n
Manningham, John, 28
Margeson, J.M.R., 33n
Marlowe, Christopher, 32, 34, 130-31
Mathers, Rev. Donald, 99
McPeek, James A. S., 184-85
medieval cycle drama, 155

Mehl, Dieter, 154n
melodrama, 197
Middleton, Thomas, 213, 275
Miller, Arthur, 31, 275
Miller, Jonathan, 277, 279-82
Milton, John, 68, 102-3, 115
Moore, Marianne, 114-15
morality play, 180
Muir, Kenneth, 45, 269
Munday, Anthony, 220

Nelson, Robert J., 154n, 156, 163-64
New York Shakespeare Festival, 185-89
North, Sir Thomas, 43-44, 45
Nosworthy, J. M., 28, 275

Olivier, Sir Laurence, 49, 275, 279-82
Osborn, James M., 156n
Ovid, 33n, 45

Palmer, John, 57-58
Papp, Joseph, 185-89, 227, 278, 282-83
paradox, 202, 220, 221, 226
parody, 140-41, 147-52, 161-62, 167, 171
Parrott, Thomas Marc, 111
Partridge, Edward, 154n
pastoral, 147-51; and comedy, 139-44; and tragedy, 139-44
Pearson, Hesketh, 304
Peele, George, 155
Petrarch, 81, 141
phenomenology, 238-39
Phialas, Peter G., 163n
Pindar, 70
Pirandello, Luigi, 155, 305
Plato, 220
Plautus, 28, 44
Plutarch, 43-45, 46, 240, 245, 264n
Poole, Roger, 238n

Pope, Alexander, 290
Prior, Moody E., 35n
Prouty, Charles T., 198, 219, 227
puns, 142, 144, 180-84
Pyles, Thomas, 180n

Quiller-Couch, Sir Arthur, 98

Rabkin, Norman, 280n
Rashomon, 305
Richard III, 177
Richardson, Tony, 276
Riggs, David, 77
Righter, Anne, 154, 165, 168
romance, 28, 77; narrative, 33n;
  and tragedy, 117-19, 127-28,
  130-37
Rose, Mark, xiii
Rosen, William, 268, 269n
Rowley, William, 213
Rymer, Thomas, 58, 195-96

Saldivar, Ramon, 46
Salingar, Leo, 33n, 77
Salvini, Tommaso, 303-4
Sanders, Norman, 61
satire, 144, 185
Scheler, Max, 238n
Schleiner, Winfried, 82n, 90n
Schutz, Alfred, 238
Scully, Malcolm G., 288n
Seneca, 33n, 300
Sexton, Joyce Hengerer, 180
Shaaber, M. A., 80n, 88-89
Shakespeare Association of
  America, 67
Shakespeare Newsletter, xv, 17
Shakespeare Quarterly, xv
Shakespeare, William
  All's Well That Ends Well:
  33, 104, 137, 179, 242
    Antony and Cleopatra: 36,
  46, 58, 60, 105, 137, 240, 252;
  Antony's suicide speech, 297-98;

Bankside production (1973),
  277; compared to source, 43-44;
  lecture topics, 55
    As You Like It: 33, 35, 104,
  107, 153; fathers and daughters,
  189; and *Lear*, 138-52; play
  within play, 168; and romance,
  88-92
    Comedy of Errors: 22, 33, 62,
  111; and *Pericles* and *Twelfth
  Night*, 27-28
    Coriolanus: 36, 46, 57-58,
  220-70; Aufidius, 259-62; hero
  as warrior, 247-50; hero's
  multiple roles, 242; patrician's
  view of hero, 242-45, 247-50;
  people's view of hero, 250-53;
  politics, 245-47; sources, 46,
  244-45; Volumnia, 253-59,
  265-66
    Cymbeline: 22, 37, 38, 44,
  114, 116, 118, 137; and *Much
  Ado* and *Winter's Tale*, 30-31
    Hamlet: 35, 38, 56, 58, 104-5,
  115-17, 118, 125, 135, 137, 142,
  145, 154, 218, 240, 276, 287,
  288, 295-96, 305-16; acting
  Hamlet, 299-302; actors and
  Hamlet, 49, 60, 278; adaptation,
  274-75; Chamberlain-Wood
  production, 282-83; dumb show,
  305-9; fathers and daughters,
  189; film versions, 275-76;
  ghost's speech, 305-9; King
  Hamlet's murder, 305-9;
  "Murder of Gonzago," 307-8;
  psychoanalysis, 61; quiz, 54
    1 Henry IV: 33, 34, 61, 106,
  167; discussion topics, 55;
  Falstaff and Benedick, 201-2;
  Falstaff and Bottom, 165; plan
  for teaching, 56-57
    2 Henry IV: 33, 34, 61;
  III.i.4-31, 293-95

Henry V: 33, 34, 35, 36;
St. Crispin speech, 296
1 Henry VI: 33; fathers and
daughters, 189, 191
Henry VIII: 33-34, 35, 38;
and *Richard III*, 33-34; and
Winter's Tale, 34
Julius Caesar: 35, 36, 45, 112;
and *Romeo and Juliet*, 34-35;
writing assignment, 40-42
King John: 311
King Lear: 31, 35, 36, 55, 59,
62, 71, 78, 104, 105, 111, 112-13,
116-17, 118, 135, 137, 138-52,
180, 195, 239-40, 299; and *As
You Like It*, 138-52; "Come,
let's away to prison," 146-50;
fathers and daughters, 189;
graduate course, 72-73; New
York Shakespeare Festival
production (1973), 283; quiz, 54
Love's Labour's Lost: 154,
168-69, 171, 172; Holofernes,
xi, xiii; Pageant of the Nine
Worthies, 157, 159-63
Macbeth: 22, 35, 36, 46, 58,
74, 105, 114-37, 153, 221, 239,
275; banquet scene, 128-30; "If
it were done," 297; opening
scenes, 119-20; optimistic view
of life, 116-18ff; porter scene,
126-28; quiz 54; and *Richard
III*, 29-31; Shaw on playing
Lady Macbeth, 298-99; witches,
120-22
Measure for Measure: 33, 57,
95-113, 137; Duke Vincentio,
106-10; Isabella, 97-103; and
Romeo and Juliet, 29; source
for Davenant's *The Law
Against Lovers*, 278; and
tragedy, 105-6
Merchant of Venice: 33, 37,
38, 44, 55, 58, 287; fathers and

daughters, 189; Miller-Olivier
production, 279-82; and *Much
Ado*, 212-13; teaching Shylock,
56; writing assignment, 40-41
Merry Wives of Windsor: 168
Midsummer Night's Dream:
33, 107, 171, 172, 180, 278n;
fathers and daughters, 189;
film (Peter Hall), 277; "Pyramis
and Thisbe," 157, 163-68; quiz,
54; and *The Tempest*, 28
Much Ado About Nothing:
115, 146, 177-227; Beatrice,
203-5; Benedick, 194-203;
Claudio's uncle, 219-225; and
Cymbeline and *Winter's Tale*,
30-31; Don Pedro, 185-89; the
Friar, 213-18; inconsistencies,
195; Leonato, 189-94; Margaret,
206-13; and *Othello*, 212-13;
Papp-Antoon production,
185-89, 196n, 227, 278, 282-83;
play within play, 168; puns on
"nothing," 182-84; the thief
"Deformed," 184-85
Othello: 35, 36n, 55, 57, 58,
101, 116-17, 118, 137, 240;
acting Othello, 302-4; and
Cymbeline, 31; fathers and
daughters, 189-91; inconsistencies, 195-96; and *Much Ado*,
31, 193-94, 212-13; Thomas
Rymer on, 195-96; and *Winter's
Tale*, 31
Pericles: 116, 118; and
Comedy of Errors, 28; fathers
and daughters, 189, 206
Richard II: 17, 33, 34, 35,
58, 59, 61, 302, 303; and
Edward II, 34; "This royal
throne of kings," 295-96
Richard III: 33, 34, 36, 61,
234; Cibber's production (1700),
278; and *de casibus* tragedy,

Shakespeare, William (*cont.*)
34, and Henry VIII, 34; and
Macbeth, 29-31
  Romeo and Juliet: 35, 36, 101,
  213, 215; fathers and daughters,
  189-91, 206; and genre, 104; and
  Julius Caesar, 34-35; *liebestod*,
  48; and *Measure for Measure*,
  29; quiz, 52-53; Zefferelli
  production, 60
  The Taming of the Shrew:
  22, 33, 35, 37, 38, 86-87, 88;
  fathers and daughters, 189;
  Induction, 157-59, 168-69;
  Kate's choler, 85-87; and
  women's studies, 79-92
  The Tempest: 33, 38, 112,
  116, 118, 138-39, 153-54, 234,
  287; and *Midsummer Night's
  Dream*, 28; and New Comedy,
  44-45
  Timon of Athens: 46, 137,
  240
  Titus Andronicus: 33n, 101,
  111
  Troilus and Cressida: 44,
  97, 137
  Twelfth Night: 33, 35, 60,
  104, 107, 146, 277, 287, 288; and
  Comedy of Errors, 28; play
  within play, 168-71
  Two Gentlemen of Verona:
  44, 101; fathers and daughters,
  189; Papp production, 278, 283
  The Winter's Tale: 33, 34,
  57, 115-16, 118, 179, 287; and
  Cymbeline and *Much Ado*,
  30-31; fathers and daughters,
  206; and *Henry VIII*, 34; and
  Othello, 31
Shaw, George Bernard, 58,
  290-91, 298-99, 301, 315
Smith, Hallett, 112-13
Spencer, T.J.B., 69-70, 76, 80

Spenser, Edmund, 147, 149, 180,
  181
Spingarn, J. E., 196n
Spurgeon, Caroline, 237
stage directions, 128-29
Stanislavsky, Konstantin, 313
Steemsma, Robert C., 79
Stevenson, David, 227
Stockholder, Katherine, 267-68
Styan, J. L., 49-50
Svendsen, Kester, 61n

teaching: audio-visual aids, 9ff,
  49-50, 273, 275-76; changing
  student-teacher relationships,
  24-26; and disaffected high
  school students, 73-74; goals,
  18-19; grading, 39-40; in the
  nineteenth century, 49;
  problems and hazards, 3-26, 27,
  49-51, 96, 114-15, 228-29, 273;
  professionalism, 78; relevance,
  importance of, 12-13, 17, 24-26,
  61
  activities in the classroom:
  discussion, 11-13, 16-19, 247,
  281; film compared with stage
  productions, 276-77; lecture,
  48-63 *passim*, 114-15, 273-74;
  performance, xii-xiii, 9, 49-51,
  62, 284-88; reading aloud, 9-10,
  17, 62, 73-75, 290-304; study of
  productions, 278
  approaches: adaptation for
  production, 274-78; affective,
  9-13; context in canon, 95-113;
  as drama, xiii-xiv, 60-61, 115-16,
  119-37 *passim*, 154, 237, 273-289,
  290-304, 305-16; genre, xiv, 22,
  31-32, 57, 103-4ff, 111, 114-37
  passim, 138, 141, 145-52, 220;
  historical context, 100-101, 264,
  277; imagery, 22, 122-23, 134-36,
  236-37; interdisciplinary, 237-39;

moral, 101ff, 144-45, 234-36; multiple perspectives on character, 230-70; New Critical, xii, 59-60, 154-55, 236-37; as poetry, 125-30, 290-304; performance, 96-99ff, 273-89, 290-304; psychological, 61, 84-96, 189-94, 309-10; "scientific," 6-9; source study, 42-47, 88-91, 98-100, 111, 180-81, 191-93, 222-23, 244-45, 264; thematic, 80-81, 154, 172, 177-227, 236-37; theological, 309-10; through play within play, 153-73; women's studies, 79-92
arrangement of readings, xiv, 27-36, 81, 138, 153; chronological, 32, 156; generic, 32
graduate, 42, 67-78; exams, 71; interdisciplinary, 68-69, 71; professionalism, 75ff
student assignments: exams and quizzes, 17-18, 36-38, 51-54, 285; memorization, 17; papers, 38-42, 167-68, 284
Terence, 34-35
Terry, Ellen, 195n
Tey, Josephine, 177
theatrum mundi, 154
Thomson, Peter, 278n
Tillyard, E.M.W., 112
time, 117-18; in *Lear*, 149; linear, in drama, 233-34; in *Macbeth*, 122, 230-31, 134-36; in pastoral, 141-42
tragedy, and comedy, 34-35, 50-52, 103-10, 142-48, 150-52, 167, 212-13, 220; Greek, 301-2; hero, 140; *Macbeth*, 116-18; and melodrama, 31; moral per-

spectives on character, 239-70; and pastoral, 139-44; resolution, 29, 116-19, 150-51; and romance, 117-19, 127-28, 130-37; tragicomic convention, 31
Traversi, D. A., 111-12, 267
Tree, Herbert Beerbohm, 304n
Turner, Robert Y., 314

Van Tieghem, Paul, 81n
Velz, John W., 35n, 40n, 45n
Velz, Sarah C., 45n
Vickers, Brian, 234n, 235n, 245n, 248n, 262n
villain, 29-30, 150

Waith, Eugene, 33n
Walter, J. H., 36n
Waterston, Sam, 186
Watson, Douglass, 186, 187
Weber, Max, 238n
Webster, John, 213
Webster, Margaret, 84n
Weisstein, Ulrich, 80n
Wellek, René, 81n
Whitaker, Virgil K., 28n
White, Richard Grant, 182-83
Widdoes, Kathleen, 186, 187
Wilder, Thornton, 155
Williams, Tennessee, 155, 275
Williamson, Nicol, 49
wit, 211
Wood, Peter, 282-83
Woolf, Virginia, 79
Wordsworth, William, 68

Yeats, W. B., 58, 145, 147, 152
Your Own Thing, 277-78

Zefferelli, Franco, 60

LIBRARY OF CONGRESS CATALOGING IN PUBLICATION DATA
Main entry under title:

Teaching Shakespeare.

Bibliography: p.
Includes index.
1. Shakespeare, William, 1564-1616—Study and teaching—
Addresses, essays, lectures. I. Edens, Walter.
PR2987.T35   822.3'3   77-71979
ISBN 0-691-06339-7

PRINTED IN U.S.A

GAYLORD